P9-BHY-218

TALES FROM BEYOND THE TAP

ALSO BY RANDY BACHMAN

Randy Bachman's Vinyl Tap Stories

RANDY BACHMAN

TALES

FROM

BEYOND

THE TAP

VIKING

VIKING

an imprint of Penguin Canada Books Inc., a Penguin Random House Company

Published by the Penguin Group

Penguin Canada Books Inc., 90 Eglinton Avenue East, Suite 700, Toronto, Ontario, Canada M4P 2Y3

Penguin Group (USA) LLC, 375 Hudson Street, New York, New York 10014, U.S.A.
Penguin Books Ltd, 80 Strand, London WC2R 0RL, England
Penguin Ireland, 25 St Stephen's Green, Dublin 2, Ireland (a division of Penguin Books Ltd)
Penguin Group (Australia), 707 Collins Street, Melbourne, Victoria 3008, Australia
(a division of Pearson Australia Group Pty Ltd)
Penguin Books India Pvt Ltd, 11 Community Centre, Panchsheel Park, New Delhi – 110 017, India
Penguin Group (NZ), 67 Apollo Drive, Rosedale, Auckland 0632, New Zealand
(a division of Pearson New Zealand Ltd)
Penguin Books (South Africa) (Pty) Ltd, 24 Sturdee Avenue, Rosebank, Johannesburg 2196,
South Africa

Penguin Books Ltd, Registered Offices: 80 Strand, London WC2R 0RL, England

First published 2014

1 2 3 4 5 6 7 8 9 10 (RRD)

Manufactured in the U.S.A.

LIBRARY AND ARCHIVES CANADA CATALOGUING IN PUBLICATION

Bachman, Randy, 1943–, author
Tales from beyond the Tap / Randy Bachman.

Includes bibliographical references and index.
ISBN 978-0-670-06763-3 (bound)

1. Bachman, Randy, 1943– —Anecdotes. 2. Rock music—
Anecdotes. 3. Vinyl Tap (Radio program)—Anecdotes. I. Title.

ML420.B113A3 2014   782.42166092   C2014-900033-2

eBook ISBN 978-0-14-319186-5

Visit the Penguin Canada website at **www.penguin.ca**

Special and corporate bulk purchase rates available; please see
www.penguin.ca/corporatesales or call 1-800-810-3104, ext. 2477.

CONTENTS

INTRODUCTION

One of the delights of doing *Randy Bachman's Vinyl Tap* is the feedback I receive from my listeners. I must have the most loyal pack of followers anywhere on radio—and many of the themes I've covered on shows have been prompted by their suggestions. These listeners really take the show to heart and feel connected to it and to me, so much so that they're quite comfortable writing in and sharing their own life experiences, the music they love, and how and why they listen to the show.

Over the years I've been asked through letters, emails, and in person many questions that don't always fit into the show's themes or context. This book is my chance to address those queries and give my fans the stories from outside the show, the tales from beyond the *Tap*. I've kept a list of these questions for several years, and together with my friend, musicologist and writer John Einarson, we've selected twenty questions that serve as chapters in the book. Some of these questions are music-related, while others are quite personal. Some are long and elaborate, while others are short snappers. Answering them here gives me the opportunity to share my experiences as well as my thoughts and insights. I've really tried to open up in these pages and give readers and my longtime listeners a glimpse beyond the public persona. You may not agree with everything I say, but you can't fault me for being honest and forthright. That's the way I am on my shows. In doing so, I hope I answer the questions and tell you about the things you've wanted to know.

Rock on!

Are there any songs in particular
that have changed your life?

Randy with Led Zeppelin's Robert Plant, 2008.

Records have always been an integral part of my life. There are many songs to choose from, but this question is an easy one for me. Each of these recordings has had a significant impact on me and my career.

"TUTTI FRUTTI"—LITTLE RICHARD, 1955

When I saw Elvis Presley for the first time on a little black-and-white TV at my friend's house, it was mind-blowing, world-shaking, and a signal of change for me as well as the rest of the world. I went out and bought the Elvis recording of "Tutti Frutti," and besides wanting to *be* Elvis, I wanted to play guitar like Scotty Moore. Then someone, I think it was one of my brother Gary's buddies from the Pro-Teen club, asked me if I'd heard the version by Little Richard, the guy who actually wrote the song and first recorded it. When I listened to his "Tutti Frutti" it was wilder, more raucous, and even more mind-blowing and world-shaking than Elvis's. Elvis sounded tame by comparison.

Whenever I hear either version of that song it takes me back to that time and rekindles my first impressions of rock 'n' roll.

Original rock 'n' roll was all about anything goes, having fun, going a little crazy, and just letting it all out. The more life-changing version for me, though, is the Little Richard one. He's an original. And, as I talked about in the first *Vinyl Tap* book, I was lucky enough to have him play on a couple of Bachman-Turner Overdrive tracks. I was thrilled when Richard agreed to play piano on "Take It Like a Man" on our *Head On* album. We'd already recorded the track, and just wanted him to overdub his signature piano style. He arrived looking every inch the star that he was. I was in awe of him. However, once in the recording studio with him, we discovered that he couldn't play in the key of the song. Apparently Little Richard played only in certain keys, and this wasn't one of them. After several attempts, he was all set to walk out, until we figured out that if we slowed down the recording speed it could be played in Little Richard's key. When we sped it up to the original speed it fit perfectly. Despite this hiccup, Little Richard was everything I expected and more. It became a learning experience for both of us and a dream come true for me, the kid from Winnipeg, playing alongside one of the rock 'n' roll pioneers.

"HOUND DOG" BACKED BY "DON'T BE CRUEL"—ELVIS PRESLEY, 1955

I also saw Elvis do this on TV, and it had the same impact on me. It expanded Elvis's wild side by including the Jordanaires on background vocals on both songs, merging gospel into rock 'n' roll along with the wild hand clapping on "Hound Dog." Again, Scotty Moore's guitar playing and solos made me want to be a guitar player. I still have the 78 rpm recording.

When Elvis decided to use TCB as his logo after hearing Bachman-Turner Overdrive's "Takin' Care of Business" on a Los Angeles radio station, I was both stunned and honoured. This is the guy who facilitated my entrance into rock 'n' roll and prompted me to start playing guitar. He used my song for his motto and his logo, which is on his headstone. Pretty awesome. That song not only changed my life but Elvis Presley's, too.

"OH BY JINGO"—CHET ATKINS, 1953

Growing up in Winnipeg in the 60s was the most amazing experience. We had the greatest radio stations that played all the latest music and also broadcast live bands. When I first heard the CKY Caravan Saturday morning show, featuring Hal Lone Pine and Betty Cody and their band, the guitar I heard behind the vocals was Lone Pine Jr., a.k.a. Lenny Breau. I first met him at one of their Saturday morning broadcasts at Gelhorn Motors, across from Kildonan Park on North Main Street, and it was a life-changing moment. There was this kid, a mere two years older than me, playing like Scotty Moore, Chet Atkins, and Merle Travis all rolled into one. He was barely seventeen but was already a professional musician, playing full-time in his parents' band and travelling with them. We became friends.

One of the first songs I heard Lenny play was the old 1920s standard "Oh By Jingo." He played it Chet Atkins style, with the bass and melody, so it sounded like more than one instrument. The following week I bought the Chet Atkins recording of "Oh By Jingo," and with Lenny's help I learned that song as well as the rest of the album. I used to skip high school in the afternoons to go over to Lenny's house and watch him practise. He'd show me how to play different things, and I gleaned so much from him. It was the greatest two years of my life (even though it resulted in my failing a couple of grades). I still play "Oh By Jingo" every day—as a warmup and as a memory of my great teenage years, playing hooky from school and spending afternoons at Lenny's house learning rock 'n' roll, rockabilly, country, and jazz. Years later, when the Guess Who signed with RCA Records and I met Chet Atkins at their New York office, our common thread was Lenny Breau and that song.

"SCHOOL DAYS" AND "JOHNNY B. GOODE"—CHUCK BERRY, 1956 AND 1957

I put these two songs together even though they were released a year apart because they were a pair of milestones for me and for rock 'n' roll in general. Unlike Elvis, Chuck Berry was a singer, songwriter, and guitar player all in one. And unlike the fun, nonsensical lyrics of "Tutti Frutti" (or at least nonsensical to my naive prairie white-boy ears), Chuck Berry told stories with great characters and fantastic lyrics interwoven with a call-and-response style between his voice and guitar. He'd sing a line, then reply to it with a great guitar lick. His backup band, with the one-and-only Johnny Johnson on piano, was an amazing entity in its own right.

Over the years I've played many gigs with Chuck Berry, and I loved every song he played. Like Elvis and Little Richard, he was a trendsetter and influenced everyone who came after him. Where would every guitar player be if it wasn't for Chuck Berry? "Johnny B. Goode" was the quintessential story of every kid who picked up a guitar and tried to play it "like ringin' a bell."

"BO DIDDLEY"—BO DIDDLEY, 1955

I still remember the chill I got when I first heard "Bo Diddley": that hambone jungle rhythm, that distorted tremolo guitar, and those lyrics so catchy you could sing along to them right away. I'd never heard anything like it. Over the years I did many shows with Bo Diddley and was always amazed at how he kicked the crowd in the face with the first notes and beats he played.

When Fred Gretsch asked me to play at the March 2005 opening of the Gretsch Museum in Savannah, Georgia, and told me I'd be on the show with Bo Diddley, I jumped at the opportunity. I'd seen Bo a couple of times years before with just Jerome Green on maracas and the Duchess on backup guitar. I'd also played on the same bill with him at the Seattle Pop Festival in July 1969. I was lucky enough to find a handbill from that festival that listed all the artists who played at the three-day event. I had that little handbill enlarged, laminated, and turned into a dozen posters. I took one to the Gretsch Museum opening and gave it to Bo. He had tears in his eyes as he thanked me. He said he'd told his children and grandchildren for years that he'd played with Led Zeppelin, the Doors, the Guess Who, Ten Years After, the Byrds, Janis Joplin, and all the rock music heavyweights. Now he had proof of the event. Many years later I gave the same poster to Led Zeppelin's Jimmy Page and Robert Plant, showing that they'd played with Bo Diddley. You could see the same pride on their faces.

At the meet 'n' greet in the green room before the Gretsch event, Bo showed up with one of his feet bandaged. He'd had a couple of toes amputated a day or two before because of a diabetic condition, yet amazingly enough, he still came to perform on the show. Bo was a real trooper. He was in great spirits despite his foot and never let the audience know that he might have been in pain, even though they could see the bandage. I opened my set at the Gretsch Museum with some Chet finger-style guitar and then played a few of my hits that had been written and recorded on my Gretsch 6120 Chet Atkins guitar, including "Shakin' All Over" and "Takin' Care of Business." It was a great set because the band backing me—Chuck Leavell from the Allman Brothers on piano and Vinnie Colaiuta from Sting's band on drums— were fabulous. Then I put my guitar on the stand by my chair and went to sit in the front row to watch Bo. When he came out onstage he pointed to my guitar on the stand and my empty chair and said, "Who's missing up here? Who's supposed to be in that chair?" I sheepishly raised my hand and replied, "Me." Bo then said, "So get up here and let's rock." I jumped up onstage and spent the next hour and a half playing alongside Bo Diddley. What a great moment in my life that was.

"BE-BOP-A-LULA"—GENE VINCENT, 1956

Much more than the Elvis clone he'd been tagged as at the time, Gene Vincent was the real deal. He wrote his own songs and created his own sound. He also had an amazing guitar player in Cliff Gallup. I bought every single, EP, and album I could find of Gene's and learned every one of his songs. Gene's music was the ultimate rockabilly rock 'n' roll. "Be-Bop-A-Lula" and every Gene Vincent single and album cut became part of my guitar repertoire. "Be-Bop-A-Lula" is even more primal, earthy, and raw than anything Elvis had recorded. I can understand why Gene Vincent was regarded as more dangerous than Elvis.

He must have made parents apoplectic with his leering and sneering.

When Gene played Winnipeg at the Dominion Theatre in 1959, he had six songs in the Top 10. In *Vinyl Tap Stories*, I told the story of how my friend Victor Zahn and I met Gene and his band over that Easter weekend and invited him to dinner at my parents' house. There was hardly anyone at the shows because of Good Friday and Easter Sunday. Victor and I attended the first night and were able to get backstage after the show to talk to Gene and his band. Gene was impressed by Victor's old army surplus Harley-Davidson motorcycle and asked Victor to give him a ride. After that, he was our friend. Although he didn't make it to dinner, he did give me an autographed Blue Caps cap, which I still have. The Blue Caps had just come from California, where they'd all acquired new Fender guitars and amps in a promotional deal with the company. Man, their gear looked cool.

I love Jeff Beck's tribute album to Gene and the Blue Caps, which he recorded several years ago—he managed to capture their authentic sound, and brought back every memory for me in vivid highlight.

"APACHE"—THE SHADOWS, 1960

There were two hit versions of this Jerry Lordan instrumental. Both rocked my world. The first one I heard on Winnipeg radio was by Jørgen Ingmann (known as "the Swedish Les Paul"), who multi-tracked his big Gibson hollow-body guitar. He used echoes, played what's known as pinch or false harmonics (where you pluck a fretted string with your thumb or index finger along the neck to achieve an overtone; Eddie Van Halen made this famous but I learned it from Lenny Breau years earlier), and blew everyone away. Les Paul was playing jazzy, Broadwayish songs, but Jørgen was rockin' out. The flip side, "Echo Boogie," was also an amazing track, and when you learned those two songs as a guitar player, you were on top. I next heard the Shadows version, which had a totally different soundscape and was a paradigm shift for my guitar brain. Bruce Welch, one of the finest rhythm guitar players in the world with a fantastic acoustic sound, set the perfect backing for Hank Marvin's incredible echoed single notes.

When I saw the Shads' fiftieth reunion gig at the Hammersmith Odeon in London, and again later with Cliff Richard at the 02 Stadium, that song rocked the whole crowd, and me along with it. At sound check, I got to hold Hank's legendary salmon-coloured Fender Stratocaster, reputed to be the first Stratocaster in the U.K. Check out the picture on my website.

"STONE FREE"—THE JIMI HENDRIX EXPERIENCE (B-SIDE OF "HEY JOE"), 1966

The Guess Who went to London in 1967 to make it big and be the next Beatles. How naive we were. Instead we went there and flopped. It was a train wreck, but we got to hang out in Soho where a lot of the rock 'n' roll clubs were. One of them was the famous Marquee Club on Wardour Street, where we met the Who and argued with them over their band name. Talk about cocky Canucks. We also met Cat Stevens, Reg Dwight (a.k.a. Elton John), who was working as a studio demo musician, and many other great songwriters and performers. Eric Clapton had started Cream by then, and Jimi Hendrix had arrived in London a few months earlier and was all the buzz in the music world. He'd put out his first single, a slow and funky rendition of "Hey Joe," which we immediately added to our repertoire.

But it was the B-side of that single that grabbed me even more. "Stone Free" was an amazing first glimpse into what was coming from Jimi Hendrix. It had a throbbing beat and a smouldering intensity that erupted when Jimi soloed. It's incredible to imagine that this was his very first recording with the Experience. The three of them had been together for only a little more than a week.

I remember buying the first Jimi Hendrix Experience album in London and taking it back to Winnipeg before it was released in Canada. Doc Steen, the program director at radio station CKRC, listened to it and said he loved the music but couldn't and wouldn't play it on AM radio. Six months later he was playing it every three hours. "Purple Haze," "Fire," "Foxy Lady"—all were game changers. AM radio was slowly overtaken by FM radio. Singles started to emerge from albums. If the tracks were too long, the deejays did their own edits, and gradually radio changed with the times.

Playing in Hendrix's style on songs like "Stone Free" ultimately helped me develop my own sound.

"I FEEL FREE"—CREAM (OFF THEIR *FRESH CREAM* ALBUM), 1966

This was an amazing track from a blues-influenced power trio— Eric Clapton, Jack Bruce, and Ginger Baker—that pushed my thinking towards wanting to sound like Clapton. They didn't get their name for nothing. They were the cream of the U.K. players. The intro to this song was unlike anything ever heard before, kind of a 50s retro doo-wop style followed by moaning vocals and a guitar solo that sounded like a haunted woman crying in the night (known as Clapton's "Woman Tone").

I'd been working on a distortion unit with Gar Gillies, who built Garnet amplifiers in Winnipeg. Because I grew up playing classical violin and loved the sound of bowed strings, especially the viola and cello, I wanted my lead guitar to sound like that. Using "I Feel Free" as a template, Gar and I built a 12AX7 tube–powered pre-amp to achieve that sound by boosting the signal to the amp via the pre-amp, which creates distortion. I named it the Herzog just because I'd seen that name somewhere and thought it was cool. Along with my 59 Gibson Les Paul Standard guitar, it became my "American Woman" sound. But it was inspired by Clapton's tone on "I Feel Free."

"WHOLE LOTTA LOVE"—LED ZEPPELIN (OFF THEIR *LED ZEPPELIN II* ALBUM), 1969

Another mind-boggling game changer. This was an album track that got played as a single, with many different edited versions out on AM radio, while the longer album version became a staple on FM radio. I'd heard Jimmy Page as a studio guitarist playing on so many singles out of London that I thought of him as an amazing chameleon and creator. To be a backdrop for so many hit singles, to play such great solos and rhythm to enhance the songs in so many different styles, was remarkable.

I met Jimmy in 1967 when the Guess Who played a television show with the Yardbirds in Cleveland. We shared a class-room as a dressing room, and Jimmy asked if he could try out my Rickenbacker guitar. I said yes, if I could play his Telecaster. So we swapped guitars for a few moments. Little did I know what incredible music that guitar would go on to create. Page with the Yardbirds was amazing.

A year or more later I heard that his new group, Led Zeppelin, had signed with Atlantic Records. When the first Led Zeppelin album came out, they played the Seattle Pop Festival with the Guess Who. I stood and watched them play for hours. It was an amazing time for music, all new sounds and styles bursting forth, and Led Zeppelin's blues-based hard rock was at the forefront. Bands were evolving at the speed of sound. "Whole Lotta Love" with its heavy power-chording riff showed off everything that Led Zeppelin was: the riffs, the shrieking vocals, the thundering drums, the solid bass playing, and, of course, Jimmy Page's superb guitar. This song and the album it came from ushered in the era of classic rock, which continues to be a vital musical force and had a profound influence on my playing and the sound of the Guess Who. Just listen to "American Woman" and you can hear that influence.

"CAUSE WE'VE ENDED AS LOVERS"—JEFF BECK (OFF HIS *BLOW BY BLOW* ALBUM), 1975

The Yardbirds can lay claim to spawning three of the greatest lead guitar players in rock music. This British Invasion band was more than merely a pop hit singles group; they were experi-menters pushing the rock 'n' roll envelope by integrating innova-tive sounds and influences into their music. I think it's fair to say that the Yardbirds invented psychedelic music, with such ground-breaking songs as "Heart Full of Soul," with its Middle Eastern–flavoured, sitar-like guitar solo; "I'm a Man," with its rave-up freak-out at the end; "Shapes of Things," featuring a unique raga rock solo using controlled feedback; and "Happenings Ten Years Time Ago," with its weird voices and droning effects. The man responsible for creating these spectacular musical innovations and soundscapes was Jeff Beck. He took blues guitar to the moon.

Jeff was the second lead guitarist in the Yardbirds, replacing Eric Clapton, whose brilliance was only hinted at during his time with the band. Later, Jeff was joined on guitar by session player extraordinaire Jimmy Page, who would carry on after Jeff quit. Clapton, Beck, and Page—a not-too-shabby alumni roster. All three guitar giants emerged from the same area of south London, where they lived within twenty minutes of each other. As a guitar player, I don't favour one over the other; I appreciate the distinctive styles of each.

After Jeff Beck left the Yardbirds, he formed the first of two Jeff Beck groups, which included two then-unknown members: Rod Stewart and Ron Wood. I loved Jeff's *Truth* album, recorded with this lineup—it was a life-changing LP for me, and still is. His use of the wah-wah pedal was far beyond any of his contemporaries. I bought every album he released, whether it was solo or with a group. In the latter 70s he moved into fusion jazz and continued his groundbreaking guitar explorations.

His 1975 *Blow by Blow* album, produced by legendary Beatles producer George Martin, was a milestone. Side two opened with a song written by Stevie Wonder and given to Jeff to record. "Cause We've Ended as Lovers" is beyond description, an emotional tour de force. On the album sleeve, Jeff dedicates this track to the great Roy Buchanan, an influential guitar player in his own right. I've seen Jeff play "Cause We've Ended as Lovers" many times and I've played it many times myself, both in concert and for fun. It's a stunning song, with great chords and a format that allows for a significant amount of freedom to improvise over. It's a guitar lesson in cool, and remains one of my favourite instrumentals of all time because of Jeff's amazing playing. Nobody plays like Jeff Beck.

"HOW HIGH THE MOON"—LES PAUL AND MARY FORD, 1951

I remember first hearing this on the radio when I was a kid and thinking it sounded so cool, all these guitar players playing together. I later learned it was just Les Paul by himself, multi-tracking his guitar. In the early 1950s, Les basically invented sound-on-sound multi-track recording, and it became his signature. Multi-track changed the very nature of recorded music. You could record the instruments first, for example, and then add the vocals over top.

The first recordings I made were on two-track recording machines. Later with the Guess Who, we moved up to three-track, four-track, and then eight-track recording. The Beatles recorded *Sgt. Pepper's Lonely Hearts Club Band* on a four-track machine. Nowadays with digital technology, forty-eight-track recording is possible.

But it all started with Les Paul. The other thing that really impressed me about "How High the Moon" was Les's rapid-fire licks. He and his wife, Mary Ford, made some landmark recordings, and even though they were playing kind of pop jazz, they included jazz and blues on them as well. Les Paul was a genius who made guitar magic. Jeff Beck once said that he learned to play lead guitar by lowering the speed on Les Paul albums from 33 1/3 to 16 2/3 rpm to slow the licks down.

I met Les Paul and Mary Ford when I was about seventeen. As I described in *Vinyl Tap Stories,* they were playing the Rancho Don Carlos supper club out on Pembina Highway in south Winnipeg, a long way from where I lived in the North End. I took the bus to see them, but with the drinking age still at twenty-one, I was too young to get in. Somehow I was allowed to stand in the kitchen and watch by the door as waiters came and went, clanging their trays. I stood beside Les's stack of Ampex tape recorders and watched in awe and amazement. He got that multi-tracked sound live by using several tape recorders and playing along to the recorded parts. Afterwards, he let me hold his guitar and showed me the cool descending lick in "How High the Moon."

Decades later, when I was with BTO opening for Van Halen on the 5150 tour, Les came to our gig at the Nassau Coliseum in New Jersey. We chatted backstage, and to my astonishment he remembered me standing at the door at the Rancho Don Carlos. He smiled and said, "'Here, kid, hold this,'" recalling the very words he'd spoken to me so long before. A few years after that, I went to the Iridium Club, where Les played every Monday night. Onstage, he told the story of our first meeting, and then invited me up to perform "How High the Moon" and to play the lick he'd shown me way back at the Rancho. Then he asked me to do one of my own songs, so I played "Takin' Care of Business," with Les and his trio backing me up. I was higher than the moon from that experience.

"I GET AROUND" BACKED BY "DON'T WORRY BABY"—THE BEACH BOYS, 1964

The Beach Boys were North America's answer to the Beatles. When I first heard this band—made up of three brothers, a cousin, and a next-door neighbour—I related to them instantly; I'd played with my own brothers for various events as kids. Beach Boys songs represented our teenage years of girls, cars, beaches, sunshine, and rock 'n' roll. They were fun songs about fun times. We didn't get into the surfing thing in Manitoba, though. Where would you surf? I was in Chad Allan and the Reflections at the time, and because I had a high falsetto voice, whenever we played a Beach Boys song I was designated to sing the high Brian Wilson parts.

Years later, I toured with the Beach Boys and became good friends with Carl Wilson and the rest of the guys. There were plenty of squabbles and pranks but lots of love and respect, too. Besides, I was used to that environment with my three brothers. I wrote some songs with Carl for the Beach Boys' *Keepin' the Summer Alive* album, including the title track, but when Carl asked me to produce the album I was in the midst of my divorce and couldn't do it. To this day, I regret saying no to him on the phone. Carl has since passed on, but I recently visited with the guys again in Toronto at their 50th Reunion Tour. We had dinner backstage together and talked about old times. They played about forty-five hit songs that night, including "I Get Around" and "Don't Worry Baby," and had everyone rockin'. I stood in the audience and sang all the falsetto parts, just like I used to.

"SHAKIN' ALL OVER"—JOHNNY KIDD AND THE PIRATES, 1960

When I first heard Johnny Kidd and the Pirates' original recording of this song on a reel-to-reel tape from the U.K., I knew I was meant to play it. That guitar riff was iconic. My band, Chad Allan and the Expressions (we'd changed our name from Reflections to Expressions by then because an American group called the Reflections had a hit with "Just Like Romeo and Juliet"), recorded it late one night with one microphone in a TV studio in Winnipeg. Bob Ashley, our keyboard player, didn't know what to play on piano, so I told him to play a Little Richard *clinkety-clink* kind of thing. I arranged that song with the drum break in the middle and all the screaming at the end. Chad Allan was sick with a bad cold that night, so he sang it lying on his back. But we managed to create a little magic with that recording. One thing that I did differently from the Johnny Kidd version was to use my Bigsby vibrato on that big E minor chord where the verses stop. That gave the chord a quivering sound that really worked. On the Pirates' version, the guitar player simply slid a metal cigarette lighter along his twelfth fret. It sounded so tinny.

We sent the song to Quality Records in Toronto, where George Struth put "Guess Who" on the label just to drum up some publicity. "Shakin' All Over" became a nationwide hit, and we got our new name. I still love that riff and play that song today.

"LIKE A HURRICANE"—NEIL YOUNG (OFF HIS *AMERICAN STARS AND BARS* ALBUM), 1977

This is Neil at his wildest guitar soloing. He's playing with complete abandon. Neil wrote this song about meeting a girl in a bar, and when he performs it in the concert video he has a giant fan directed at him, trying to blow him down. Alongside "Cinnamon Girl" and "Down by the River," it's become one of his signature songs. When I first heard it, I was blown away, and it didn't take a giant fan. It's Neil at his electric best. I saw him once with Crazy Horse in a small bar in Half Moon Bay near his ranch outside San Francisco; they played "Like a Hurricane" for about forty-five minutes, in a John Coltrane kind of jazz trance, on and on, taking themselves and the crowd to new musical heights. When I hear it on the radio, I still crank it up. And if I'm gigging with Toronto band the Sadies, which I do from time to time, we do this song and in our own way pretend that we're Neil and the Horse, just as I used to pretend I was Elvis, Hank, Jeff, Jimmy, Chet, Eric, and all my idols. I recorded an extended version of "Like a Hurricane" during sessions for *Jukebox*, the covers album that Burton Cummings and I did back in 2007, paying homage to another fellow Winnipeg rocker. It didn't make the album, but someday I'll release it.

While all these recordings played a major role in my musical evolution, I'm still being influenced by music I hear today. It's an ongoing process, and I continue to listen for new sounds and styles. Music evolves and you have to evolve with it. As a songwriter, I can't remain static—I'm always on the lookout for what's new and different, and I allow new sounds to influence my writing and playing.

Who are the people who've had the
greatest influence on you,
or played a pivotal role in shaping
you as a person or your career?

Bachman family photograph, circa late-1950s.
Back row (left to right): Charles, Gary, Randy;
front row: Robin, Anne, and Tim.

The first person who influenced and shaped me was my dad, Charles Bachman. He taught me by example a work ethic that has served me well and defined my career. He was an honest, honourable businessman who always sought to please his customers. Beyond that, he tried to make a difference in the lives of the people in the community by serving for many years as an alderman in West Kildonan. He spent time on a number of civic committees in a variety of capacities—as deputy mayor, police commissioner, fire commissioner, justice of the peace, and, following the incorporation of West Kildonan into Winnipeg's Unicity concept, as chairman of the provincial lotteries board. In nine years of service, my dad demonstrated a strong sense of civic duty and community responsibility. He seemed to have a purpose, and that was to make life better for people. Many wanted him to run for mayor, but he wasn't interested.

He worked for years to have a hospital built in the Garden City area. His father had passed away from a burst appendix— when his family had called for an ambulance, what eventually came was a horse and buggy to take him into Winnipeg proper; he could have been saved if there'd been a hospital in the north end of the city. My dad and others finally succeeded in building Seven Oaks Hospital. The community wanted to name it after him, but he wouldn't have anything like that. He was a very humble man. But there is a street named after him: Bachman Bay, in Mandalay West, a fairly recent subdivision of West Kildonan. As I got older I saw how respected he was in the community. I was immensely proud of him, and still am.

My dad had a tough life growing up without a father, but he had high standards for himself. He expected the same from his boys. I was the oldest and was supposed to set an example for my younger brothers. I wanted to please my father, but that wasn't always easy. Especially when you're the oldest son, you want to earn your dad's approval. When I ran over my foot the last time I ever drank (more about that later), he told me he was ashamed to call me his son. I never had another alcoholic drink from that day on. It had nothing to do with joining the Mormon Church, since this was months before that happened. I just never wanted to displease my dad.

I don't think he ever told me he was proud of me; he wasn't the kind of person to show affection. I hardly recall getting a hug from him, and I don't think he ever told us he loved us. But I think that was a generational thing, having grown up in hard times, with the Great Depression and World War II. His own father died when he was about five or six, so he never got to experience having a dad around to teach him or demonstrate how to be a father. He never thought I could make a career out of being a musician, and believed I should be working a regular job because that was the culture in which he was raised and lived. You finish school and you get a job for life until you retire. It wasn't until I bought that big house on Scotia Street that he came to realize that being a musician could actually be a gainful occupation.

He worked long hours as a dispensing optician at Imperial Optical on South Osborne Street in Fort Rouge, travelling by bus five days a week. He later founded Benson Law Opticians on Kennedy Street downtown before setting up his own business, Charles Bachman Optical, in the Boyd Building on Edmonton Street. But when he came home from work he'd have dinner then go downstairs and continue working. Every single night he'd be downstairs fixing a window or a door, repairing furniture, or building replacements for the house. He even created a basement. Our house at 356 Seven Oaks Avenue, on the corner of Powers Street, was built on cinder blocks. My dad wanted a basement but couldn't afford one, so he and my uncle Jack dug it out by hand, carting the dirt and mud outside in a wheelbarrow, building the support beams, pouring the concrete. It took them two years to complete it. For one whole summer, my brother Gary and I shovelled sand into a little cement mixer outside. After that, he built a porch on the front of the house. Later, he built the house we moved to at 655 Hartford in Garden City, and built a garage for it, too. He never had any training as a carpenter or a plumber; he just did it. He was one of these do-it-yourself guys—he'd even fix the car if it broke down. My dad was such an industrious man. He'd also take us camping every summer with this little tent we had and all the camping gear. We always roughed it, and he taught us a lot about how to look after ourselves.

I've never been afraid of hard work or a challenge, and I've never played it safe in my career. I credit that to my dad's example. My brother Gary, who's two years younger, and I both acquired a strong work ethic from my dad. Gary has worked hard to build one of the most successful real estate businesses in Winnipeg. Our brothers Timmy and Robbie, who are about ten years younger, never had that same work ethic. Although we were a close family growing up, the age difference between the two sets of brothers created a sense of two families within one.

When I got my first big royalty cheque from "These Eyes," I bought a car for my dad and another car for my first wife Lorayne's dad, Bob Stevenson. I also gave my dad some money for his mortgage. I wasn't able to pay it off, but I gave him about $10,000 to put a dent in it. I never knew until just before he died that he hadn't used that money for the mortgage. In the early 90s, when he was dying of pancreatic cancer, I'd take my kids out of school early every day for the ninety-minute drive to visit him in Abbotsford, B.C., because I never knew if this might be the last day we'd see him alive. After one of these visits, he called me back into the room alone. "Remember that $10,000 you gave me?" he asked. "I put it in the bank and it's been collecting interest ever since. I want you to take it out and each of you boys split it between you." It was worth about $40,000 by then. I thought about it that night, and the next day I told him, "This money was for you to help pay off your house. I can't take it." Gary had planned to take him to Rochester to the Mayo Clinic, so I told my dad that the money could be used for that or in some other way to make the last days of his life on this earth easier for him. I didn't need it and didn't want it. None of us needed it. I don't know what he did with it, but I hope he used it.

It was around the same time that I discovered he'd had a dream to buy some land, four acres out near Winnipeg's perimeter, near McPhillips Street in the North End. His dream was to build houses there for his four sons and him and my mom, and that we'd all live together. The grandkids would all be living there, too, like a Bachman enclave. But he never sat us down and shared this dream with any of us. So when I announced in 1972 that I was moving to Vancouver because I just couldn't get work for Brave Belt in Winnipeg, and that I was taking Timmy and Robbie with me, along with his grandchildren Tally and Kezia, it must have broken his heart. I was shattering this dream of his that none of us even knew about. When I found out about it years later, I asked him why he'd never told us. That was just the way he was. I felt the same pain when Tally moved away to Maui and later Los Angeles and took away my grandson. I thought I'd never see them again. My parents were just pleased that I didn't take Gary, too. My dad later sold the land and he and my mom moved out to British Columbia to be closer to us.

They bought a piece of land in Surrey and built a West Kildonan–style house complete with a full basement. A whole band could practise there it was so big. My dad was used to that kind of house. I lived not far from them, so we'd all go over and spend Christmases together, just as we had back in Winnipeg. A few years later he became restless, and to no one's surprise bought another parcel of land and built another house. This was his life. He was always working around the house. When he went out to B.C., he simply continued doing what he'd always done.

When my dad was diagnosed with cancer, his doctor gave him two or three months to live. But ever the fighter, he lived another eleven years. I was on the road a lot then, but Gary would fly in from Winnipeg once a month to be with him for a week, and later Timmy moved in to look after him. That was a wonderful thing Timmy did. It was heartbreaking to see my dad in his final months in such a weakened condition after being so strong and vital all his life. When he died in January 1993 it was devastating for me. Now I was the head of the Bachman clan. It certainly made me realize even more the importance of family. My son Tal wrote a song inspired by his grandfather entitled "If You Sleep." That song about my dad's passing touched so many people. It's very moving.

Before he died, my dad called the four boys in to see him and handed us each an envelope with a cheque. When he'd sold his dream property, those four acres in north Winnipeg, he put that money in the bank. Now he was giving it to each of us equally. Here he was giving his children their inheritance while he was still able to see us enjoy some of it. It was a lesson I've applied to my own children: every Christmas, besides the usual presents, I give them each a little dividend on their future inheritance. I really enjoy sharing that money with my kids and seeing them use it now rather than when I'm gone. Thank you, Dad.

Another person who had a significant influence on me was Ted Holdaway. He was my grade 11 teacher at West Kildonan Collegiate back in the late 1950s. Ted, who was from Australia, had come to Winnipeg for a competition years earlier as a member of the Australian water polo team. He liked it here so much that after returning to Australia to earn his teaching degree, he came back to Winnipeg to teach.

I'd failed grade 11 because I'd spent too much time at Lenny Breau's house watching and learning guitar from him. I credit those two years with Lenny for providing me with the foundation for my later career as both a guitar player and a songwriter. But it cost me two years of high school. Up until then, I'd been an A student. My daily routine was to go over to twins Carol and Karen Schmolinger's house for lunch, and then when they headed back to school I'd make my way over to Lenny's parents' house for a different kind of class. When I returned to West Kildonan Collegiate, having flunked my previous year, I was put in a room full of Fonzies, guys in leather jackets older than me. They were considered "hard rocks." Some of these guys were in their late teens, even early twenties; they couldn't get a job without a high school diploma and had come back to complete their senior matriculation. I was tall for my age, so I didn't look that out of place, even though I definitely was. Mr. Holdaway was our homeroom teacher. He was in his early thirties, but was a big guy in excellent physical condition from having been a water polo player. Nobody messed with him.

On one of the first days in this class, we were trying to vote in a class president for the student council. None of the Fonzies was interested, so Mr. Holdaway called me up to the front of the class. "All right, you bloke," he said (he used all these cool Australian slang terms). "I don't think you're such a bad bloke. I think you'd make a good class president. Does everybody agree that Randy would make a good class president?" They all put up their hands, thrilled to have finally found a sucker, and so I became the president. I said to him after class that I didn't know if I had it in me, and he replied, "I think you're a leader. You just haven't had the chance to show it yet, but I think you have that ability within you." He also spoke to me about my grades and why I was doing poorly in school. "Your IQ is high but you haven't been applying yourself. You've got another chance now. You've been getting forties and forty-fives. It's not that hard to get another 5 or 10 percent. That's all you need. You just have to pass and get your senior matriculation. No one will ever look at your marks, just the fact that you completed high school and have your diploma. You can at least finish something you started." He also knew that I played guitar. "I see that you have another love, and that's music. If you get your high school diploma you can go off and play your guitar and at least people will know you can read and write and finished high school."

When other teachers had already written me off, Mr. Holdaway really hammered the message home to me that I could succeed if I set my mind to it. He gave me a chance and inspired me to believe in myself. He showed me that I could be a leader, something I hadn't really thought I could do before then. He saw something in me. He never discouraged me from pursuing music; he just wanted to make sure I completed high school first. If it wasn't for him I'd probably never have finished school. I've never forgotten his words. Being class president meant meeting with the student council once a month and deciding when things like dances and pep rallies would be held and helping organize these things. No big deal, but it did mean that I had to report back to my class on student council business and speak out at council meetings on their behalf.

Ted Holdaway went even further in supporting and encouraging me. I was expelled from West Kildonan Collegiate near the end of that year for playing hangman. Well, not just playing it once, but all year long. There was a teacher from England named Mr. Battershill, one of those old-school types who always carried a riding crop. If you were asleep or daydreaming, he'd whack your desk to get your attention. I sat at the back of the classroom with my buddy Dennis Tkach right across from me, and during every literature class with Mr. Battershill, Dennis and I would play hangman. We'd use a notebook and pass it back and forth between us, one of us trying to guess the letter and the other adding another part to the scaffold when that letter was incorrect. Foolishly I'd kept all these in one notebook, a whole school year's full of hangman in literature class. We'd even included the dates and who'd won. One day late in the school year, I think it was May by then, Mr. Battershill caught us. When he looked through my notebook, he saw that we'd been doing it during double English literature classes, the last two periods of every Monday, Wednesday, and Friday, all year since September. He threw us out. My mother made me return to school, but they wouldn't take me back. The principal, O.V. Jewett, a sour old guy, told my mom I wasn't worth it. He said I was shiftless. He did the same thing to comedian David Steinberg, who was two years ahead of me.

So I went to St. John's High School, a notoriously tough school where Burton Cummings and the other guys in the Deverons went. I lasted only a day. When the St. John's principal called O.V. Jewett for a reference check on me, O.V. told him I was a bum and that he wouldn't let me back into

West K. So I was immediately bounced from St. John's. I ended up at Garden City Collegiate—my mother knew Bobby Bend, who was the principal there; Bobby called Ted Holdaway and Ted convinced him that I was worth taking a chance on. Since my year was shot, Bobby told me to come back in the fall and he'd give me another chance.

That's where I completed my high school education. I even became the Garden City Collegiate prom king in grade 12, along with my then girlfriend, Claudia, as prom queen. What a moment. Here we are being introduced as the prom king and queen and we're supposed to go out in front of the entire student body and dance the first waltz. But Chad Allan and the Reflections was the band that night, so instead of dancing I had to get up onstage and play Santo and Johnny's "Sleep Walk" while someone else danced that first big waltz with Claudia.

If not for Mr. Holdaway's belief in me, I wouldn't have finished high school and gone on to community college at the Manitoba Institute of Technology (I didn't graduate from there, but that's a whole other story). After so many decades, I received an email from Mr. Holdaway three years ago or so. He's retired and living in Edmonton and listens to my radio show every week.

In 2007, West Kildonan Collegiate—now relocated in the former Edmund Partridge Junior High School on Main Street where Garry Peterson and I once played our first-ever live performance as the Embers—invited me back for the opening of their new music room named in my honour. Latter-day Guess Who member Bill Wallace was the band teacher at the time and conducted the school band through "Takin' Care of Business." The Seven Oaks School Division superintendent, Brian O'Leary, introduced me, and as I stepped forward to speak I looked up to the sky, or at least the ceiling, and declared, "See, O.V., I made it!"

In *Vinyl Tap Stories,* I wrote at length about the influence and impact Lenny Breau had on me, but suffice it to say that I wouldn't be where I am today if I hadn't met him. It's a given that he was perhaps the most important musician in my life. Not a native-born Winnipegger (Lenny was born in Maine), he moved to the city with his parents, whose country band, the Hal Lone Pine and Betty Cody Show, he'd been playing in since the age of thirteen. By the time I met him he was still in his teens but already far and away the best guitar player in the city, and on his way to becoming a virtuoso who would redefine the instrument and how to play it. He took the Merle Travis/ Chet Atkins' fingerpicking style and blended it with jazz, flamenco, classical, and rockabilly to create his own distinctive style and sound. You need only hear a few notes to recognize Lenny's playing. Despite his tragic death in 1984, his legend and legacy live on, and guitar players continue to discover his genius. I feel very privileged to have met him so early in my guitar-playing career.

Lenny wasn't much older than me, but he knew a lifetime of guitar licks and technique. In just those two short years, he taught me a vocabulary on the guitar that has taken me all over the world. I could never be the guitar player he was, but I'd never have become the guitar player I am without his taking an interest in me. It was never a formal-lesson situation and I never paid him. He was simply kind enough to let me watch him practising and to occasionally show me some of his technique. Beyond the fretboard, Lenny also taught me a valuable lesson that made me who I am today: no matter how hard you practise guitar, someone will always come along who's better than you. So write good songs. They last forever. I've taken that advice to the bank many times over my career. I wanted to be like him, a dedicated musician, and so I'd practise four and five hours a day before school, after school, weekends, even playing in the dark in my bedroom after lights-out. He was already a professional musician and I aspired to be one, too.

I learned another valuable life lesson from Lenny, and that was to not get involved with drugs. Lenny was smoking pot at age sixteen. When he moved to Toronto in the early 60s he got into heavier drugs, LSD and ultimately heroin, and was never able to shake free. Lenny was brought down by drugs, his career ruined by them. I saw drugs take control of him and vowed never to allow that to happen to me.

When you listen to my songs "Undun" and "Looking Out for #1," you hear chord patterns I gleaned from my time with Lenny. I've paid him back by releasing his studio recordings and live tapes on my Guitarchives record label. For years, Lenny kept asking me when I was going to do a jazz album. My success in the rock-music world had no cachet with him— jazz was the real deal as far as he was concerned. "When are you going to do a jazz thing, man?" I finally took the leap in 2004, recording my jazz-influenced album with a title inspired by Lenny: *JazzThing*. Through the power of digital technology and computers, I was able to duet with Lenny on George Gershwin's immortal "Summertime." We never had the opportunity to perform together back in the day, so this was the closest I could get to sharing a song with the master. It was a thrill beyond words.

Burton Cummings joining the Guess Who in January 1966 changed my life forever. It's been a complicated affiliation, no doubt. One journalist once described our relationship as the longest-running soap opera in Canadian history. That may be a bit oversimplified. Burton and I are very different people, that's a given, but we were able to bring those differences together to create a body of music that will outlive us. I had a drive and a passion back in the early 60s and I saw that same drive in Burton, along with a guy who was willing to commit and hang in for the ups and the inevitable downs. I also saw a young man who had raw talent bursting from him as well as a tremendous voice. The Deverons, Burton's high school band, were cool and had a lot of fans, but they were never going to go anywhere. I think Burton knew that, too, because when we invited him to join the Guess Who, he didn't hesitate. He didn't think about the other guys in the Deverons. He always says it was a gift and that you don't look a gift horse in the mouth. I'd seen the Deverons playing several times, and I knew he could sing rockers just like Eric Burdon, as well as ballads.

I forged an alliance with Burton soon after he joined in early 1966 because, being the main songwriter in the band at the time, I wrote for the lead voice. I'd written songs to suit Chad Allan's voice, and now I could write for Burton's grittier voice. And because of that, the sound of the band changed. We went from "And She's Mine" to "Clock on the Wall." I wrote "Believe Me" as a Kinks or Paul Revere and the Raiders song, but it just didn't suit Chad's voice and style, and you can hear that on the record. In Burton's hands, though, it was right. Later, songs like "These Eyes," "Laughing," "No Sugar Tonight," and "No Time" were conceived with Burton's voice in mind.

When Burton joined the Guess Who, he'd just turned eighteen and had dropped out of St. John's High School. His mother, Rhoda, knew my dad because he was so well respected in the community as an alderman and prominent mover 'n' shaker. Before she'd allow her son to join the band, Rhoda called me up and said that if I'd be like a big brother to Burton, who was an only child raised without a father, and take him under my wing, she'd let him join the Guess Who. I don't think Burton was aware at the time of that caveat. I agreed, and for a time I'd pick him up before gigs and take him home afterwards. But like any fraternal relationship, ultimately the younger sibling rebels against the older sibling's restrictions. After a while, I'd take Burton home as his mother expected only to have him sneak out of the house to carouse with his buddies until all hours and get into whatever shenanigans they could find. Burton was an adult now and not about to be constrained by a big brother figure. I'm sure the resentment he may have harboured towards me in serving that role lay at the base of our often thorny relationship.

Nonetheless, there was one aspect of our relationship that I was able to cultivate. With a half-dozen singles and two albums under my belt, I tutored Burton on songwriting. What came from that was a collaboration that drew on our individual personalities and combined musical tastes. We'd meet on Saturday mornings at his grandmother's house on Bannerman, where Burton and his mother lived, and share our ideas. Whether it was a line for a verse or chorus, a cool riff or chord pattern, a clever song title, or even a few words strung together, we'd give it equal attention, searching for the germ of an idea for a song. We'd combine ideas and stimulate each other's creativity or shoot down an idea that might be deemed weak or silly (in its initial incarnation, "White Collar Worker" was one such song thread I had that was judged as not up to our standards; it later found life under the title, "Takin' Care of Business"). We wanted to be like the great songwriting teams of pop—Bacharach and David, Leiber and Stoller, Goffin and King, Lennon and McCartney, Jagger and Richards. Those were our inspirations and our heroes. From those lofty dreams we ultimately created a songwriting partnership that gave the world such songs as "These Eyes," "Laughing," and "No Time," as well as many of the songs on our first three RCA albums. Not bad for a couple of naive prairie kids.

I was more often the chorus guy and Burton the verse guy. I'd bring in guitar riffs and he'd add maybe chords or a bridge idea. As time went on, though, it became a more balanced collaboration. I can remember writing part of "Share the Land" with him, but I've never been given any credit for it. I had that line "Have you heard the news" and the guitar riffs, which I'd taken from Neil Young's "Down by the River."

In my solo shows, I always introduce "These Eyes" as the song that changed our lives, and it's so true. I had the distinctive D minor 7 to C major 7 piano riff. Burton liked it but didn't like my lyric idea of starting with "these arms." Instead he suggested we start with the eyes, then move to the arms in the second verse. The song came together quickly. "These Eyes" went on to sell over a million copies, and was followed by several more million-sellers. My life was, indeed, forever changed. Burton and I were ultimately anointed as Canada's Lennon and McCartney.

When I left the Guess Who in May 1970, it was a rancorous parting, and I took a shellacking not only from the media but also from Burton. I was vilified in every interview he gave and written off as a spent force that would never make it in the music business drug free. Drugs had already driven a wedge between him and me long before we parted company. But for several years afterwards, I was subjected to a litany of ridicule and verbal potshots, some of them of a very personal nature. The reality was that the pressure was now squarely on Burton's shoulders to deliver the goods without the collaboration we had enjoyed. Burton doesn't react well to pressure and generally avoids stressful situations. He never liked business meetings or making the big decisions. I just let the music do the talking as Bachman-Turner Overdrive rose to the top, outselling the Guess Who.

Since then we've had an on-again, off-again relationship, culminating in the Guess Who reunion and the Bachman-Cummings partnering that followed. Neither were without their hurdles (more on that later, too). But the bottom line is that meeting Burton Cummings was a pivotal moment in my life.

Neil Young has come in and out of my life since we first met back in the early 60s. He remains an inspiration and an influence on me as well as a close friend. As I did with Lenny Breau, I wrote about our relationship in *Vinyl Tap Stories*. I admired his enduring stick-to-it-iveness and his spirit of adventure, which he has way more of than I do. Damn the torpedoes and full speed ahead, that's Neil. He does whatever he wants, whether it's a country album or a techno album or a tour with a rock-abilly band. No one tells Neil Young he can't or shouldn't do something. I've never had that kind of confidence to do whatever I want, and I envy that quality in Neil. I was too afraid to be that way, maybe because I had a wife and kids when I was very young. I was focused on cultivating a more commercial appeal and writing hit songs. I've notched up more hits than he has, and he's reminded me of that on a few occasions. I think Neil's only #1 hit single was "Heart of Gold." But he was never focused on hit singles. He has integrity for always charting his own course. If it sells, it sells; if it doesn't, so what. At least he's honest with himself, whether the music industry or his fans like it or not. I envy his body of work and his ability to switch things up at will.

Back in the mid 60s, we were travelling to the same destination but following our dreams on different highways. Somehow our paths managed to cross from time to time. I was a musical inspiration for him back in Winnipeg. He acknowledges that in his recent autobiography, *Waging Heavy Peace,* and I'm flattered. He's my hero. Our early success with "Shakin' All Over" in 1965 inspired Neil to shoot for something beyond Winnipeg's perimeter highway.

I'm older than Neil by a couple of years, but when I first met him, not long after he moved to Winnipeg from Toronto, I saw in him a dream and a determination that a lot of other guys on the local scene didn't have. No matter what it took, he was willing to dig deep inside and find what was needed to succeed. It was the same determination that I had, and it was nurtured in both of us beginning with Elvis and Buddy Holly through to the Beatles: to live a rock 'n' roll life playing and writing songs. Even at that young age, he was able to see beyond Winnipeg and even beyond Canada. The Guess Who had been recording and were already travelling on the road by then, but we shared a vision that was bigger than the local community club and teen dance circuit. Back then, there were several guys on the local scene who had the talent to go somewhere in music, guys like Mike Hanford of the Shondels, but they were content to be big fish in a small pond. Winnipeg is an isolated city, and taking a chance at making it in Toronto or Vancouver, let alone New York or Los Angeles, took a lot of confidence and chutzpah that Neil and I, and the other guys in the Reflections/Guess Who, had. He recognized early on, as I had, too, that if you wanted to make it you had to be writing songs. In the Reflections and the early Guess Who, I was the principal songwriter. Neil's lyrics were deep and esoteric compared to mine. I could never have written a song like "Sugar Mountain" or "Nowadays Clancy Can't Even Sing," and he was still in his teens when he wrote those. His career moved in incremental steps, going from playing all over Winnipeg to moving on to Thunder Bay where he met Stephen Stills, and from there to Toronto where he played with Rick James and Bruce Palmer, and ultimately to success in Los Angeles.

He told me recently that having an aneurysm a few years ago made him realize how precious life is and how much he wants to stick around for it as long as possible. He came to the conclusion that he no longer needed drugs or alcohol. The last time we were together we talked for over two hours, reminiscing about the old days in Winnipeg, Gretsch guitars, my echo unit from the Reflections. It was wonderful. He's in a really good space now. He hadn't written any new songs at that point and was worried that he might not be able to without any chemical enhancement, but I told him not to worry. When the inspiration came he'd feel it in his head and in his heart. A few weeks later I got an email from him, excitedly telling me that he'd been writing songs again and it felt really great.

Beyond the music we're both pretty simple guys. He collected antique cars, I collected antique guitars. He recently sold his car collection and I sold my Gretsches. We both spent our money on things we knew, and even though Neil used drugs he never ever became an addict or a casualty like David Crosby or Crazy Horse guitarist Danny Whitten. We also never got distracted by all the trappings of success and acclaim, like living in Beverly Hills mansions or travelling in private jets. Maybe that's just the Winnipegger in us.

One thing Neil has always enjoyed and benefited from and that I missed is the consistency of a longtime manager. Elliot Roberts has been the man behind Neil's career since 1968. He believes in Neil and has done so from day one. Neil will say, "I want to make this happen," and Elliot will do it. He never questions Neil's artistic vision; he supports it, and that allows it to flourish. They're a team in the best sense of what that means. Each brings his individual strength to the relationship: Neil's talent and Elliot's business acumen. My own managers or record labels could take me only so far. I could have broken through in more countries around the world, but they were unable to make that next step. If I'd had Gilles Paquin as my manager throughout my career, that career might have been a lot different. However, I'm eternally grateful that I have him with me now.

Like me, Gilles Paquin is a Winnipeg product, although he grew up in the francophone community while I was on the other side of the Red River. Early in his career, he worked for five years in the CBC's French- and English-language departments as a director/producer, producing music and variety television. Starting in the mid 70s, Gilles partnered with Sam Katz in Nite Out Entertainment, and the pair went on to become major concert promoters in western Canada (Sam Katz is currently Winnipeg's mayor). Throughout his career, Gilles has worked with some of the world's greatest entertainers, including Billy Joel, Alabama, Muddy Waters, and Bill Cosby. Like me, Gilles never stops. He went on to build his own entertainment empire, Paquin Entertainment, with offices in Winnipeg and Toronto. With his wife, Patti, he also operates Koba Entertainment, which produces family-oriented television and touring stage productions. His affinity for live performance and theatrical production as well as family entertainment is unmatched. Besides me, he also manages Canadian singer/songwriter icon Buffy Sainte-Marie. Gilles is widely respected in the entertainment business and has an impressive track record. And he's one of the good guys in the shark pool.

Gilles came into my life and career much later; we've been together about ten years now. Here's my reality: I wake up every morning or sometimes in the middle of the night with one, two, or ten ideas. I have a head full of ideas. But nobody, whether it's been managers or wives, has ever helped me with those ideas until Gilles Paquin. It's always been a fight upstream to get someone to listen seriously to them. Until Gilles, they'd all say, "You can't do that." Whereas he'll listen and say something like, "Okay, this idea is crazy, those two will never work, but this other one we might be able to make work, so let's get started on it." And the next day I'll have more ideas and he'll look at those. He's my dream maker, but he's also the guy who's able to say, "You can't juggle twelve balls in the air at once, so let's just focus on these three ideas." Gilles listens and gives me the kind of straightforward advice I need, without just shooting everything down or saying that none of my ideas will work, however fanciful or out there they may be. And it's more than just a business partnership; he's the friend and confidant I never had. Over the years I've made some terrible mistakes, trusting people whom I thought could be trusted. Gilles is the antithesis of all that. He's the friend and manager I wish I'd had guiding me throughout my entire career. For a lot of reasons, I didn't have that consistency, but now I just want to extend my life and career ten years further to be able to enjoy this relationship we have and to keep it working.

But that isn't to say I haven't known fantastic people in the music industry. One of them was Charlie Fach. I first met Charlie in New York while I was still in the Guess Who. He was a label executive at Mercury Records, and he impressed me as a nice guy, someone I hoped I might work with down the road. He was already a veteran of the music business, having worked for the RCA Camden and Smash labels. During that brief encounter, Charlie gave me a bit of advice that helped to change my life. He told me to always label my demo tapes with my name written prominently in red ink. That way my tape would stand out immediately in a pile of other demo tapes, and if it fell into the trash can they'd see your name and hopefully recognize it and give the tape a listen.

That's kind of what happened to ultimately bring Bachman-Turner Overdrive to his attention at Mercury Records: he recognized my name among a pile of tapes. His advice to me a few years earlier paid off. Otherwise we might have ended up in that trash can with god knows who else. Brave Belt, my post–Guess Who country-rock experiment, was on its last legs. I'd kept it alive using my Guess Who nest egg to the tune of some $97,000. We'd been signed to Reprise Records on Neil Young's recommendation, but our debut album was too mellow to attract a wider audience. Also, no one knew it was that Guess Who "American Woman" guy behind the band. We'd recorded a second album, but by then I'd recruited Fred Turner into the group. It was me, former Guess Who lead singer Chad Allan, Fred Turner, and my youngest brother, Robbie, on drums. Chad Allan quit the group in the midst of those sessions, though, because with Fred's booming voice we were moving into more of a rock direction, away from the mellow Gordon Lightfootish stuff that Chad preferred. After a baptism of fire in Thunder Bay, where we discovered that what we did best was straightforward meat 'n' potatoes rock 'n' roll, Brave Belt had transformed into what would become BTO.

Reprise dropped us after the second Brave Belt album, so I financed the recording sessions for what was intended to be *Brave Belt III*, featuring our harder-edged sound. But the album was rejected by more than twenty record labels. Dispirited and almost bankrupt, I'd decided to break up the band in the face of what seemed like universal indifference. Then I got a phone call from Charlie Fach at Mercury Records in Chicago. I could hear "Gimme Your Money Please" playing in the background as we talked. He'd spotted my name on the tape box, given the tape a listen, and liked what he heard. "Is the whole album like this?" he asked. He was calling to offer us a contract. Talk about in the nick of time or right down to the wire.

Without Charlie deciding to give me a shot, I don't know where I'd be right now. I was blackballed in Canada after my exit from the Guess Who. That band exerted considerable influence in the Canadian music scene and wasted little time in getting the industry up here to write me off. I couldn't even get any bookings. But Charlie knew none of that, and made the decision to sign me and the band based exclusively on the music and my reputation in the States as a hit songwriter. "I'll give you a chance, kid." (He always called me kid.) That was another life-altering moment.

When he signed us, Charlie told me that I should include "Bachman" in our name. Given my track record, he said, it would generate some interest in the band, which would open up promotional opportunities as well as establish me as the leader. It was wise advice. We weren't Brave Belt anymore, although we'd still get the occasional country-rock booking and end up blowing the walls off the place. So we became Bachman-Turner Overdrive.

Charlie always dealt fairly with us, and we respected him. Mercury had the ability to get our name and our records out there. We reciprocated by touring relentlessly, playing anywhere and everywhere there was interest in the group. Wherever we went, the records were there and on the radio, and as a result, sales spiked.

Near the end of 1975, I heard that the federal government was about to close a tax loophole that allowed you to buy guaranteed annual annuities. These deferred your tax burden by paying out in smaller amounts in later years; you'd be taxed on those reduced sums rather than on the larger total. As investments, they also accrued interest. Our financial adviser had suggested that BTO take advantage of this before it was too late. Now, Mercury Records owed us roughly $925,000 in royalties for that year, but they'd be payable after the loophole closed. So I phoned Charlie and explained the situation, and he agreed to fly up to Vancouver with the cheque. But when he arrived he presented us with a cheque for $1 million, saying he'd take the additional amount from our next royalty period. That's the kind of guy he was. He said he was absolutely beside himself on the plane ride carrying a million-dollar cheque in his pocket. We combined the royalty cheque with our tour earnings and were able to take advantage of the annuities, and to this day each of us still receives an annual six-figure cheque. Ironically, none of the guys in the band wanted to go with the annuities. If we hadn't we would have forfeited more than half of our multi-million dollars to the taxman.

Charlie was one of the key ingredients in BTO's massive success. Years later, when he started Compleat Records in the 1980s, I was the first act to call him, and we continued our relationship.

The other component of BTO's mega-success in the 1970s was Bruce Allen. He came into my life at a time when Brave Belt couldn't get any bookings based out of Winnipeg. Bruce was a booking agent on the West Coast who I was vaguely aware of, so I called him out of the blue to see if he could find us some work. He said he could keep us busy out there, so I made the decision to relocate the group to Vancouver. A week before that, we'd driven all the way to Toronto in January—from 40 below zero to 40 below zero—to play some club in Etobicoke for two nights. We'd just broken even on that trip. Bruce got us two weeks in a Vancouver club for good money, so we drove out, this time going from 40 below to 50 above. Moving to Vancouver was a no-brainer. Now I knew why prairie people sold the farm and moved to the West Coast.

When Charlie Fach offered to sign the band, he asked that we bring along our manager when we signed the contract. We didn't have a manager. For all intents and purposes I had that role, but Mercury Records was expecting the band to have a separate manager; it was the tried-and-true way of the music business. So, with no one else to turn to, I asked Bruce—who as our booking agent was keeping us busy with gigs in and around Vancouver—if he'd like a free trip to Chicago. I offered to throw in a steak dinner at a fancy restaurant and a couple of tickets to a Cubs game. "Sure" was his immediate reply. The only condition I then laid on him was that he act as the band's manager. He had no idea what that entailed, but I assured him I'd fill him in on the way. All I needed, I told him, was a guy to say to the record label, "They want … They need … They have to have." I taught Bruce how to be a manager. He took only 10 percent, but since I'd already secured the record contract, he stepped on board a train that was already leaving the station full speed ahead. Bruce learned how to drive that train by riding with us. And he took those lessons with him to Loverboy and Bryan Adams on his way to becoming one of the biggest managers in the business.

We promised Mercury we'd work our asses off, and in that first year we logged over three hundred gigs, criss-crossing the continent. Bruce went on the road with us to every single date. After each gig, I'd tell him everything that went wrong and everything that went right. We roomed together on the road and would debrief each other on the show back at the hotel. He ultimately left his booking agency with partner Sam Feldman, but before that he'd call Sam every night no matter where we were, and we were constantly on the move, giving Sam instructions over the phone. Then he'd hang up, turn to me, and say, "Okay, Randy, what went wrong tonight?" He was the epitome of the hands-on manager, not the kind at the end of a long-distance call. He was in the trenches getting dirty with us. Bruce's determination to make BTO a success was as great as mine. Eventually, he got bored standing in the wings during our sets, so he started calling the lighting cues to the light man because he knew the songs and when to have a spot on so-and-so for a solo, all of that. He really busted his hump for the band.

My only regret with Bruce is that when I left BTO after a heated meeting in 1977, he chose not to stay with me. There are plenty of examples of managers who continue to work with the band as well as a member who leaves for a solo career; Peter Gabriel and Genesis is just one. But it was an emotionally charged situation, and Bruce opted to stick with the band. He was betting on Fred being able to carry the load as BTO's front man, singer, and principal songwriter, but Fred couldn't do it all. I wish Bruce had had a wider perspective or scope to see that the music business was evolving and we needed to evolve, too. We were overworked and needed to take a break. Take six months or a year off, do whatever we needed to do to recharge our batteries—whether that was buying a boat and sailing off for a while, or in Robbie's case, buying guns and a tank—then come back together renewed and refreshed. But it was a tread-mill and we were caught on it. We'd run out of steam. I thought I had a big solo career ahead of me and figured I didn't need Bruce Allen, and he figured BTO could still carry on successfully without me. We were both wrong. Instead it was one of those situations where someone says, "F you, I know better than you."

Bruce and I were a formidable team, and BTO wouldn't have become what it was without him. Together we made BTO unstoppable. He told me years later that his mistake was in underestimating me. He also said that I'm the only guy he once managed who he doesn't have to chase for his royalties. I've always paid him.

Songwriter and record producer Ralph Murphy has been a dear friend of mine for many decades. We first met in London on the ill-fated Guess Who trip in February 1967. Even in the brief time we were there, Ralph and I managed to write a song or two together. That was our initial connection, but it's grown far beyond that since. Like us, Ralph was a Canadian musician in London. Somehow, we met on a street after I noticed this guy wearing a Canadian flag pin on his jacket. That was Ralph. At age nineteen, he was signed to Mills Music and writing songs for British recording artists. Even though he now lives in Nashville, where he's worked for ASCAP (American Society of Composers,

Authors and Publishers, an organization that collects royalties for songwriters from public performances) for many years, and I'm out on the West Coast or in Toronto, we keep in touch and run into each other often. He and I always go to the annual ASCAP awards together.

Ralph has written songs for the likes of Randy Travis, Ray Price, Don Williams, Kathy Mattea, Little Texas, Shania Twain, Brotherhood of Man, Jeannie C. Riley, Crystal Gayle, and Ronnie Milsap, among others, and has published the how-to book *Murphy's Laws of Songwriting*. He also produced hit records by April Wine, Mashmakan, and Brutus, to name a few.

What's also amazing about our relationship is that as a boy he lived on the same property I now own on Salt Spring Island. Ralph's mother came to Canada as a young woman after answering an ad in a British newspaper for a nanny. She was employed by a family who originally lived on that island property. Although born in Britain, Ralph spent his early years on Salt Spring with his mother before the family relocated to Ottawa. I found this out years later when we were at a big music industry event on Vancouver Island. He and I and his mother were travelling on the ferry to the island when she pointed and said, "Oh, look, Ralph, it's Salt Spring Island, where we used to live." So I said to her, "That's where I live now." She then pulled out this old black-and-white photo of Ralph as a youngster dressed like Little Lord Fauntleroy, very British schoolboy–looking, taken by a lake. I told her that the tree in the background looked like the tree still on my property. So she asked me what my address was, and when I told her she replied, "That's where we lived!" Talk about coincidence. Ralph and I are still friends with Tony Hiller of Mills Music in the U.K., who I also met on that 1967 Guess Who trip. Tony's now in his eighties. These guys are old and dear friends, and that friendship is all about music.

I'd never heard of a mixer until I met Phil Ramone. Up to that point, the record producer simply mixed the recorded tracks at the end of a session to balance the instruments and vocals. When we came to Toronto to record the album *A Wild Pair* for Coca-Cola in the fall of 1967, our producer, Jack Richardson, told us after the recording sessions were completed that he wanted a fresh set of ears to mix the tracks. So he brought in the boy with the golden ears, Phil Ramone from New York. Phil hadn't attended any of the recording sessions and hadn't heard the songs until he listened to the completed tapes. He then objectively mixed the instruments and voices to get an optimum sound. It was a challenging job, too, because we'd been working with a lot of additional players on the tracks, some of Toronto's top jazz players. The result was phenomenal. *A Wild Pair* still sounds great. It was such a step up for us hearing Phil's work; it sounded like a professional recording.

Phil Ramone was a classically trained violinist who'd studied at Juilliard, the top music school in North America. In 1959, he and his partner, Jack Arnold, opened A&R (Arnold and Ramone) Studios in New York, and it quickly became a popular studio for jazz and pop artists. When Jack Richardson made the decision to sign us to his production company, Nimbus 9, after the success of *A Wild Pair,* he took us down to A&R Studios in September 1968 to record what would become *Wheatfield Soul,* which included the single "These Eyes." We loved working at

A&R Studios, and the sound we achieved there remains impressive. Just listen to "These Eyes" if you don't believe me. Pretty damn awesome, even some forty-five years later. That was the magic Phil created at A&R Studios and the reason why everyone wanted to record there.

Because I got to know Phil, I'd go in during our off-hours and watch him recording people like Dionne Warwick with Burt Bacharach there. I observed everything and soaked it up like a sponge, just sitting in a corner quietly watching. I applied the lessons learned from that experience when recording Brave Belt and later BTO. From Phil Ramone, I learned about things like microphone placement and mixing, all things I needed to know to be a producer.

Phil Ramone went on to produce several of Paul Simon's solo albums, winning a Grammy for *Still Crazy After All These Years*. The list of artists who've had the pleasure of working with Phil reads like a who's who of contemporary music from the last forty years, and includes Ray Charles, Chicago, Natalie Cole, Bob Dylan, Gloria Estefan, Aretha Franklin, Billy Joel, Elton John, Quincy Jones, Julian Lennon, Madonna, Barry Manilow, Paul McCartney, George Michael, Luciano Pavarotti, and Carly Simon, as well as Canadian teenage jazz pop sensation Nikki Yanofsky. Phil Ramone has left a real legacy. Sadly, he passed away in early 2013. All of us who worked with him and knew him are forever grateful to have had the opportunity.

I owe Larry Brown an enormous debt of gratitude for helping the Guess Who land a steady gig when we really needed a break. After our disastrous trip to London to tour and promote the band, we returned to Winnipeg humiliated and staggering under the weight of a $25,000 debt. That's in 1967 dollars, so you can imagine how much that would be today. Besides all the costs of shipping our newly purchased gear and new clothes overseas, we found out we had to pay back King Records owner Rita King for all the money she'd spent promoting our record in the U.K. Her partner, Philip Solomon, who owned Radio Caroline, had had her buying airtime from him for "His Girl"—and as soon as she stopped buying it, the single fell off the charts. The way pirate radio worked was that you bought the airtime for your record just as you'd buy air time for a commercial. That's the way it was, and the owners of the pirate stations made a fortune. We were paying the same rates as a commercial for toothpaste or Corn Flakes. And if your record happened to be longer than that, it would cost you more for airtime. It was extortion, but we didn't know it at the time. So when we refused to sign an exclusive contract with Rita, she charged all that money back to us. In other words, we got royally screwed.

Rather than break up and assume a quarter of the debt each, we were determined to soldier on. Coming to our rescue was CBC Winnipeg, who asked us to perform weekly as the house band on their nationally televised *Let's Go*. The show was the Winnipeg edition of the *Music Hop* series, which ran weekdays at five-thirty p.m. from different cities. Winnipeg's day was Thursday. Larry Brown was the show's producer, and over the two years we acted as house band, we developed a close relationship with him. *Let's Go* gave us a national audience, and besides that it paid us $1100 a week, which we put directly towards our debt payments. We supported ourselves with gigs on weekends.

Just before the second season began, Larry approached Burton and me with an offer. If we wrote some songs and he liked what we came up with, we could perform them on the show. His suggestion was the catalyst for the creation of the Bachman-Cummings songwriting partnership. We now had a goal to motivate us, and we accepted the challenge with the utmost earnestness. In due time, we were debuting several of our compositions on *Let's Go,* including an early version of "These Eyes" as well as several of the songs that would end up on our *Wheatfield Soul* and *Canned Wheat* albums. Without that generous offer from Larry Brown, our songwriting partnership may not have developed or flourished to the extent that it did, yielding gold records for the Guess Who. I owe Larry a deep debt of gratitude for nurturing in Burton and me the dream that we could become songwriters.

Songwriting is my life. I've been fortunate to have written or co-written a number of hits over my career, and I never tire of telling the stories about how those songs were born. But I never thought of turning those stories and those songs into a concert. It was Ray Davies, the Kinks' leader, visionary, and songwriter, who gave me the inspiration for my Every Song Tells a Story concert series, album, and DVD. Back in the late 1990s, I was in London when a friend I knew there, Rupert Perry, who was head of EMI/Capitol Records in Europe, called me up and invited me to see Ray Davies's Storyteller show at the Drury Lane Theatre. I arrived a bit late because, although it was only a few minutes away from my apartment, I got lost. (By the way, owning my own apartment in London was a giant step up from sharing a

hotel room with the other guys in the Guess Who back in 1967.)
The thing about London is that there's no grid—streets go every
which way and start and end wherever. So I lost my way walking
to the theatre. Finally I hailed a cab and said to the driver, "Can
you take me to the Drury Lane Theatre?" and he says, "Sure"
and drives me around the corner. There it was. Cost me £4 to go
around the corner. When I arrived the show had already started
and the opening act was on. In the lobby, one of the attendants
was taking down the show's posters because this was the final
night of the concert series. I asked him for a couple and he gave
them to me, no problem. Ray followed the opening act; he had
another guitar player with him, just the two of them onstage. He
talked about each song and then the two of them would play that
song on acoustic guitars. It was very enjoyable getting the inside
scoop on songs I loved.

After the show, Rupert took me backstage to meet Ray
Davies. He signed one of the posters for me and one for my son
Tal, who's a major Kinks aficionado. I told Ray what a fascinating show it had been and what a great concept he had of telling
all the stories behind his best-known songs like "You Really Got
Me," "Sunny Afternoon," "Lola," and "Come Dancing." Ray
replied, "You can do that, too, mate. You've got stories to tell
about your songs." I thought it was a terrific idea, but instead of
calling it "Storyteller" I decided on "Every Song Tells a Story"—I
had this book on guitars that included the line "Every guitar tells
a story," so I simply adapted that. Unlike Ray's production, I
didn't want it to be an acoustic show. After the story, I wanted a
band to present the song as people remember it rather than as a
stripped-down rearrangement. It completes the memory for the

audience. So I went out with this concept, backed by my band, and it's been extremely successful.

Throughout my life and my career I've been fortunate to know or meet people who've been able to provide me with either valuable life lessons or a step up in my musical endeavours. No one ever accomplishes anything alone. I've made mistakes and I've trusted the wrong people sometimes, but it's all part of life's experiences. I am eternally grateful to the above-mentioned people, who've provided many of the all-important pieces to the puzzle and helped me achieve my goals and dreams. To each of them, I tip my hat in sincere appreciation.

You've met so many of your
musical heroes over the years.
Is there anyone you would like
to have met or meet?

Jimi Hendrix at the Marquee Club in London, 1967.

It's true, I've been very fortunate throughout my career to have met a lot of my personal musical heroes, like Chuck Berry, Little Richard, Bo Diddley, B.B. King, Gene Vincent, Hank Marvin from the Shadows, and guitar great Jeff Beck. I've even had the opportunity to play alongside or record with many of them. Still, there are some I never had the chance to meet.

I would have liked to have met Jimi Hendrix. He virtually reinvented rock guitar playing back in the 60s. He's the guy who took blues and psychedelic music, put it all together, and popularized it for everyone, black or white. He was a guitar innovator who wasn't just copping old blues licks, as many of his contemporaries were doing at the time. I read somewhere that Eric Burdon once said Jimi Hendrix took the blues from the Mississippi Delta to Venus, and that's so true. He broke down boundaries and pushed the envelope until it didn't look like an envelope anymore.

I saw him once when he was Jimmy James playing the Cafe Wha in New York. He wasn't Jimi Hendrix yet. As Jimmy James, he'd been playing for years throughout the southern U.S.

on what was known as the chitlin' circuit, backing a variety of black performers, including for a time Little Richard as well as the Isley Brothers. But every time he'd step forward to take a solo he'd be fired afterwards because his playing was so flamboyant that he upstaged the star performer. There was no holding him back.

Linda Keith, Rolling Stones guitarist Keith Richards's girl-friend at the time, spotted Jimi playing a Greenwich Village club with a band called the Blue Flames, and although she failed to convince Stones manager Andrew Loog Oldham of Jimi's star potential (rumour has it Mick and Keith were nonplussed when they saw him perform), she did succeed in getting Animals bass player Chas Chandler to check him out. The Animals had just completed their final U.S. tour before breaking up (Eric Burdon would put together a new lineup shortly thereafter back in the U.K.), so Chas was looking to move into artist management. Suitably bowled over by Jimi's prodigious talent, Chas convinced him to come to London, and even bought him the plane ticket. Hendrix had one qualifier: he wanted to meet his personal guitar heroes Eric Clapton and Jeff Beck. Chas knew both guitar-ists. Within days of his arrival, Jimi Hendrix was a sensation in London.

When the Guess Who was in London in February 1967, Hendrix was the talk of the town. We heard him on the radio over there. This was six months before he made his triumphant return to America at the Monterey Pop Festival. In London, everyone was frizzing their hair like him, playing Stratocasters, cranking up their Marshall stacks. We didn't see him then, but we were aware of his influence. When I heard the first Jimi

Hendrix Experience album, it absolutely blew me away. It was revolutionary. And they're still releasing his recordings: they keep digging up more studio jams and putting them out for newer generations to discover his magic. Hendrix loved to play with anyone. If he'd lived, I think he'd have moved more into the kind of fusion jazz that became popular soon after he died. But he had so much management conflict and so many personal issues surrounding him at the time that it's no surprise he died young. He's another example of an incredible talent lost to drugs.

Jimi Hendrix's guitar tone and approach to the instrument was so unique and distinctive. His music was much less cluttered than Cream's, where Jack Bruce was very busy on bass and Clapton had a denser tone to his guitar because he used a Gibson. There was much less space in Cream's sound compared to Hendrix, who was playing a Fender Stratocaster, which gave him a sharper, trebly sound when played through a Marshall amp. When he cuts into the solo in "Hey Joe" it's so biting and compelling. I'd heard the Leaves doing a fast jingle-jangle folk-rock version of "Hey Joe," and Tim Rose had done a slow folkie version, but Hendrix rearranged it with a funky tempo, adding that Shadows kind of ending where the bass and the guitar do these single-note climbs together. That was very cool.

After the Guess Who came back from the U.K., we'd play "Hey Joe" and other Hendrix songs. Burton would back-comb his hair to make it all frizzy and Garry Peterson, Jim Kale, and I would play as a three-piece behind him. We used to really sound like Hendrix with my Herzog and the giant whammy bar Gar Gillies made me for my Strat. Garry Peterson could play that busy jazzy stuff like Mitch Mitchell. We introduced Hendrix's music to Winnipeg audiences months before his debut album came out there. It was cool to be ahead of that curve.

Listen to Jimi Hendrix with Buddy Miles on drums and it's not the same. It's a funk beat. He may have felt more of an affinity with Buddy and his playing, being a black guy, but Hendrix's true sound was with Mitch Mitchell on drums. Mitch did all that busy drumming, but it fit underneath Hendrix's playing. It filled the holes. The best Hendrix is the original Jimi Hendrix Experience. Noel Redding, a guitar player who picked up the bass for the first time when he joined the band, wasn't comfortable or confident about being a Jack Bruce–style virtuoso bass player soloing against the guitar playing. He'd been auditioning for Eric Burdon's new Animals on guitar when Eric suggested he meet Jimi's manager, Chas Chandler. Chas suggested Noel try bass and jam with Hendrix, who was still a complete unknown. With Jimi and Mitch flying on their instruments, Noel Redding's job was to hold it together and be the underpinning of the song structure, nothing more. He also created spaces in the music, not just fill for fill's sake. They each had a role and they each fit it perfectly. When Hendrix started playing with his black buddies it got funky, but he lost some of the sonic exploration and experimentation that the Experience had. They were all great players who brought their own style and sound, and that affected what Hendrix was playing. Those first three Jimi Hendrix Experience albums—*Are You Experienced, Axis: Bold as Love,* and *Electric Ladyland*—remain definitive.

Jimi Hendrix never regarded himself as a singer and didn't like his voice; he'd always ask his producers to bury it in the mix. But the fact is that he had a very distinctive vocal style. Sure, he wasn't Paul McCartney or Eric Burdon, but you recognize his voice as soon as you hear it. It's soulful and sincere. I can identify with him on this. I never saw myself as a lead singer and never sang lead in any of my bands, including the Guess Who, until I formed Brave Belt. That's when I found my voice, so to speak. But I could never shake the belief that it wasn't a lead voice. When we went into the studio to record *BTO II* and I gave Fred Turner the lyrics to "Takin' Care of Business," he handed them right back to me: "No, you sing it. It's your song." He wasn't saying that in a nasty way, just recognizing that when we'd conceived the song onstage at a Vancouver club after Fred lost his voice, it was me singing it. All I was doing was singing the lyrics to my old Guess Who–era composition "White Collar Worker" over a simple three-chord progression and adding a new chorus based on a radio deejay I'd heard on the way to the gig, who'd shouted out, "This is Darryl B on CFUN radio, takin' care of business!" Even though "You Ain't Seen Nothing Yet" became our biggest hit by far all over the world, I was still uncomfortable with my voice on it and would turn the radio off whenever it came on. But you can't argue with a hit record, so I became a lead singer. Hey, everyone said Neil Young couldn't sing, but he's done okay.

What a lot of people don't know is that Jimi Hendrix spent time in Canada. He had relatives in Vancouver and had lived with them as a youngster, and had even done some gigging there early in his music career, playing lead guitar with Bobby Taylor and the Vancouvers in 1962 alongside guitarist Tommy Chong, later of Cheech and Chong fame. The band had a residency at a club called Dante's Inferno before Jimi returned to Seattle.

I wish I'd met Texas blues guitarist Stevie Ray Vaughan. Although influenced by Hendrix and Clapton, he took the blues back to its roots and played with such intensity and fire. Every note came from deep within him; he really felt what he was playing. Stevie Ray was rootsier than Hendrix, more Albert and Freddy King–influenced, and he was dedicated to that authentic style and sound. But like Hendrix, he had a distinctive sound playing an old battered Strat, except he used a cleaner, more top-end trebly tone that bit your head off. He could bend two and three strings at a time to great effect. Stevie Ray was so well respected in the guitar fraternity that even guitar gods like Eric Clapton, Buddy Guy, and Robert Cray were fans. He recorded some outstanding albums backed by his band Double Trouble, but one of his best performances was backing David Bowie on "Let's Dance." That's the recording that brought Stevie Ray Vaughan to public prominence. The real tragedy was that after years of substance abuse—he had a weakness for Crown Royal and cocaine—he'd straightened out and turned his life around only to die soon after in a tragic helicopter accident. Eric Clapton was supposed to be on that same helicopter.

I've never met Eric Clapton. He's kind of my ideal of the cool guitar player. The tone from my Herzog on "American Woman" is based on what's called Clapton's "Woman Tone" that he used with Cream. "I Feel Free" was one of my and Burton's favourite songs back in 1967. That's his Woman Tone on that recording: a Marshall turned on full, the treble on his Gibson guitar turned all the way off, and the pickup selector set on the neck pickup. It's very bassy and distorted, but the notes still pierce that dense sound fog. You can hear that tone to great effect on Cream's big hit "Sunshine of Your Love." I'd love to meet Clapton and maybe even play on a track with him. But we've never crossed paths, and I don't even know if he knows who I am. We don't travel in the same circles.

Clapton got his start with the Yardbirds, who were a South London blues quintet until they recorded a pop song, "For Your Love," in early 1965. This was not the music Clapton wanted to play, and in fact he plays only on the middle eight section that gets chunky on the guitar chords. Incidentally, that's Brian Auger on the harpsichord on that track. He quit the band following the session to dedicate himself to playing the blues. Jeff Beck replaced him. Talk about putting in your thumb and pulling out a plum. Jeff took the Yardbirds into sonic explorations with songs like "Shapes of Things" and "Over Under Sideways Down."

Meanwhile, Clapton joined blues stalwart John Mayall, and together they recorded the classic Clapton blues album *John Mayall's Bluesbreakers with Eric Clapton*. Often called the Beano album after the comic book Clapton is reading on the cover, that's the album that earned him the epithet "God"—you'd see "Clapton is God" written on walls in London. The Clapton sound was born: a 1960 Gibson Les Paul guitar through a Marshall amp. That sound would go on to define lead guitar for the next forty years.

Clapton later formed Cream with bassist Jack Bruce and Ginger Baker on drums, taking that name because they were regarded as the cream of the crop on their respective instruments. Their debut album, *Fresh Cream*, knocked my socks off when I heard it in late 1966. *Disraeli Gears* was their big 1967 breakthrough album, but Cream was best as a live act. They were known to jam up to twenty-five minutes on some songs onstage, each guy in his own musical world yet still bringing it all back together. That's the jazz aesthetic: beginning with a familiar song then going off into jam land before bringing it back to that same familiar refrain. Cream applied that to blues rock. *Wheels of Fire* was a brilliant album because it included an entire disc recorded live along with a studio album. "Crossroads" remains a Clapton classic, and it's a bit of a rite of passage for novice guitar players to learn the solos in that song.

Although Clapton went on to great success with Blind Faith, Derek and the Dominos (the electric "Layla" anyone?), and in his solo career, he's never burned with the same intensity as he did with Cream. When they reunited in 2005 at the Royal Albert Hall, where they'd played their farewell gig in 1968, it wasn't the same because they'd changed their equipment. Clapton wasn't playing a Gibson through a Marshall stack. That's the definitive Clapton sound.

I have met Jeff Beck and Jimmy Page, who joined the Yardbirds with Jeff before replacing him on lead guitar, so two out of three Yardbirds guitarists ain't bad. Page later transformed what was left of the band into Led Zeppelin, and the rest is history. I loved the Yardbirds. Clapton, Beck, and Page are still out there doing it, too. They each play in a distinctive style and sound that's instantly recognizable.

I first met Jimmy Page in Cleveland in 1967 when he was still in the Yardbirds. I next ran into him two years later in Led Zepplin when we both played the Seattle Pop Festival in July

1969, a weekend-long event that drew over 150,000 people. We were on the bill with all these amazing artists like the Doors, Ike and Tina Turner, the Byrds, Chicago, Santana, the Flying Burrito Brothers, Lonnie Mack, and Chuck Berry. Led Zeppelin was also on the bill; they were still building their name and reputation in America at the time, and it might have even been their first U.S. tour. One thing I remember about them was that after their set, they quickly changed their clothes and went out to the back of the crowd, this massive sea of humanity, to watch all the other acts perform. No pretensions or star trips; they were genuinely interested in seeing and experiencing all the other artists. Even before their set they'd be out there in the audience digging the bands. I thought that was very cool. How many artists of their calibre do that today?

I wish I'd met Buddy Holly, one of my early heroes. I remember the announcement of his death and being stunned. On February 3, 1959, my friends and I had been planning to drive down to Moorhead, Minnesota, where Winnipeggers often went to shop, until we saw the headline in the newspaper that morning and heard the news on the radio. I can't say it was the day the music died, as Don McLean wrote in "(Bye Bye Miss) American Pie," but I do know that it affected me deeply. Buddy could have been as big or bigger than Elvis, and had the edge over the King because he wrote his own songs and had begun producing his own recordings. His last session was "True Love Ways," where he incorporated orchestration and jazz sax. It was an indication of where he might have gone had he lived. The first record Chad Allan and the Reflections ever recorded and released was entitled "Tribute to Buddy Holly," concerning his fateful airplane crash. It was written by U.K. songwriter Geoff Goddard and had been recorded there by Mike Berry and the Outlaws.

To my eternal regret, I missed meeting Elvis Presley. BTO's manager, Bruce Allen, and my brother Robbie didn't tell me that the band had been invited to meet Elvis. This was in 1975. We'd been endlessly on tour and finally had a few days off. I wanted to go home and see my wife and kids; I'd been away for months and was convinced my kids wouldn't know me if I didn't get back soon. The other guys in the band knew I wanted to go home, so they didn't tell me we had an opportunity to meet the King himself. Elvis was my first introduction to rock 'n' roll—the first record I ever bought was "Hound Dog" backed by "Don't Be Cruel" after seeing him on *The Ed Sullivan Show* on my friend's television (we still didn't own one). As I mentioned earlier, Elvis had adopted Takin' Care of Business as his logo and I'd heard that he loved our song. Years later, I learned that he actually sang "Takin' Care of Business" once and that it was recorded at a rehearsal or sound check. It's in the vaults somewhere. I'd love to hear that.

So I flew home, and unbeknownst to me, the guys flew to Las Vegas to meet Elvis at his request. The way it went down was that the guys were ushered into a room, Elvis walked in and looked at them all, and then asked, "Which one of you guys wrote 'Takin' Care of Business'?" And I wasn't there. So I never got to meet the King. Two years later he was dead.

Beyond his music, I always felt an affinity to Elvis because he was a twin whose sibling, Jesse Garon Presley, died in childbirth. He was haunted by that throughout his life, the fact that he lived and his brother didn't. The same thing happened with me: I was a twin but my sibling died at birth. I've often felt that same "Why me" and "What if" emotion.

I briefly met Mick Jagger when the Guess Who played the giant SARS festival north of Toronto in July 2003, but it was so insane backstage around the Stones that it was merely a quick hello and handshake. I'd love to be able to sit down and chat with him, but he's so busy that it's not likely to happen. I do have a fabulous painting of Mick Jagger that I'd wanted to get signed, and when I went to the Stones concert at Toronto's Air Canada Centre in the summer of 2013, although I didn't get to meet him in person, through the band's road manager, Mick signed the painting and personalized it. I'm grateful to Randy Phillips from AGI and Lorne Saifer, who called in favours to get that done for me.

I would someday like to meet Paul McCartney. He's someone I'd be humbled to be in the presence of. I'm not sure he knows who I am, although I did hear that he once told the CBC he was a Guess Who fan. That would mean the world to me, being the original Beatlemaniac who sat through a half-dozen showings of *A Hard Day's Night* at the Garrick Theatre in Winnipeg back in August 1964. My dad had to send the West Kildonan police to find me. I don't know how many years Sir Paul will be touring, but he's certainly worth seeing. He's a real live Beatle who still plays Beatles songs. I've met and played with Ringo Starr, and that was a thrill beyond belief, but Paul was part of the creative team that wrote all those Beatles songs and sang many of them. I also wish I'd met John Lennon, as he was my favourite Beatle—their leader, the captain of the ship. Lennon's songs were always edgy rock 'n' roll. I modelled the way I stood onstage and bounced to the beat after him. John did that to keep Ringo in time, and in Brave Belt and BTO, I used the same trick to keep my brother Robbie in time as well.

Musicians often complain about
life on the road in a band.
You've lived that life for decades.
What was life like on the road for you?

Loading the station wagon for a Chad Allan
and the Reflections gig, circa 1964.

People generally assume that being a musician is a glamorous life, and it is—for one, maybe two hours a day at the most when you're onstage. It's the same thing as being an actor in the theatre. For those two hours onstage, you're rockin'. It doesn't matter whether it's an arena or a bar; you live for those two hours. But the rest of the time it's a lonely, tedious job. You're away from your family and your friends. Nowadays you can Skype, which is a bit better but never the same.

Back in the early days, I'd write letters home and then often get back before the letters arrived. Also, in those days long-distance calling was expensive. You had to go through an operator. So you didn't do that very often unless it was an emergency or a special occasion. You'd arrange a time each week, usually a Sunday evening, to call, but that would only make you lonelier because you'd just want to be home with the family. Because of the expense, you didn't waste a lot of time. You had to give each kid a few minutes on the phone so that it didn't appear as if Daddy didn't care. And, of course, you'd hear from your wife about the toilet that's leaking or the dog that ran away or the fight in the schoolyard or little Johnny's playing hockey now or there's no money to pay the hydro bill. You miss all this, and being so far away, there's nothing you can do. It was very hard on wives and kids: they had to hold down the fort sometimes for months on end. I missed so many of my kids' birthdays, I can't even count how many. I was on the road when our first child, Tal, was born in 1968. Lorne Saifer, who was my business partner at the time and later managed the Guess Who reunion band from 2000 to 2003, drove my wife to the hospital and held Tal. I didn't get to hold him for several days because we were on tour. I missed other births as well. The problem is you never know for certain when the baby is going to arrive.

For my son Brigham's birth, I took some time off before the due date so I'd be home. Then our manager, Bruce Allen, called us to say we had an offer for a big one-nighter in Portland, Oregon, with Heart and Steve Miller. We could fly down, play the gig, and fly back that same day. I didn't want to do it; Fred didn't want to do it. But the three single guys, Robbie and Blair and Bruce Allen, had no commitments, and together they managed to get Fred onside. So we end up doing the gig. Onstage, I was so preoccupied thinking about Lorayne and the baby. She was due that weekend. We were in the middle of "Roll On Down the Highway" and I lost where I was in the song. So I started to play a solo, only I wasn't sure if I was in the right spot. Fred and Blair were both looking at me, puzzled. I played the solo for about two or three minutes but didn't know how to come out of it, so I walked over to Fred in the midst of the song and hollered in his ear, "Where are we?" He looked at me with surprise and shouted back, "Portland!"

I came offstage shaking, then got into the car and drove straight home to Lynden, Washington. Brigham was born the next day. I told the guys I never wanted to do that again. We were rolling in money by that point, so we didn't need that one more gig.

It was heartbreaking on the road sometimes, looking into the audience and seeing guys just like me with their arm around their girlfriend or wife, knowing they were going home to some loving together and I was going back to an empty hotel room. Add to that all the travel—planes, trains, and automobiles— and the monotony of hotel rooms, truck stops, restaurants, and having to be cheery backstage at concert venues while meeting radio people or record-promotion people who've brought fans who won a contest to meet you. Then there were the scuzzy drug dealers hanging around backstage.

So as a musician, you live for those moments when you're actually onstage, and hopefully that gets you through the other twenty-two hours of the day. Then you finally get home from the tour, you kiss your wife and kids, you get to know each other again, and before you know it, you're looking to get back out on the road. It's this weird addiction. That's why I wrote "Rock Is My Life, This Is My Song."

Rock is my life and this is my song.
When we come into a new town,
Everybody's there.
When we play our music,
Candles light the air

When the music's over, over,
You wonder where we are.
I'm standing in the silence,
With my old guitar, my only friend.
Rock is my life and this is my song.

—RANDY BACHMAN, 1974

Robbie Robertson from the Band once said, "The road has taken many of the great ones: Hank Williams, Otis, Jimi, Janis, Elvis. It's a goddamn impossible way of life." It most certainly is. I can honestly say that on my way up and on my way down in many different bands, I've played almost every town, city, village, and crossroads in Canada, whether at a concert, a hockey arena, a high school dance, a wedding, or a social.

Back in 1973, when we first hit the road as Bachman-Turner Overdrive promoting our debut album, we played some three hundred shows in one year. If you allow for travel days, we had no time off that year. None. But I knew that the only way we were going to break the band was through sheer determination and a gruelling touring regimen. It was the tried-and-true method of getting your name out there: get yourselves out there. Looking back, I don't know how I did it. In the end, we achieved our goal, but we paid a steep price for it. For most of my children, I was away during much of their early lives and I missed seeing their development day by day. I wasn't there for the birth of several of them. I was in and out of their lives and their mother raised them. I never had a birthday at home from the age of nineteen until I was thirty-eight. As a travelling musician, you learn to adjust, to celebrate those kinds of events on days off, to have a birthday party on the next available night.

There's an awful lot of monotony being on the road. You don't know where you are or what hotel you're in; you put last night's hotel key into tonight's hotel lock; you try to get into your room only to find that it's another guy's room; you lose track of the daily routine of breakfast, lunch, and dinner. Your whole day is spent preparing for those two hours onstage that night. Everything else is both a blur and a distraction. You get up and you don't know where you are or what day it is. A road manager is knocking on your door telling you that the bus or the limo is leaving in ten minutes, so you throw everything together, including yourself, and head out the door. You arrive in the next town, the next stop on the tour, get to the hotel, throw your stuff in the room, maybe catch a couple of hours' sleep, get up and go do the sound check then back to the hotel and again try to get some sleep or a bite to eat (unless you chose to eat with the crew at the venue before the gig), then back in the bus or limo to the gig, play, the crowd goes nuts, you wave goodbye, back in the limo or bus and back to the hotel. Now take that whole routine and multiply it by twenty or fifty or a hundred. No wonder musicians don't know where they are.

Imagine going camping with your family. One kid cuts his finger and another gets sick from eating too much; your teenage daughter broke up with her boyfriend; the dog gets lost and you have to go find him; it rains and the tent leaks; the Coleman stove runs out of propane; you get a flat tire. Now picture all these things happening at the same time every night for ninety days, and that's what it's like being in a band on the road. There's always something you have to deal with, and nothing goes smoothly. You're waiting in the van because two of the guys slept past their wakeup call; you get up at four in the afternoon and want breakfast but the hotel stopped serving it at eleven. On and on. It's a circus played out on a daily basis.

I had my first experiences on the road back in the early 60s with Chad Allan and the Reflections. We'd leave school after four on Friday, drive to somewhere like Sioux Lookout, Ontario, to play a high school dance, do four one-hour sets, pack up, and drive right back, getting home the next morning, all for $150. The first few times we borrowed my dad's station wagon, but we ended up ripping the ceiling liner by pushing the drums into the back—we didn't have drum cases, so the legs and lug nuts would poke into the ceiling material.

Around this time, I dated a girl named Claudia, whose father, Glenn Senton, was the vehicle maintenance manager at Birchwood Motors in Winnipeg. I think I became the son Glenn never had. He was so generous and kind to me, a really sweet guy. He used to let us take cars off Birchwood's lot if we had to go out of town for a gig or to Minneapolis to record. No deposit, just have it back by Monday morning. I'd borrow my uncle Jack's trailer for the equipment, collapse our family tent over it by tying a rope around everything, and off we'd go. When we started making a bit more money, Glenn showed us the advantages of leasing a new car. So we leased two Buick station wagons and literally drove them into the ground. It was great because you could bring them back the following week and they'd have to fix them because they were leased. The

Guess Who went all the way to New York in those Buicks in the spring of 1965.

When Paul Cantor called us from New York to come down and tour in the U.S. with the Kingsmen and Dion and the Belmonts, we didn't hesitate. When opportunity knocks, if you choose not to answer, it may not knock again. Neil Young was willing to take that chance, and so were we. When we started touring farther afield, Neil asked us what it was like beyond Winnipeg. And those who weren't willing or able to see beyond Winnipeg are still there. I'll run into these guys and they'll say, "Remember me? I was in the Fifth?" or some other band. There were a lot of talented guys, contemporaries of ours on the Winnipeg scene, who were content to remain the local heroes and not take a chance somewhere else. But we seized every opportunity, and by the time we made it big with "These Eyes," we were already seasoned road warriors.

I remember I'd mail my old underwear home; my mom would wash it and give it to my younger brothers. I'd go out to JC Penney and buy three or four packages of white underwear and T-shirts every two weeks. I'd do this for months while we were on the road.

There were very few black people in Winnipeg when I was growing up—and when you did see a black person they were somebody famous, like an entertainer or a sports personality. So when we travelled through the southern United States in 1965 I was astonished to see the way black people lived and were treated. It was such an eye-opener for us innocent prairie kids. I grew up Ukrainian in the North End of Winnipeg, and we were subjected to some prejudice, being called Bohunks or Hunkies, but it was nothing like what we witnessed in the South. That was our first big tour and quite an experience.

As tour demands increased, our road manager, Russell Gillies, found us a green GMC half-ton panel truck for the equipment while we travelled in one of the leased station wagons. One time, the Buick broke down in the middle of the prairies and we ended up towing it behind the GMC truck. Burton and I stayed in the Buick, which was hooked up to the truck with a chain. So there we were, being pulled in a Buick down the Trans-Canada Highway. Somewhere in the night the chain broke and we careened off the highway into a ditch. We watched as the truck receded into the distance ahead, oblivious to the fact that they were no longer towing us. Burton and I managed to push the car onto the shoulder, and sat inside waiting for the other guys to discover we weren't behind them anymore. They must have gone at least ten miles before that realization hit them and, panicked, they turned around. They finally found us, but the chain had been thrown somewhere along the highway when it broke. Our roadie, Jim "Jumbo" Martin, had to lie on the hood of the truck, looking for the lost chain in the glow of headlights as one of the guys slowly drove it down the highway. Finally the chain was located and the Buick was hooked up again.

But the truck itself kept breaking down, and with no cell phones back then, we'd never know where Jumbo was; we'd arrive at a gig and the equipment wouldn't be there. So we decided to get an old Greyhound bus. At least we and the equipment would arrive at the same time. Grey Goose Bus Lines in Emerson, Manitoba, at the Canada–U.S. border was selling old buses, so we bought a blue one for $10,000. It's pictured in the background on that famous photo of us in a wheat field. Russell and the guys at Garnet amplifiers fitted it out with bunks and places for the equipment. We each had a bunk and a locker, with a little sitting area at the back and space for the stand-up amps, which we could load in from the back door. There was no bathroom and no air conditioning, but the windows opened. It was nothing like the $500,000 land cruisers artists use these days that are like luxury suites at the Hilton on wheels. We had a radio and a table up front where we played cribbage or poker or sat with guitars.

During the summer of 1966, the Guess Who undertook a gruelling four-week tour of one-night stands in Saskatchewan. Using Regina's Westward Inn as a base, we'd venture out every afternoon in our bus to destinations like Weyburn, Estevan, Yorkton, Melford, and Moosomin, and even as far as into Alberta, returning to Regina in the wee hours. It was twenty-eight nights in a row in twenty-eight different Saskatchewan towns, four one-hour sets a night with a ten-minute break between each set. We were paid $400 per night, and had to cover all our own expenses. A Kentucky Fried Chicken outlet adjacent to the hotel provided our main source of sustenance. We each had a $6 per diem and had to get through the day's meals on that. We rented two rooms and shared beds.

Another time, near Trail, British Columbia, the brakes failed on our bus and we almost went over the rails and down a cliff. Trail is in a valley, so as you come in you're driving down from the mountains. There's a big left turn, almost a hairpin turn, before you enter the main street. They have these roll-off roads for trucks that can't gear down fast enough and are burning out their brakes. So we were driving along the highway, coming into

Trail in the evening, when the bus's brakes started smoking and squealing because we were going too fast before Jumbo, who was driving, could hit the brakes. We were all in our bunks resting. Jumbo couldn't slow down enough to make the turn, and we were about to fall off this cliff on top of a row of houses below. So Jumbo yelled out that we'd have to jump from the bus. Jim Kale leapt from his bunk, ran to the door, and jumped out, followed by Burton. I wouldn't go without my '59 Les Paul guitar, so I grabbed it, wrapped it in a towel, and was about to jump out with it when Jumbo somehow miraculously managed to slide the bus into a lower gear. At that moment, the whole transmission fell out on the road, smoking, with burning oil and bent metal everywhere. Thankfully the bus came to a stop before Garry and I had to jump out. Jim was all cut up because he landed on the gravel shoulder. But we survived.

The most amazing coincidence was that a car pulled up behind us, a guy came out to see if we were okay, and it turned out to be Ben McPeek, who'd done the orchestral arrangements for "These Eyes." He's originally from Trail and was coming home for a holiday; he was going to take in our concert that night. So Ben drove on to Trail and recruited a bunch of cabs to take us and our gear into town. We played the gig that night. No one in Trail could fix the bus, though, and we ended up shipping its pathetic carcass back to Winnipeg on a railroad flat car. We rented a couple of station wagons and made it home, but the bus wasn't repairable, so we had to buy another one. The new bus was chrome-sided, and we kept it until I left the band.

Having enjoyed a modicum of comfortable travel with the Guess Who, Brave Belt was back to basics for me. We were a country-rock band initially, meaning we were all using smaller amps and didn't travel with a lot of gear, so we started out with an American Motors station wagon. Then we moved up to a Ford Econoline van, the workhorse for mid-level bands. After we flipped it into the ditch, we couldn't afford to get it repainted, so we just touched up the scratches with brown paint. Fred Turner said it looked like Tonto's horse, Scout, from the *Lone Ranger* TV show, so that's what we called it. It became our little in-joke: "I'll pick you up in Scout." Scout was like a sieve on the highway, with all these holes and cracks where the wind whistled in. The heater and defroster couldn't keep the windows clear. If it was forty below outside it was the same temperature inside. We had a giant leather glove–like cover for the front of the van to keep the draft out and some of the heat from the engine in. My father-in-law, Bob Stevenson, made us large Sterno cans from Empress Jam pails with a toilet paper roll soaked in alcohol and a wick in the middle. We'd put two of these on our dash to keep the windows clear and a couple on the floor to keep our feet from freezing. That's how we travelled back and forth across western Canada in winter, with these burning cans of alcohol all over the van. When I think back on that now, it's a wonder we never caught fire or exploded.

Brave Belt could rarely afford a hotel room, so we'd drive to a gig then pack up and drive home. Thunder Bay, Regina, even as far away as Toronto or Vancouver—we'd turn around and drive home, taking turns at the wheel. If we absolutely had to stop overnight, we'd pitch a tent off the side of the road. A couple of times we were embarrassed when fans who'd just seen us playing somewhere would spot us a few hours later in our little tent with a Coleman stove, eating peanut butter sandwiches. Not the glamorous rock 'n' roll lifestyle they'd imagined. There were few luxuries. We later referred to it as Brave Belt boot camp, and it prepared us well for the rigours of touring in BTO.

We were once trapped by an avalanche in Scout as we were travelling through the Rocky Mountains on our way to Vancouver. We heard a rumbling outside the car and looked up in time to see the side of a mountain sliding down towards us. There was no place to go, no side of the road, only a steep dropoff. Fortunately, the avalanche stopped just in front of and to the rear of our line of vehicles, trapping us between massive piles of snow. The highway was a whiteout on both sides. We had our peanut butter sandwiches and our Sterno cans, so we were okay for a short period. Food was later dropped from a helicopter for everyone, and the next day snowplows cleared the highway behind us.

Another time, we were north of Edmonton, on the way to Grande Prairie, and we flipped Scout. We were doing seventy miles an hour when Fred leaned down to pick up a sandwich and lost control of the wheel; the van careened into a snow-packed ditch, where it flipped over onto its roof. But it didn't stop there. It continued to plow through the snowy ditch, sinking farther and farther with the weight of all the amplifiers now turned upside down, until it finally came to a halt. We found ourselves upside down, too, but we managed to get out through the windows.

With BTO, we started off with a station wagon and a van for the gear. Only much later, when we had to make giant leaps across country, did we fly, renting vans once we arrived. But we always maintained a frugal road regimen. Some of our opening acts would be flying in on jets and staying in the fanciest hotels, while we'd arrive in an Ambassador station wagon. We never had a bus in BTO and never used a private jet. When we flew, we flew commercial. Only in the very last days did we end up with semi-trailers. We stayed in Holiday Inns and didn't travel with huge entourages. That's why BTO made really good money: we didn't waste it. My philosophy was to keep it simple. Why waste your hard-earned money on frivolous expenses? We didn't use huge stage sets or props; all we took with us were lights and a really good sound system. By reducing our overhead, travelling frugally, and staying in comfortable, if not glamorous, accommodations, we maximized our bottom line. Some of the most successful artists of that decade lost money on their tours simply because of needless expense—flying in Learjets, accompanied by a retinue of hangers-on, all paid for by the artist, carrying massive sets and backdrops, snorting profits up their noses. Not BTO. We were the only band of the time that was in the black on the road.

In the early months with BTO, we'd play anywhere and everywhere. We'd do drive-in theatres with a stage in front of the screen on a Saturday afternoon. People would sit out on their car hoods like it was a picnic. We did those kinds of gigs with Styx, Peter Frampton—anyone who was trying to get started in the early 70s. We'd play St. Louis today, Boston tomorrow, Buffalo one night, Portland two nights later, wherever there was airplay for our album. "The album's breaking in Louisville! Can you get there?" Zigzagging across the country wherever the record was breaking was costly—Bruce Allen and I maxed out our American Express cards to the tune of $20,000—but Mercury bailed us out. They knew they had to provide tour support to get the album off the ground. They needed us to get out there and work the album.

It took its toll on us personally, though. We'd be told we could go home in two weeks only to get close to that point and be told we had to do three more weeks. Then those three weeks turned into three months. At one point, Fred had Bruce pinned on a hotel bed, choking him, because he kept extending the tour and we couldn't go home. Bruce, Robbie, and Blair were single, so it didn't matter to them being on the road, but Fred and I had wives and kids. It was tough phoning our wives to tell them we wouldn't be home now for another month. In terms of breaking the band wide open, it was the correct strategy and it paid off in the long run. We became the premier touring band in the States. But that relentless touring was hard on the home front, and no amount of money could salve some of those wounds.

When BTO started out, we were an opening act for anyone and everyone. Once we got bigger, though, we had artists like Bob Seger, Thin Lizzy, Brownsville Station, ZZ Top, and REO Speedwagon opening for us. We kicked REO Speedwagon off one of our tours because they were trying to upstage us, the headline act. They did this thing in their show where they stopped the band and yelled out to the crowd, "We want to hear you make some noise—we want to hear St. Louis make some noise!" or wherever we were. The problem was that this was our shtick, which we did every night just before we played "Takin' Care of Business." These guys were cocky enough to steal from us. They were gone.

I remember we didn't know who Aerosmith was when they were opening for us on a tour. On the first night, this guy comes swishing into our dressing room wearing all these colourful scarves, looking like Barbara Eden in *I Dream of Jeannie*. We didn't know who he was, so we threw him out. Turned out it was Steven Tyler, Aerosmith's lead singer.

Now, things are different. With the Guess Who reunion and Bachman-Cummings, we toured at a more reasonable pace; we were all older, and Burton's voice couldn't handle belting it out night after night. We also travelled in luxury tour buses, with the equipment going out ahead of the band in semi-trailers. It was a smooth-running operation. Bachman and Turner is very much like that, too. We're not out to kill ourselves.

One thing you learn in the music business is that every-thing is on your dime, whether it's extra equipment or a truck or even the food backstage. It's all charged back to the artist. So if they're taking $200 off for backstage food and it's a couple of grey-looking salami cold cuts and a bag of chips, they're ripping you off. You arrive in town for the gig and you don't have time to go shopping, nor do you know where to go to shop for food, so you rely on a decent backstage spread. You can specify particular foods in your rider, but you're likely going to be overcharged. Sometimes you're better off checking out decent food outlets in advance using the internet and pre-ordering what you want to be delivered backstage. I've seen people backstage look appalled when after a gig we've grabbed a box and scooped up all the remaining food to take onto the tour bus, but we paid for it, so we might as well take it.

Bachman and Turner recently toured New Zealand. It was my first time there, and Fred's, too. My band and crew brought their spouses or girlfriends on the tour, which made it a great experience, like one big wonderful extended family. We played four gigs in fourteen days, and so we were able to take in a lot of sightseeing. In every city or town we went to, we were the guests of the mayor or the local chamber of commerce. Bungee jumping, water skiing, surfing, white water rafting, massages, restaurants—everything was free. And the food was phenomenal. Sushi on the street that would knock you out. Along with America and Pat Benatar, we were treated like royalty everywhere we went. Festivals numbered fifteen to twenty thousand people and were geared to bringing the whole family. They went from noon to early evening—it stays light in New Zealand until ten o'clock—and they had free food wagons for the kids. The parents could even buy jugs of wine because the festivals were sponsored by wine companies. You saw everyone from toddlers to grandparents, and there was no violence and nobody drunk. None of the usual rock festival nonsense. Everybody had a good time. It was wonderful, one of the best tour experiences I've ever had. I'm glad we were able to talk Fred into it, because he didn't want to go just to New Zealand; he thought that if we were going that far we should do Hawaii, Japan, Australia, and other places out there. But the reality is we're not thirty-five anymore. We went, did the gigs, and enjoyed the days off. We got paid well for those four gigs, and all our expenses were paid by the wineries. It was a win-win for us. How could we turn it down?

As soon as we returned from New Zealand, I hit the road with my band for a cross-Canada tour, doing my Every Song Tells a Story shows. It was ninety days out and really hard on me. Not only was I singing and playing, but I was also talking a lot, too. And I did it all with a guitar strapped to me, so physically it was arduous. The easy part was that I was able to sit down throughout the shows instead of standing, hitting foot pedals, moving up to the mic and stepping back and dancing around as you do while holding a guitar on my shoulder. But I had to see a chiropractor every couple of days just to get straightened out for the next couple of gigs. When I got home after the tour, I was exhausted. It took me a solid ten days to get back in shape. I told my manager, Gilles Paquin, that I just couldn't do another tour that long.

After all, I'm not that kid in a Buick station wagon anymore.

You've played thousands of gigs in your career.
What are your most memorable performances?

Randy playing Live 8, Molson Park,
Barrie, Ontario, July 2, 2005.

This is a question I'm frequently asked, and I never intend to sound flippant, but the reality is that when you've played as many shows as I have over some fifty years, they become a blur, especially if you're on the road constantly. It's like that old joke about the band coming onstage to the crowd going nuts and yelling out, "Hello, Cincinnati!" and from the side of the stage the road manager frantically yells, "No stupid, it's Oakland!" It's a whirlwind, and you're right in the centre of it.

I do have snatches of moments that I recall. Playing Madison Square Garden was big, but it's such a vague impression that I don't remember it because it came at the end of a ninety-five-date tour. It was a major moment in my career, since everybody who was anybody in popular music plays Madison Square Garden. So I do recall feeling that it was significant, but the reality is that it was just another stage and another screaming audience. I'm sure it was the same for the Beatles or the Stones; all these gigs become a blur in the day-to-day touring routine. When I reflect on it now, it was a milestone and I should have stopped to smell the roses, invited my parents to attend, shared the moment. But

BTO was so huge by then that all the arenas seemed the same. And it wasn't our first New York show—we'd played there several times at different venues, beginning with theatres and working our way up to places like the Nassau Coliseum and ultimately Madison Square Garden. We worked our asses off to get where we were and were rewarded with the opportunity to headline such a revered venue. As in all our shows, we ran on adrenaline.

The famous Budokan Arena in Japan was a cool moment. The crowd was so excited to see us, yet it remained polite throughout the show. The Beatles had played that venue back in 1966. No one spoke English, yet they were all singing the words to our songs. We recorded a couple of dates in Japan for BTO's live album. And we had the opportunity to take in some of the Japanese culture, which was an amazing experience for a bunch of prairie dogs like us.

Playing before fifteen thousand people at the Long Beach Arena, where the original Buffalo Springfield had played their final gig, and being called back for five encores was memorable. The Hammersmith Odeon was also a major gig for us, wrapping up BTO's first U.K. tour. We ended up doing two shows there because ticket demand was insane. Selling out Detroit's Cobo Hall, the Spectrum in Philadelphia, and Three Rivers Stadium in Pittsburgh was amazing. There were riots outside Three Rivers Stadium because so many people wanted to see us. I remember those big ones.

Cobo Hall was a triumph because CKLW radio in Windsor had been *the* radio station that initially broke "These Eyes" and many other hits for the Guess Who. That station also jumped on Bachman-Turner Overdrive songs. Records played on CKLW's

50,000-watt stations were heard in Detroit, Toledo, Cleveland, St. Louis, and surrounding areas. So to headline at Cobo Hall supported by local hero Bob Seger was a great feat for us—and I know there were many Canadians in the crowd from Windsor who came to cheer on the home country boys. The Spectrum in Philly was also a highlight gig. As kids growing up in Winnipeg, we'd hear of these legendary arenas for hockey games, rock concerts, and other major events, so to actually play one and sell it out was an amazing experience.

BTO broke the attendance record at Toronto's CNE in 1975, drawing 23,000 people. They had to add more bleachers. To be the opening act for the Beach Boys one year at the outdoor CNE bandshell and then to come back a few years later as headliners was a thrill. When we played "Welcome Home" and everyone lit up their lighters, it was tear-jerking to say the least. The boys were back in town, and they'd been rocking the world. Words cannot express what we felt. Our summer 1975 Canadian tour became the highest-grossing tour in Canadian music history up to that point and the first million-dollar tour by a Canadian band, pulling in $1.5 million in just thirteen days. I remember there was a bit of a backlash against us by some in the Canadian music media because we were earning so much money. I guess they thought that wasn't the Canadian way.

We played a lot of outdoor festivals in BTO. And sometimes there were so many cars jamming the road into these gigs that the promoter had to hire helicopters to get us there. That was pretty awesome. I remember one in Kansas, where a windstorm lifted the stage right off the ground while we were playing. It was insane. Stagehands ran out, locked arms, and pushed us right off the stage just in time, or we might have been killed. All our gear was mangled.

The Seattle Pop Festival in July 1969 was the largest audience I'd ever played for until very recently. It was a star-studded event featuring the biggest artists in rock music at the time. The Guess Who were one of the only acts booked for all three days at the festival, so we were at the site each day, wandering around backstage and catching all the acts. The Doors were there, Ten Years After, Led Zeppelin, It's a Beautiful Day, Chicago, Alice Cooper, Procol Harum, Ike and Tina Turner. We were doing our psychedelic thing with "Friends of Mine"; among all these cool acts we wanted to be regarded as hip, not the "These Eyes" guys. In a tent backstage, I jammed with the Byrds as well as the Flying Burrito Brothers with Gram Parsons. They were both doing glorious country rock, and I loved it. I also got to see Tina Turner naked. We were seated on a scaffold watching the other acts onstage, and during Ike and Tina Turner's set she ducked inside a little enclosed space at the side of the stage to change costumes, unaware that we were sitting right above and she was in full view. I met Tina Turner years later but refrained from mentioning it.

The Guess Who gig in Kitchener, Ontario, in the summer of 1969 is one of those performances I recall clearly. I broke a string, and to tune up after changing it, I started playing B to D to E power chords over and over. I was really enjoying that chord progression, so kept going with it, and the onstage jam that followed yielded the seed for "American Woman." How I came up with those chords together I'll never know, but that gig most certainly changed my life. Another one that's indelibly printed on my brain is appearing on *American Bandstand* in August of that year and being presented with our first gold record for "These Eyes" by none other than Dick Clark himself. That was quite a moment for us as a Canadian band. Dick was extremely friendly and congratulatory, and made us feel at ease even though this was a huge milestone in our career.

There's one gig with the Guess Who that I'll never forget. On May 16, 1970, we played the Fillmore East, an old vaudeville theatre built in the 1920s in New York's East Village. "American Woman" had just hit #1 in *Billboard*, and so there we were, the premier group in North America that week, headlining a show at promoter Bill Graham's legendary venue. And I was leaving the band. It was my last show with the original Guess Who.

Before that night, I'd been back in Winnipeg getting my health in order after suffering several gallbladder attacks during our American tour. Our road manager, Jumbo Martin, would take me to a hospital in different cities each night, but the doctors thought I was just some drugged-out rock musician and didn't take it seriously. The pain was excruciating, though, and I knew I had to get home to see my family doctor to get the medical attention I needed. So the band found a temporary replacement for me for the remainder of our East Coast tour dates, a guy we met in Philadelphia named Bob Sabellico. He knew all my guitar parts from listening to our records. The plan was for me to rejoin the group in New York for the Fillmore East gig, the final date of the tour. I paid Bob out of my end, although the band also gave him a sports car following the tour.

Earlier I had agreed to produce an album for the Mongrels, a Winnipeg band that had just signed with RCA. So, in order to get the contracts all taken care of—and to get my Guess Who side project, my guitar instrumental album *Axe*, all squared away—I flew into New York a day early to meet with Don Birkhimer at RCA's offices. The Guess Who was playing in the Boston area, and when they heard I was in New York a day early and meeting with RCA, the guys got very upset. In their eyes, here they were keeping the band going by fulfilling our contractual obligations on the road with a replacement, and yet there I was, their leader, in New York negotiating contracts for my own personal projects. They were incensed, and a nasty confrontation took place at our hotel a few hours before the gig that night. They viewed it as my sabotaging the Guess Who for my own agenda, betraying them, when that wasn't the case. It was a problem we couldn't resolve, and as a result, I was out of the band. But I still had to play the Fillmore East gig that night.

I was feeling under the weather, physically, and now emotionally too, but sufficiently pumped to play. Buddy Miles and Bloodrock were the opening acts. Then we took the stage to a rousing response. Our first set was incredible. Between sets I suffered yet another gallbladder attack that doubled me over in the filthy Fillmore East washroom, down on my hands and knees in the dirt, before we took the stage again. Nevertheless, we performed another inspired set. I played my ass off that night. I'd been so hungry on the plane because I was afraid to eat— every time I did the attacks would hit me—so I came out of the bathroom high on my body's adrenaline, praying to God to get me through this because I knew it was my last night with the band. None of the guys talked to me backstage between sets. Onstage, I played a solo, and when it was supposed to end I didn't stop. I went into another solo, doing sixty-bar guitar breaks in songs. I looked over and Garry Peterson was digging it, encouraging me to keep going. I did this in every song, taking extra-long solos, flying on my adrenaline rush. The crowd went nuts and called us back for several encores. I wish I had a tape of that performance. As I recall, Burton's expression throughout our show that night was one of amazement because of how I played.

I'll never forget that night, and there are so many other big shows to look back on, too. But, for all that crazy life of touring, it's the more recent gigs that stand out in my memory. Fred Turner and I reunited onstage for the first time in fifteen years when we played the Red River Flood Relief concert at The Forks in Winnipeg in May 1997. Anyone who's grown up in Winnipeg knows about floods. Living not far from the Red River, I remember the 1950 flood: much of West Kildonan, right up to Main Street, was under water, and I was let out of school to fill sandbags with my dad. Later we floated in a boat down Inkster Boulevard all the way to the front porch of my grandmother's house. The 1997 flood was called "The Flood of the Century" because it had surpassed even the 1950 mark. Singer/actor/activist Tom Jackson joined forces with Gilles Paquin to produce a fund-raising concert, and they invited me to perform. CBC televised the event nationally. I suggested that Fred be invited since he was back living in Winnipeg; no one had thought to ask him. Backstage it was a bit uneasy because Fred and I hadn't spoken in several years, but once we got onstage we rocked, bringing the crowd to its feet. During our set, Burton Cummings joined us, and we could see the emotion on the faces of the crowd when we played those BTO and Guess Who songs. It obviously meant something special to them, and did to us as well.

On the evening of June 30, 2000, the reunited Guess Who played CanWest Global Park, home of the Winnipeg Goldeyes baseball team, before thirteen thousand adoring hometown fans. The show was being filmed for a CBC special and later a DVD release. However, the threat of rain that day had everyone nervous, especially Burton, who always gets anxious playing before a local crowd. We took the stage around nine-thirty and received a lengthy standing ovation just for walking out. The rain held off for about an hour before we had to leave the stage for fear of being electrocuted. Surprisingly, or maybe unsurprisingly for a Winnipeg audience, no one left their seats, determined to wait out the rain. It was definitely a festive atmosphere, one that the rain failed to dampen. When it started letting up we returned to the stage to one of the most rousing welcomes I think I've ever experienced. "Only in Winnipeg would the crowd stay!" shouted Burton. Lightning overhead provided a heavenly light show as we finished our set.

Back in early 2003, the whole SARS scare had people staying away from Toronto in droves, afraid they might contract the SARS (severe acute respiratory syndrome) flu, which had first appeared in China. There were fears of a pandemic in and around Toronto, where hundreds had been hospitalized. Conferences, conventions, and concerts had been cancelled and hotel bookings were way down. In an effort to show the world that there was nothing to be afraid of and to attract people back to Toronto, local politicians organized a massive outdoor concert just north of the city. The Rolling Stones were rehearsing in

Toronto at that time at a private school, and since their concert promoter, Michael Cohl, is a Torontonian, they were asked to headline the concert. Rush and AC/DC were also booked, along with a long list of other acts, including Justin Timberlake, an odd choice for this kind of outdoor rock festival.

The reunited Guess Who had been rolling along for three years by then and were invited to perform. But by that point the wheels were starting to fall off the cart, and it would end up being our last performance together. Ironically, it was before the largest audience in the band's history. Neither Burton Cummings nor I with BTO had played for that many people in one spot ever. On July 30, more than 450,000 people showed up at the Downsview Military Base for the SARS concert. It was like Canada's very own Woodstock: SARStock.

To be offered a spot on the bill with Rush, AC/DC, and the Stones, to be spoken of in the same breath as those artists as our peers, was very gratifying indeed. Walking out on that stage and seeing nothing but people in all directions was my very own Woodstock moment. It was like an ocean of bodies under the waning sunlight. Doing our set was among the highlights of my life. We really rocked that day, and in the middle of the set, to do my song "Takin' Care of Business" while half a million pairs of hands clapped along was something I'll never forget. It was very emotional for me. Justin Timberlake had gone on before us and received a rough reception from the audience. They booed and hurled bottles and garbage at him, but he persevered, even dueting with Mick Jagger at one point. The Stones closed the concert with a ninety-minute set that proved why they're the greatest rock 'n' roll band in the world.

The next day, the *The Globe and Mail* declared our performance a "resounding triumph," citing me in particular for rousing the lethargic and sun-stroked crowd. "What Mr. Timberlake and the others could not do, the Guess Who managed, shaking the sun-induced malaise from an unfocused crowd, sparking the first crowd–performer connection of the day. 'See you havin' fun, just a-lyin' in the sun' sung by Mr. Bachman triggered a response from the crowd, many of whom were arriving from work themselves." That was the icing on the cake.

But even after all that, I can still get nervous before a show— as I did in early 2004, when the CBC contacted me about taping a live jazz concert for their late-night jazz program *After Hours* at Winnipeg's Windsor Hotel. My album *Jazz Thing* had just been released, and while the jazz snobs weren't impressed, my fans loved it. I worked with some great writers and players on that album, and it opened up new doors for me, and I received new respect. It wasn't about writing and playing jazz instrumentals; I wanted to write jazz songs with lyrics and melodies, to write another jazz standard. Rock 'n' roll had always been my comfort zone, so jazz was frightening. I was taking a gigantic step into the unknown. And so when the CBC said that I'd be backed by bass player Ron Halldorson and drummer Reg Kelln—Lenny Breau's longtime musicians back in the day in Winnipeg—not surprisingly, I was nervous. Lenny will always be my guitar idol, and I'm forever in his debt for the knowledge and technique he imparted. And these guys were in a whole different league from me. Every player in Winnipeg looked up to them: they'd been living, breathing, eating, and sleeping jazz their whole careers.

So playing live with Lenny Breau's sidemen was intimidating. But they put me at ease, as did the packed club. Even the premier of Manitoba, Gary Doer, was in attendance, along with a lot of local guitar players.

I opened with a solo performance that mixed some jazz noodling with some rock, just to ease the crowd, and myself, into the set. But the ice was broken at the end of my little solo bit when someone whispered to me that my fly had been open the whole time and the entire audience knew. After that, Ron and Reg, along with my keyboard player, Chris Gestrin, played a set of songs from the *Jazz Thing* album, plus numbers like "Blue Collar," "Looking Out for #1," and even a jazzy "Takin' Care of Business." In the end, it was a delightful evening of music. I had fun and it was a dream come true for me.

After the Guess Who reunion had run its course, Burton and I decided to team up and tour as Bachman-Cummings. It made sense, since we were the guys who wrote the hit songs, and by billing ourselves under our own names we could do non–Guess Who material from BTO and Burton's solo career as well. We toured Canada and did some gigs in the States, and it was a big success. In June 2005, we were invited to play Sir Bob Geldof's Live Aid updated event, Live 8. With concerts held simultaneously on four continents, the event was broadcast live to some three billion people worldwide on July 2. The Canadian concert, held in Barrie just north of Toronto, boasted an impressive lineup, including Neil Young, the Tragically Hip, Bryan Adams, Gordon Lightfoot, Bruce Cockburn, Barenaked Ladies, Tom Cochrane, Great Big Sea, and Jann Arden. Mötley Crüe and Deep Purple were also included.

When I arrived there, the crowd numbered over thirty-five thousand; Burton, however, was nowhere to be found. I finally received word that he was ill back in Toronto and wouldn't be performing. The expectation was that our set would be cancelled, but I wasn't about to walk away. I just figured, "If Burton's not here I'm going out anyway." I gathered together his backing band, the Carpet Frogs, and with an acoustic guitar backstage we ran through three BTO numbers, "Hey You," "You Ain't Seen Nothing Yet," and "Takin' Care of Business." When they announced my name we hit the stage running. We did the three songs and the audience went crazy. Afterwards, Steve Morse, who was playing with Deep Purple that day and is one of the best guitarists in the world, came up to me and said, "Man, you were incredible!" That was a great moment for me.

Burton and I were approached several years ago to do a symphony show of our greatest hits, but he wouldn't do it. Ever since the Guess Who played with the Winnipeg Symphony Orchestra back in January 1968, he's regarded symphony players as snobs. It had been a great experience hearing our songs accompanied by a full ninety-piece orchestra, but Burton was disgusted when he saw a couple of symphony players putting their fingers in their ears while we were playing. He vowed never to play again with a symphony orchestra. But I don't think they were doing that to be snobs; I just think they weren't used to the volume of rock instruments and amplifiers. Nowadays, many symphony players are younger people who grew up with rock 'n' roll and are pretty hip. They may not play it with the symphony orchestra, but they know it and can appreciate it. For the gala opening of the new MTS Centre arena in downtown Winnipeg back in

November 2004, Burton and I performed on a bill that included the Winnipeg Symphony Orchestra. They were supposed to back us on "His Girl," but unfortunately their tuning wasn't in synch with Burton's electric keyboard, so they had to sit there while we played the song alone. But I'll never forget standing in the hallway outside my dressing room and hearing one of the symphony players, a double bass player, warming up on his big acoustic bass by playing Jimi Hendrix's "Purple Haze." It was very cool. He had long hair and little John Sebastian glasses. I told him I'd love to do an album with him, and he gave me his card. A lot of symphony players today aren't the stuffy pricks that Burton claimed they were.

I'd love to do a symphony concert tour, playing with different symphonies across the continent. If it happens, I'm sure these concerts would be memorable. I'd come in a few days ahead to rehearse with the orchestra, and then do a couple of shows with them. It would be called Randy Bachman's Symphonic Overdrive concert series, and would feature songs like "These Eyes," "Laughing," "Undun," a couple of my favourite Jeff Beck numbers, the Beatles' "Tomorrow Never Knows," and maybe a cool bossa nova version of "American Woman" that I've recently worked up. I want to take the symphony players out of their comfort zone and really challenge them.

Even though many of the gigs I've played over more than fifty years as a musician are now a vague recollection, I always take each and every performance seriously and go out there with the utmost professionalism. And I demand the same from the musicians onstage with me. I know what it's like to be the fan in the audience watching your own musical hero, and I never take that lightly. I also remain after each show, meeting fans and signing whatever they place in front of me. I'm keenly aware that it's because of them that I'm able to do what I love doing, and to continue doing it for as long as I'm able. I'm always thinking about that next gig.

Throughout your career you've written
hundreds of songs, many of them huge hits.
You've written alone and in collaboration.
Which do you prefer?
What's your songwriting process?

Randy at the RCA Studio, Chicago,
recording with the Mongrels, August 1970.

My favourite part of being a musician is songwriting. I love writing songs and recording. If all I could do was tour playing classic rock, it would offer only limited satisfaction. It would be like a job, and one thing I've never wanted is to make music a job. Going out on the road with my band or with Fred Turner as Bachman and Turner is a fun thing to do and it generates income, but the creative side is really what stimulates me and keeps me going. I get up every day and work on songs. It's a craft, and the more you do it, the better you get. But you have to work at it.

Early on, I made it my business to analyze what made a song a hit, studying the craft of songwriting and arranging. I was fortunate that we had Top 40 radio in Winnipeg, which was all hit songs in a variety of genres. You could hear a Beatles track followed by an Ian and Sylvia folk song, a Dean Martin hit, and maybe a country instrumental by Floyd Cramer. It was wonderful to have such a wide range of styles. I'd listen to a hit song and deconstruct it for the key elements that made it a hit. There was always a certain magic in those hit songs. And back then, the best of the best songwriters were on commercial radio.

The first time I heard Bo Diddley—with that "shave and a haircut, two bits" beat, his tremolo guitar sound, his playing a whole song in one chord—it was a revelation. I'd never heard anything like it before. Its unique beat and feel was the key element in his sound. And then Chuck Berry taking country blues ("Maybelline" was based on an old country/bluegrass song called "Ida Red") and turning it into a rockin' style with lyrics that teenagers, white or black, could relate to was a further revelation. Chuck Berry is the poet laureate of rock 'n' roll. The rhymes he created were astounding: he could conjure up word pictures that depicted the white teenage experience perfectly. Also, every Chuck Berry record I bought was a guitar lesson. My favourite album to this day is *One Dozen Berrys,* originally released in 1958. I'd listen to that album over and over for how basic rock 'n' roll should sound and how the lyrics should tell a story. I tried to make "Takin' Care of Business" like a Chuck Berry song, telling a story about commuters going to work in New York.

I wanted to write hit songs, but I wasn't very good at it initially. I learned that you might write ten songs and one of them could be decent. So having one of my first compositions, "Stop Teasing Me," become a hit single in Winnipeg was a huge boost to my confidence as a songwriter. When we arrived at Scepter Records in New York in June 1965, they listened to all our original material and selected only one track to re-record: "Stop Teasing Me." They thought it was a great song, and yet all I was trying to do was write another "Do You Want to Know a Secret" by the Beatles.

Back in the early days, before "These Eyes," I was the principal songwriter in the Guess Who (and in Chad Allan and the Reflections, and later Expressions). Chad also wrote, but not as prolifically. I composed songs like "Stop Teasing Me," "And She's Mine," "Clock on the Wall," and "Believe Me," all early Guess Who hits. I also wrote for other artists in Winnipeg, like the Mongrels, the Eternals, and Sugar and Spice. What had stuck in my brain was Lenny Breau's lesson: there'll always be another guitar player better than you, so write good songs because they'll last. At that point I was writing alone. Chad and I didn't collaborate, and the other guys in the band weren't that interested in songwriting.

Here's the thing: if you want to be a basketball player, you watch the pros, study their moves, and copy them until you start to develop your own style. Songwriting is a similar process. You have to study the masters and learn from them initially by copying them. I'd listen carefully to the songs on the radio and try to write the follow-up based on that hit song. "What would he or she write next?" It's not going to have the same progression but it's going to have a similar feel and sound that will be recognizable enough to the listener as that artist's style. It's like when Rocco Laginestra, the head of RCA Records at the time, asked Burton and me to write another soft, ballady song like "These Eyes": he wasn't asking for the same chord pattern and progression, a "These Eyes Part 2"; he wanted the same mood that would touch people. So, using the Bee Gees' "New York Mining Disaster 1941" and the Dave Clark Five's "Because" as a chord template, we wrote "Laughing." Burton used that same Dave Clark Five chord progression for his solo hit "Stand Tall."

Songs like "Believe Me" and "Clock on the Wall" were obvious clones of the artists I was listening to, in those cases the Kinks, Paul Revere and the Raiders, and the Animals ("Clock on the Wall" is derivative of "House of the Rising Sun" even to the point of borrowing some of the chord progressions). That's how you start out. When I'm teaching people the basics of how to write songs, first I suggest they list their ten favourite songs. Then I tell them to pick one song from the list, and keep the whole song and chorus but sing a different melody over it using the same lyrics. Add a new guitar solo as well. Once they have a new melody, change the lyrics. For example, if it was about a girl, make it about a car. Then change the phrasing and breaths. Finally, take the chord progression they've been using and alter the tempo. Now they have a new song derived from their influences. That's how you deconstruct a song and create a new one from it. One of the things I learned from the Beach Boys' Brian Wilson is to have what's known as a fake book, a music book with the charts for all the standards and Broadway show tunes. You take the chords off the top line—the chords and patterns that have been proven to stick in people's minds. Then, instead of playing the chord for, say, two beats like that standard, you play it for four, or vice versa. But keep the chords' linear progression. Play around with the way you use that progression, and keep playing it over and over until you come up with a melody that fits over those particular chords and some lyrics that work. Suddenly you've got a song. This becomes part of your songwriting practice. It may be how you get started.

Although I'd been writing alone, and would continue to do so from time to time, when Burton Cummings joined the band I found an eager and willing collaborator. As I said earlier, he and I wanted to be like the hit songwriting teams we so admired. We found that we each had a particular musical perspective we could bring to the collaboration and, given our shared musical history growing up in Winnipeg, similar musical references as well. It was like an intuitive language we had, a way of communicating exactly what we meant by cutting through all the superficialities. In other words, even though we were and still are very different personalities, we spoke the same musical language.

Burton and I each brought ideas to the table. I was a good hook-and-chorus guy, and Burton, with all his poems, saw himself as something like his hero, Jim Morrison. But he would sometimes ramble, his lyrics becoming long poetry, so I'd suggest we cut it off here, put in a chorus, repeat the guitar hook. Make it more concise and focused. Sometimes he'd write a middle eight or bridge (that's the changeover part in a song following the usual verse-chorus, verse-chorus pattern; think "And when I touch you I feel happy inside" in the Beatles' "I Want to Hold Your Hand") and I'd write an intro. Or we'd change the key. Every song we collaborated on differed in who brought what to the table and who suggested what changes. It wasn't like Elton John and Bernie Taupin, where Bernie provided Elton with sheets of lyrics and Elton would miraculously write music that fit those lyrics perfectly. I don't know how they did that, because they never sat down together to collaborate. Bernie would mail Elton the lyrics, and the next time he'd hear them they were completed songs. Lennon and McCartney were true collaborators in the first few years, sitting down together with ideas that each brought the other. Sometimes it might be an almost fully formed song that the other contributed the final ingredient to, and on other occasions it was a germ of an idea, a hook, a line or a chorus, and they'd finish it collaboratively. It's often been said that Lennon was the words man and McCartney the melody guy, but that's not true, and far too simplistic. Each guy complemented the other. That's what Burton and I did.

When we wrote "These Eyes," for example, I had the intro piano part and the line "These arms long to hold you," and I played it for Burton. He saw potential in this seed of an idea, but, as I mentioned earlier, he suggested that it start with eyes first then go to arms in the next line, and he was right. It made sense. As we worked on the song further, he suddenly came up with that long line of strung-together lyrics, "These eyes have seen a lot of loves but they're never gonna see another one like I had with you," and it fit perfectly. That's how a true collaboration works. It's a give-and-take process.

There were some song ideas I brought to Burton that he rejected, so I'd often complete them myself and then take them to other groups in the city who were eager to get a Bachman composition. "Not to Return" for Sugar and Spice and "Good Good Man" and "Funny Day" for the Mongrels are examples of that. When I played Burton my song about commuters in New York entitled "White Collar Worker," he hated it. But I resurrected it later and it became "Takin' Care of Business." That's another songwriting lesson: never throw anything away. You might find another context for it sometime later. It wouldn't have worked for the Guess Who at the time, but in reworking it live onstage, simplifying it from four hundred chords to three and adding a catchy chorus, it became a hit song. Similarly, when

Fred Turner first played "Blue Collar" for me he had way too many chords and chord changes in it, so we simplified it and made it a better song by doing so. Often simpler is better.

Once Burton and I hit our stride, we developed our own style—and our influences, while still there, were less obvious to the listener. I don't think anyone listening to "No Time" hears the Buffalo Springfield's "Hung Upside Down" from their second album, but that's where the idea for the riff and verse structure came from. It's obvious to me because I had that song in mind when I wrote "No Time." The main thing, though, was that I was writing songs to fit Burton's voice, to complement his amazing vocal talent.

The Guess Who sound was quite varied because of the diverse influences we each had. You hear the band Traffic in "Talisman" and Jethro Tull in our use of the flute. There's the Doors and Cream in some songs and Georgie Fame in others. Look at "No Time" or "American Woman": they don't sound like "These Eyes," and nothing else we did sounded like "Undun." We really did have a wide range of styles, and had we stayed together with that original lineup I think we could have become one of the biggest bands in the world. The potential was there. The band limited that potential after I left when they brought in other guys and narrowed their sound and style. Two more albums and we'd have been around the world (there were still major international markets we had yet to crack). We had the ability to appeal to a wide constituency of listeners because we had the psychedelic hippie thing, the hard blues rock, jazz rock, soft ballads, country rock. We could do it all. We could have been the next Beatles. If we'd kept going, it would have been amazing. "Palmyra" had the potential to be a monster song, had we been able to go back in the studio and finish it—but as it was, there were no overdubs on the version ultimately released. "Miss Frizzy" was one of my greatest guitar riffs. Those two songs were abandoned in the studio until a few years later, after I was long gone.

While our collaboration was the principal source of the Guess Who's material, Burton and I each still came up with songs on our own. Burton composed "I Found Her in a Star" on *Wheatfield Soul* and "Heygoode Hardy" on *A Wild Pair*. "A Wednesday in Your Garden" was written by me alone, as was "No Sugar Tonight," but the best example of my writing on my own is "Undun." It's what happens when a song practically pours forth straight out of you as if from somewhere else and you're just the conduit. You have to catch it before it's too late and the inspiration is gone. Neil Young often writes like that, where the song comes through him almost fully formed and he doesn't even know where it came from. "Cowgirl in the Sand" and "Down by the River" were like that. "Undun" was that kind of experience for me; the inspiration or seed of an idea came with a line from Bob Dylan's "Ballad in Plain D" where he sings, "She was easily undone." I was sitting in my hotel room in Vancouver listening to FM radio when I heard that song with that line. I just switched the radio off and immediately started writing verses. Before I knew it I had half a dozen verses written out over this jazzy, Lenny Breau chord pattern I'd been playing around with. The lyrics didn't even rhyme. Burton edited the lyrics down to a couple of verses, and I had the song. That was his only contribution to the creation of it. "Undun" was kind of given to me by the angel of song. Every once in a while that happens, but more often you have to work at a song, polish and refine it.

Everyone always thinks Bob Dylan's songs come to him in some divine inspiration. But if you've seen the movie *Don't Look Back,* about his last solo acoustic tour of the U.K. in 1965, there's a scene where Bob's sitting at a typewriter pondering each word and phrase as he types out the lyrics to a song idea he has. Meanwhile there's all manner of noise and distraction around him in the room, including Joan Baez annoyingly singing a song, yet he's completely oblivious to it all. He's so focused on songwriting and polishing a rough diamond into a gem. Gordon Lightfoot agonizes over every word and line in his songs. It's all part of the individual creative process.

In Bachman-Turner Overdrive there was very rarely any collaboration. I was a songwriter when I left the Guess Who and was looking to create another vehicle for my songs. I wanted to keep writing. I was also the record producer, so I knew that the albums needed good songs and I knew I could write them. I virtually financed the band with my Guess Who nest egg, right down to the last dollars I had, so I wasn't about to give up that vehicle to other drivers who had no experience. A band is not a democracy. No band is. It's a benevolent dictatorship. There are always one or two guys who write the songs and the other guys who play them. Fred had some songwriting experience, and he came into the band with some good songs that offered a changeup on the albums. But the bottom line was that BTO was created for my songs. Fred and I did collaborate on "Let It Ride," but I found that writing with Fred was difficult. There wasn't the same flow that there'd been with Burton. Still, if Fred had an idea, I'd listen to it and maybe work with him to shape it into something we could record. Or if Blair or Robbie had a riff or a rhythm that was interesting, I'd take it and work it into something. As the producer that was my role as well.

Robbie and Blair were good sailors, but neither was a captain. None of the guys in BTO was as prolific a songwriter as I was. I had a decade of experience writing songs behind me. Blair wasn't a songwriter; he was sold to us as such, but he came in with songs and fragments from his previous band, Crosstown Bus, that were just riffs and blues numbers. Robbie has a co-writing credit on "Roll On Down the Highway," but it was just a blues pattern that I shaped into a song by adding the Shadows-style riff and sorting out the arrangement. So why would these guys think they should be entitled to an equal number of songs on an album? That became one of the issues that divided us and forced me to leave. John Fogerty was the principal songwriter in Creedence Clearwater Revival and had a stellar track record with songs like "Proud Mary," "Down on the Corner," "Who'll Stop the Rain," and "Bad Moon Rising." When the other guys in the band pushed for equal songwriting space he relented, and the result, *Mardi Gras*, was both an artistic and a commercial disaster. Critics savaged the album and fans avoided it. The reality was that the other guys just weren't skilled or experienced songwriters on the same level as John Fogerty. It broke up the band. And it ultimately broke up BTO, too, even though they recorded two more albums without me that went nowhere.

Collaborating in Nashville with another songwriter is a totally different experience. You meet an absolute stranger for the first time at the writing session. You have no idea if you have anything in common. With Burton and me, even though we're different personalities and a few years apart in age, we had a lot in common in terms of our musical vocabulary. We basically liked the same music, and if I said I wanted a Georgie Fame–like bridge he knew exactly what I meant. We were lifting bits and pieces from songs and writers we both loved and connected with at that common level. But the Nashville experience is quite the opposite. I really pursued writing in Nashville for about ten years, going down there for ten-day stretches every couple of months. Woody Bomar at Sony Music set me up with some of the best writers in Nashville. You walk into the room with a stranger, it might be male or female, anywhere from seventeen to seventy years of age, and you say to each other, "Okay, what do you want to write about?" And they might say, "Driving to the studio today I heard on the radio about a dog that was run over. My dog was run over when I was a kid and I never got over it." So you decide to write a song about that feeling or emotion, whatever they want to write about. You might decide to write a song about heartbreak, and so you start sharing feelings and experiences until you find a common ground, and that becomes the germ of your song. You work for an hour or maybe three, and in the end you emerge with a completed song, you sign the sheet with the music and lyrics, and then you shake hands and say goodbye. You might not see that person again. That's the way they do it in Nashville; they might have three or four people in that room throwing around ideas and chords until they come out with something. It's not organic. It's a contrived situation intended to produce a result. Still, it can be cathartic as you share your experiences and feelings with one another. And it did teach me a lot about songwriting.

It was interesting for me to go to Nashville to write because I'm not from that milieu. I don't wear the Nashville Toupee, meaning the big cowboy hat (I never knew Dwight Yoakum was bald until he started doing movies because he never took his hat off), and I don't come from a country music background, even though I love the genre. I assumed that my rock 'n' roll pedigree would be an impediment, but it was nothing of the kind. You see all these country artists in Stetsons and you figure they were all weaned on George Jones and Tammy Wynette, but they grew up on rock 'n' roll. When they were kids they were screaming to all the hard rock bands, and now they're Mr. or Ms. Middle of the Road. Everyone in Nashville was very conscious of my rock 'n' roll background. They all knew who I was. Listen to country music today and it's all distorted guitar riffs, not whiny pedal steel guitars. Unfortunately, country music is in a rut these days. It's all these women who look and sound the same and all these guys in the big cowboy hats. And they're still stuck in that cookie-cutter concept: what's the latest hit, let's clone it. There's not a lot of originality in country music anymore.

I've gone to London to write with other songwriters with maybe two song ideas—just ideas, a line or a chord progression—and come away with fourteen different songs from those two ideas because each writer brings his or her own background to the collaboration. That background can be their personal experiences or their particular style of music. The idea you had coming in can be totally different by the end of the writing session. One collaborator could take my riff or idea and go totally somewhere else with it, a place I might never have thought to go. Then you take that same germ of an idea to another collaborator and come away with another completely different song. They want something different from the idea. In London, I wrote dance music with a black guy from Trinidad. It's all about experience.

When I was recording my *Jazz Thing* album in 2003, I didn't want it to be a jazz guitar album. I just wanted to write good jazz songs. One of the collaborators I worked with was Stephan Moccio, who was riding high (and still is) with his songs, which have been recorded by Celine Dion, Josh Groban, Seal, and Sarah Brightman, among an illustrious list of other megastars. We first spoke on the phone, and he knew who I was. Then we met at his studio in Toronto to attempt to write together. We were from two distinctly different musical backgrounds, so we needed to find some common ground. We noodled around a bit, just throwing out ideas back and forth, before he started playing a melody that caught my attention. I told him to keep going, and I started thinking of lyrics that fit the melody and the mood it created in me. It was a very emotional and cathartic moment as we pulled a song out of thin air. It was as if the song was writing itself. Sometimes you don't know where they come from; they just come through you. What emerged was a poignant song called "Our Leaves Are Green Again," about the memory of a relationship. The sentiment of the song touched both of us deeply. We recorded the demo that same day, just the two of us, guitar, piano, and voice. I think that song has a special quality to it that could make it a standard. I'm hoping someday it will be.

As a songwriter, I'm fearless. I'll try anything. I've written hard rock, pop, country, jazz, dance, techno-pop, ballads, you name it. It's all a challenge for me. Writing with a variety of people all around the world who are pretty much the best in their profession has been an incredible learning experience. It's made me a better writer, better at my craft. The odds of my landing another #1 at my age are slim, but that doesn't deter me from continuing to write. It's what I do. I know I'm not the greatest songwriter in the world, but I'm not the worst. I believe in myself and my songs. I like both writing on my own and collaborating because they're two very different situations.

I love doing my Every Song Tells a Story shows because it provides people with insight into the songs they already know. What was the inspiration, motivation, collaboration, and writing process involved with that song? It's fun to share those stories. People have told me afterwards that hearing the background stories to their favourite songs casts those songs in a whole new light.

When I was inducted into Canada's Walk of Fame recently, I told the crowd that I was grateful to be there honouring my home runs, but that I also had to honour my strikeouts. Without those I wouldn't have had those home runs. If you look at guys like Babe Ruth, Hank Aaron, or Mickey Mantle, not only were they the home-run kings, but they also struck out more often than their contemporaries did. When they went up to bat, they swung as hard as they could with every fibre of their being. If they hit a home run then everybody loved them. But if they struck out they still came back up to bat next time, with that same determination to knock the ball out of the park. It's the same with me as a songwriter. Without the failures, I might not have had the grand slams. When I said that, the audience gave me a standing ovation. I've written hundreds of songs in my career, but I'm being honoured for a few songs that transcended the others and went on to become something special.

What has your experience been recording
over the years, and how has recording changed?
What are your favourite recording studios?

The Guess Who recording *Wheatfield Soul* at
A&R Studios, New York, September 1968.

E very studio has its own character, feel, and sound. No two studios are the same. And a studio's dynamic can impact not only the experience of the artist but the resulting recording as well. I've recorded under the most primitive circumstances and the most elaborate and high tech. Each situation has been unique.

My inaugural recording session was at Arbuthnot Studios in Winnipeg. That tiny two-track recording facility was located inside Arbuthnot Audio Electronics on Taché Avenue in St. Boniface, just across the Red River from downtown Winnipeg. Two-track recording meant you could record sound on sound, overdubbing a second track onto the first. Many Winnipeg musicians started their recording careers at Arbuthnot Studios. I was still a teenager playing with Mickey Brown and the Velvetones when we were approached by a shoe salesman from Portage la Prairie named Gary Cooper to back him up on a rock 'n' roll recording. I cut a couple of singles with Gary (he also recorded as Gary Andrews so as not to be confused with the actor), and in 1961, those two singles—"Come On Pretty

Baby" backed by "Heartaches and Disappointments"—marked my recording debut.

After I joined Allan's Silvertones and we became Chad Allan and the Reflections, we cut our first single at Kay Bank studios in Minneapolis. I was excited to be moving up to three-track recording. Tommy Jong, the engineer on the session, would go on to an illustrious career in recording engineering and production. And although the studio wasn't much bigger than Arbuthnot's, it offered one more track. But the volume pod on my Gretsch 6120 hollow-body electric guitar wouldn't work, and since we'd gone down there on a Saturday and were due home Sunday evening, I didn't have time to get it fixed. I was forced to play Chad's Fender Jazzmaster solid-body guitar, which I wasn't used to playing, and I was never satisfied with the results. Nonetheless, we ended up recording at Kay Bank several more times between 1964 and 1966; it was a professional studio, something Winnipeg still lacked.

With "Shakin' All Over" in December 1964, we took a step backwards by recording in mono, meaning one track, because we couldn't afford the trip to Minneapolis, nor did we relish making the eight-hour drive in the dead of winter. Our manager, Bob Burns, hosted an *American Bandstand*–like show called *Teen Dance Party* every Saturday afternoon on a large sound stage at CJAY TV behind Polo Park shopping mall. We'd played a gig there on a Saturday evening, four one-hour sets, and decided we'd use the empty TV studio to record our next single. Bob paid the security guard a few bucks to let us in (it was about two in the morning), and had arranged for the station's recording engineer to operate the tape recorder. We had one microphone for everything, instruments and vocals, so we set up in a semi-circle in the middle of the studio and hung the microphone from the ceiling to capture the sound. Everyone plugged into Jim Kale's Fender Concert amp, which had four ten-inch speakers. If one instrument was too loud, we just turned the channel down. Garry Peterson's drums were set up beside the Concert amp, and if they were deemed too loud we had to move the entire kit a few feet back: there were no baffles (moveable soundproof walls) to separate the sound.

On one of the takes, by mistake or just from being sleepy, the engineer forgot to unpatch the speakers from the tape recorder when we were recording, and as a result we had what's known as a slapback echo on that take. The track had a dense sound and a reverb quality, as if it had been recorded in a cave. It sounded like one of Elvis's early Sun Records. When we heard it, we knew that was *the* take. There are mistakes on it, but the sound is alive. There's barely any bass on it, just a bottom-end rumble because there was no separation. But it's a perfect rock 'n' roll record from an imperfect recording session.

When we went to New York in the early summer of 1965, we recorded at Scepter Studios in an office building at 254 West 54th Street. Florence Greenberg owned the studio as part of Scepter Records, which had licensed "Shakin' All Over" in the U.S. Florence, who'd been a songwriter herself, started the Scepter and Wand record labels; they'd recorded the likes of Dionne Warwick, Chuck Jackson, the Shirelles, the Kingsmen, and B.J. Thomas, among others. We were surprised to discover that the recording engineer, her son Stanley, was blind. He knew the recording console by feel and had an acutely attuned ear for sound and mixing. Stanley was an accomplished arranger and a mainstay of the studio staff for many years. Incidentally, the same building that housed Scepter would later become the notorious Studio 54 during the whole decadent disco scene. We recorded several tracks there, including the later singles "Hey Ho (What You Do to Me)" and "Hurting Each Other."

Every recording experience for us involved incremental improvements in facilities and technology, and the resulting tracks demonstrated that. Scepter had four-track recording, which meant we could overdub more backing vocals and other instruments. Then, when we went to London in February 1967, we had the opportunity to record at IBC Studios at 35 Portland Place in central London. Mills Music had made a lot of money from our recording of "Shakin' All Over," more than we did, so they allowed us to record over two days in early March under the direction of producer Tony Hiller and arranger Cy Payne. IBC was a four-track facility that the Beatles had used at one time. The Bee Gees recorded there, as did Jimi Hendrix, Cream, the Kinks, and even the Stones, as I later learned. Tony Hiller was both a proper British gentleman and an experienced record producer who took our four-piece sound and expanded it with the use of strings, flugelhorn, and additional percussion. He also brought in a tambourine player, which we thought was insane. Garry or any of us could play tambourine. But this tambourine player was a real character, and it turned out to be Ray Cooper, who's worked with Elton John forever. Ostensibly, Tony was using us to cut a couple of demos for a songwriting team named Jerome Langely and Jerry Stewart ("This Time Long Ago" and "Miss Felicity Grey"), but he also allowed us to record a couple of tracks. IBC pressed acetates right there in the building for us to take home. I still have one.

What Tony did with us as a producer was quite impressive in terms of sound and style. Working with additional instruments allowed our music to expand and gave us a very polished sound. It was a real boost for us. Tony and I remain friends to this day, and I see him whenever I'm in London. He helped the Guess Who on our journey.

After we came back to Winnipeg, CBC-TV hired us to be the house band on their weekly *Let's Go* show. We'd record the music the day before and then lip-sync during the show's actual taping. It was back to two-track recording, but since they wanted loud vocals, we did the vocals as overdubs. They also didn't like any distortion, so it was difficult to get them to accept my Herzog or any fuzz-tone sound. Still though, we learned a lot about recording for the two years we did that show, and became very efficient at being able to lay down tracks and overdub. We had to know the songs in advance and be able to knock them out quickly with a minimum of fuss or tinkering. That's when we really became a top-notch cover band—we had to play virtually anything and everything, from Simon & Garfunkel's "Mrs. Robinson" to Jose Feliciano's "Light My Fire" along with the Doors' version as well. We also learned how to double our vocals to give them more depth. It was like a day job, with a strict routine: get the names of the songs on Monday and go buy the 45s. Have a band rehearsal Tuesday to learn the songs, record them on Wednesday, lip-sync them on the show Thursday. Then we'd play gigs on Friday and Saturday. We played the Top 40 each week for those two years, any song, any genre.

Jack Richardson, having seen us on *Let's Go,* brought us to Toronto in the fall of 1967 to record our *Wild Pair* album at Hallmark Studios. Hallmark was four tracks and probably the top studio in Canada at the time—one of those old-style recording studios with a large room and a high ceiling built to accommodate orchestras and big bands. We got to work with the top session players in Toronto, guys like Guido Basso, Jack Zaza, Hagood Hardy, Moe Kaufman, and Peter Appleyard—the A-list players, not only in Toronto but in Canada. These were the guys Lenny Breau wanted to play with, and here I was in the studio with them. The entire situation, the room and the players, was intimidating for us. But again, in another incremental step, we recorded with additional instruments that expanded our range and sharpened our focus on a more commercial sound. The *Wild Pair* tracks still sound impressive today.

After we cut the tracks, however, Jack wasn't satisfied with them, so we had to re-record everything. We'd never experienced that before, and were impressed that he believed in us so much that he'd double the recording budget by having us start all over again. Once that was done, Jack took the tracks to Phil Ramone in New York to mix them. That, too, was new to us. In the past we would record and whoever was producing the session would do a quick balance of the instruments and vocals right there, and that was it. Not having been there for the sessions, Phil was able to provide a different perspective.

After Jack signed us to his Nimbus 9 production company, he took us to A&R Studios in New York, Phil Ramone's studio, to record the *Wheatfield Soul* album. It was a wonderful facility with great sound—they had a four-track recorder in one room, and then if they felt the track needed more, they'd transfer it to the eight-track machine in another room. We loved the sound we got from that studio. Just listen to "These Eyes" and you can hear the magic in that recording. I remember that after we completed our track we watched Ben McPeek conduct the string players, just four guys, and they doubled it. Ben had written out all the charts for them. He also brought in a flugelhorn player—everyone was doing a Burt Bacharach thing by then. Burton and I didn't want the horn on it, but in the end I think they were right, because it works. The way the strings make that transition back to the first verse in the song is so majestic. That was a special moment.

Unencumbered, we were able to record the songs and album the way we wanted them to sound. Besides Phil Ramone's presence, we had some great engineers—Shelley Yakus, David Greene, Elliot Scheiner—who all went on to become big guys in the recording business, as did Phil.

One evening during the recording, we were goofing around, overdubbing the hand clapping on "When You Touch Me" and not taking it seriously. We kept blowing it, and Jack had finally had enough—he told us to go back to the hotel and get some sleep. The next day we arrived at the studio to discover that Jack and Phil had hired three professional clappers. These guys were studio clappers who made their living that way. They arrived in dark trench coats, all wearing white Mickey Mouse gloves, which they proceeded to remove one finger at a time like magicians. After they asked Jack what kind of clapping rhythm he wanted, they demonstrated the different clapping patterns and sounds just by the way they held their hands. Phil actually had a clapping music chart written out for them. So they went into the big studio room, the engineer played the track, and they clapped exactly in the right spots with the right timing, rhythm, and sound. After they left, Jack turned to us and said, "Okay, you guys, that just cost you a hundred bucks per guy. Three hundred bucks. Let that be a lesson to you about goofing around in the studio. Everything you do costs you money." From then on, we didn't fool around. The track on that album still has those professional clappers on it.

During the sessions, Phil brought in Robert Moog, who invented the Moog synthesizer, the very first synthesizer. It was a gigantic gizmo with all these dials and patch cords set up in another studio in the facility. When we went in to see him and this big thing that looked like an old-style telephone switchboard times a hundred, he demonstrated all these whizzing and farting noises, saying, "Listen to this—it's the sound of a cymbal." We were thinking, "Why do we need that? We *have* cymbals." So we didn't use it on the album. He took his contraption to two guys named Paul Beaver and Bernie Krause, who recorded several rock albums using the Moog synthesizer on jazzy numbers with spoken-word passages. These recordings predate the whole New Age electronic music genre by a couple of decades.

Because I got to know Phil, I'd go in during our off-hours and watch him record. I observed everything, soaking it up like a sponge as I sat in a corner quietly watching. When they'd take a break I'd ask whoever was producing questions about what they did. I knew I wanted to produce records someday.

Wheatfield Soul was recorded on spec for Nimbus 9, who paid for the sessions and then sold it to RCA, so we were able to record where we wanted to. But when we signed with RCA it was stipulated in our contract that we had to record in RCA's own studios. So for the *Canned Wheat* album sessions, we recorded at their studio at 155 East 24th Street in Manhattan. We stayed at the Gramercy Park Hotel near the Village and were brought to this big old studio with a huge ceiling and no baffles, a couple of microphones suspended from the ceiling. It was built for orchestras; we were told Bing Crosby had recorded there. But no matter how hard we tried we just couldn't get a decent sound. The drums sounded so dry in that cavernous room—Garry would hit a drum and you'd hear a tiny click rather than a solid thump. We had ten days to do the album, and spent the first two frustratingly trying to find a comfortable sound. We were dying to go back to A&R Studios; "These Eyes" and the whole *Wheatfield Soul* album had sounded so good. It had a wet sound with a natural reverb to it. So Jack told us to keep recording at RCA and at the end of the week to tell RCA that we had gigs to play. We then packed up our gear as if to go play a gig but instead we went to Phil Ramone's A&R Studios. We could record only two songs because of the limited time we had, so we picked "Laughing" and "Undun." Jack was able to secretly substitute those two tracks for the ones we cut at RCA. Those two tracks comprised our next single—not only were they good songs and what RCA wanted from us, but they also had a wonderfully warm, wet sound. If you listen to the original *Canned Wheat* album you can hear the difference between those two tracks and the others done at RCA. There's a depth and a presence on those two tracks that are missing on the others. That's why we decided to re-record "No Time" on the following *American Woman* album:

we knew it was a good song, but on *Canned Wheat* the sound quality was lacking. And we were proven correct.

We expressed so much dissatisfaction with recording at RCA's studio in New York and having to go all that way that they built a studio in Chicago, RCA Mid-America Recording Center on Wacker Drive, largely for us. We were the first band to try it out; workers were still finishing it when we went in to record the *American Woman* album. "No Time" sounded amazing in that studio. They had a great engineer there, Brian Christian. I used him on my *Axe* album, and I brought the Mongrels there to record with him as well. We also did the tracks that became the post–Guess Who album, *The Way They Were*, at Mid-America. After I left, the Guess Who went back there several more times. That studio was eight tracks with great monitors and a 3M tracking machine.

The first Brave Belt album was recorded on eight tracks at Century 21—the city's first professional recording studio, built by two sets of brothers, the Paleys and the Hildebrands, in the local band the Eternals. Since we hadn't yet signed with Reprise, we did the album on spec. I took the completed tracks to A&R Studios in New York, where Dave Green helped me mix them because Phil was busy, probably doing Billy Joel or someone.

I'd wanted to use Garry Peterson on drums for the album, but that would have been too difficult for him; the other guys in the Guess Who would have viewed it as changing sides. Feelings were still very tender at that point. So instead I asked my youngest brother, Robbie, who was still a teenager and had never really played in a band before. He'd started out playing a set of Ogilvy Oats porridge boxes cut down to different sizes with the lids glued back on, but by the time I approached him to record with us he had an old set of Garry drums. He was scared to death. At our first recording session, all I told him was "Play like Ringo Starr!" He did okay on the sessions and in BTO, but it would have sounded much better with Garry Peterson. Garry did, though, play in a later version of BTO.

Brave Belt II was recorded in Toronto at RCA Studios on sixteen tracks with Mark Smith engineering. This time, Reprise Records was footing the bill. Mark and I got along well at the time, and he ended up working with BTO on several albums. But I didn't like the sound on that record. They had a bad speaker system with 604E Altec Super Reds, which had great big tweeters and a crossover so that everything was very trebly. When you mix while listening through these speakers you don't add any top because the speakers are giving you that. As a result, the *Brave Belt II* tracks have no top end. We were trying to sound like Creedence Clearwater Revival but missing the mark. We should have gotten down to the meat and potatoes of it. When I played the mix for Don Schmitzerle and Mo Ostin it sounded muffled, and they insisted that we remix it. I didn't want to do that, though—I was the producer and I was stubborn—so they ultimately dropped the band.

Chad Allan contributed only two songs to the album. One of them was "Dunrobin's Gone," which he wrote with Barry Erickson. I still regard that recording as one of the finest country-rock songs to come out of western Canada until that point. And I'd double-tracked our vocals on the album, which gave "Dunrobin's Gone" a further boost. On that track, I played the bass parts sitting on my knees on the floor while I hit the organ's bass pedals with my hands. I also did that Beatles and Beach Boys thing of introducing more instruments with each verse, along with my Red Shea acoustic picking thing between verses like Gordon Lightfoot's records. The acoustic guitar— my Yamaha Hummingbird—sounds so clear on that song. "Dunrobin's Gone" should have been called "She's Gone and She Won't Be Back," and that hurt the record's chances because no one knew what the title meant unless you were from East Kildonan in Winnipeg and knew it was a street. When people would phone in to radio stations asking them to play "She's Gone and She Won't Be Back," they'd look at their playlists and say, "We don't have that record."

After Reprise dropped us, I returned to RCA Studios in Toronto to do what was intended to be *Brave Belt III* on my own dime. By then, Mark Smith had the monitors changed and they'd just installed a new Neve board. That was the magic. We were the first band to use that board, and out of that came *BTO I* with amazing sound and presence. The Foo Fighters' Dave Grohl recently produced *Sound City,* a documentary film about the legendary L.A. recording studio, and it's his contention, and mine as well, that tape, tubes, and the Neve recording console are the reasons why classic rock still sounds so good on radio. The sound is warm, even though it's now been digitized on CD. The original recordings had tape saturation, which has two or three harmonics on every note, and which you don't hear on a digital recording. You can't push CD to get distortion. There's no bigness on CD, whereas on tape the track would saturate and affect every sound around it. That's why *BTO I* still sounds good.

BTO II and *Not Fragile* were both recorded at Seattle's Kaye Smith Studios, which had been built by Danny Kaye and Lester Smith. I loved recording at Kaye Smith. Steve Miller and War were also recording there at the time we did *BTO II.* It was sixteen tracks with an API board, which was phenomenal. That studio and that board are the sound of "Let It Ride," my Stratocaster and Fred's bass both plugged directly into the API board with a limiter on each one. No amps. That's a beautiful sound. My rhythm guitar sound is very crisp on that song and throughout that album; you couldn't get that anywhere else. I'm playing my big Martin D 45 acoustic guitar on the bottom of it, but since Martins are built for bluegrass and too boomy to cut through the other instruments, I took a piece of cardboard and taped it over the sound hole. Instead of getting the oomph of the guitar from the sound box, I was just getting the strings. I mixed that under two Strats, one playing the chords high and the other playing lower. All three mixed together, and that's the rhythm on "Let It Ride."

My brother Tim had joined BTO after Chad Allan left because our gig contracts stipulated four guys in the band. He played nothing on that recording, though. Tim was great onstage and great to have in the band, but we had an understanding: when it came time to laying down the basic tracks, Tim went out and got everyone lunch. And when he returned, the guitar parts were done. Sometimes he played on them, sometimes he didn't. I even replaced some of Fred's bass parts if they weren't as precise as I wanted them. And, because Robbie kept speeding up, I brought in another sixteen-track machine and copied "Let It Ride" over to it so that I could take the first verse and splice it three times for a more precise tempo. "Let It Ride" was like the Indianapolis 500 by the time we got to the end. I never told those guys what I did—it would have been ego shattering and caused infighting. In my role as producer, I wanted the job done right, and I'd come in an hour earlier or stay later to get the sound I was looking for. I saw BTO as my vehicle to do my songs, so it was all on me.

Before going into the studio to produce a BTO album, I'd always listen to Chuck Berry's *One Dozen Berrys* as well as to the Beatles' *Revolver* and *Rubber Soul*—just to remind myself how four guys could be made to sound different, and how the Beatles cleverly integrated percussion to make their sound unique.

Besides the great sound at Kaye Smith Studios, when I worked there I could drive home every night. It was easy to cross the border back then. I'd leave the studio at nine every night, get home around eleven-thirty, sleep in my own bed with Lorayne, get up the next morning with the kids for breakfast, leave around eight-thirty, and be at the studio before noon. I did this several times a week. Other days, I'd stay longer to finish things up. But it was ideal: a great-sounding studio and home at night. I produced the Trooper albums there as well.

But while *BTO II* (which has both "Let It Ride" and "Takin' Care of Business" on it) was mixed at Kaye Smith Studios, *Not Fragile* was mixed at Sound City in Van Nuys, California, because Mark Smith had moved there. The tape machines weren't working at Kaye Smith and we couldn't wait for them to be fixed. We mixed *Not Fragile* in a week.

After we'd notched up several hit records, we could no longer get the time we wanted at Kaye Smith because now everyone wanted to record there. Heart had moved back to Seattle and was recording at the studio; in fact, they ended up buying it and renaming it Bad Animals. Then the whole grunge thing emerged from Seattle and was recorded there. Things just evolved. So for *Four Wheel Drive* we went back to Toronto to Phase One Studio, a brand-new facility built in 1974 with all Neve equipment. Bob Ezrin had recorded Alice Cooper and KISS there. They gave us a great rate, and it worked out well. We did the next albums, *Head On* and *Freeways*, at Phase One also. I had a new engineer, George Semkiw, who'd worked under Mark Smith at RCA in Toronto.

When I left BTO in 1977, I recorded my solo album *Survivor* at Richard Perry's Studio 55 on Melrose Avenue in Los Angeles. Burton had been recording his second solo album, *My Own Way to Rock*, there, and I was impressed with the facilities as well as the clients, which included Toto, the Pointer Sisters, Boz Scaggs, Diana Ross, and Ringo Starr. Phil Spector had also worked at Studio 55 after Gold Star Studios closed down. I later built my own sixteen-track studio in Lynden, Washington, in an outbuilding I named The Barn. Ironhorse and Union recorded there.

Since then, recording studios have pretty much gone digital. No tape anymore, and easy edits. With programs like Pro Tools you can make anyone sound like Celine Dion. My daughter Calliannne has a band, Techromancer, and she mixes their recordings on iPod headphones, not on speakers, because that's how their audience listens to their music. In the 60s, you'd mix for a car radio, since that was the most likely way your audience would hear your single. Having a big studio and paying fifty grand to mix a record is a waste of money nowadays because you're mixing to speakers that no one will be listening to the music on—you're missing your target market, who are listening on iPods or some other dinky little digital player. Interestingly enough, I've heard that cassettes are making a comeback in the U.K. Tape always sounds better than digital. Dolby tape has no hiss and a better fidelity than a CD. I'm not sure it'll catch on over here, though.

The reality is that home digital recording is replacing the big studios, many of which are closing up due to lack of interest. This DIY approach is bringing music back to a grassroots level. Artists are actually making more money by marketing their own music to digitally download; in doing so they're bypassing the old record label system, which took the bulk of the money and left you crumbs, if that. It's a whole new universe.

If you couldn't be a musician,
what would you be?
And have you ever had any other jobs?

Randy recording in 1979 with Ironhorse
in The Barn studio, Lynden, Washington.

I've often been asked what I'd have become if I weren't a musician, but it's not the right question. The real question is, If I hadn't been a *successful* musician, what would I have become? Answer: an unsuccessful musician. I knew from the time I was three that I was going to be a musician. I never considered anything else. I still love it. I get up every day and play guitar and write songs. That's my life and I wouldn't have it any other way. Will I have another #1 record? It's highly unlikely, but that doesn't deter me from still getting up to bat and writing songs. I have nothing to prove to anyone. I've had two worldwide #1 singles as well as albums. I've been to the top with two entirely different bands. But it's not about the success; it's about the creative process, and that's ongoing.

On my *Vinyl Tap* radio show, I once did an episode on jobs, using Johnny Paycheck's classic personal empowerment song, "Take This Job and Shove It," as the theme throughout. I'd say, "If you don't like your job just tell 'em to ..." and then I'd play the song again. It was a lot of fun. I focused on the key jobs that we depend on in our society, like doctors, nurses, teachers, and garbage collectors. If it's between teachers and bankers, who do you think is more essential?

It was difficult for my dad to accept his eldest son's dream of being a professional musician. The prevailing sentiment among postwar, 50s-era parents who'd lived through the Great Depression was, "It's a nice hobby but you'll never make a living from it. Have something to fall back on." My parents encouraged my music, but being a musician wasn't considered a real job in those days; it offered no security or financial stability. To their way of thinking you had to finish school and then get a real job. To them, a musician was like an artist, a painter, who lived hand to mouth and never made anything of himself. No one had the slightest notion of the scope or magnitude a band could rise to at that time. They just figured I'd be playing beer parlours all my life.

That's not to say I never had other jobs, though. After seeing Lenny Breau playing an orange Gretsch 6120 hollow-body electric guitar, I knew I had to have one, too. But they were expensive. Luckily, when I was about sixteen my dad got me a Saturday job as a messenger boy for Imperial Optical on Osborne Street. With it came a bus pass. I could go anywhere, any time with that pass. I'd take the bus to Osborne, pick up the lenses and glasses, then hop on the bus to Portage, where the optometrists' offices were. I'd make my deliveries, pick up the orders, the prescriptions, and the frames from them, and then take them back to Imperial. I did five or six trips a day. It wasn't big pay, but the job demanded a lot of responsibility for someone at that age. On weekends I would babysit, and I also delivered the *Kildonan Post* twice a week, Wednesdays and

Saturdays. I scrimped and saved up for that guitar. Finally, I was able to save up the $400 and acquire my beloved Gretsch.

I was already playing in a band, but once I had my Gretsch I needed money to buy a new amplifier. A friend of mine from West Kildonan, Marvin Hoffer, whose uncle owned the North Main Car Wash at Inkster and Main, got me a job there. He said, "Be at work at five-thirty in the morning." I arrived at the crack of dawn and worked like a wet dog, soaping down and chamoising cars until eight that night. When I was done, the boss handed me $15. I never went back. I could make more money playing wedding socials with a polka band, which Garry Peterson and I did.

I had no interest in working a regular job, but my parents thought differently. When I was a bit older, maybe eighteen or so, my dad got me a job at Bata Shoes, a retail store around the corner from his office downtown. He and his partner, Lorne Walsh, had opened Benson & Law Opticians on Kennedy Street south from Portage Avenue. There's nothing worse than your dad getting you a job, because you feel obligated. At Bata Shoes, when you were the new guy you got the worst customers or the toughest tasks, just to see if you could handle it. So when a big farm Baba with gigantic feet like Goofy's came in, her nylons rolled down to her calf and her feet not washed in a month, I was the one who got to fit her for shoes while the other guys watched. Swallowing my pride, I managed to sell her the shoes she wanted, so I passed the test. But I knew this wasn't for me. It was an evening shift, and when I took my break at seven p.m. I never went back. I got on a bus to East Kildonan, where the band was playing a dance that night, and made $25.

In those days, most parents were earning maybe $50 to $70 a week. I could make $50 playing two nights. But as I said, being a musician wasn't a real job to them. Only jazz musicians did that, and as far as they were concerned they were all on dope.

Again to placate my father, I briefly worked at Simpson-Sears at Polo Park in the menswear department. The sales philosophy there was that if someone came in looking for a shoelace, you tried to sell them a suit. If they wanted a tie, you tried to get them into a matching jacket. It was all about the upsell. "Would you like fries with that?" But I couldn't hustle people to buy things they didn't want. I lasted two days, standing on my feet for hours on end, trying to squeeze Bigfoot into a new suit. It made no sense doing that for maybe $20 a weekend while still playing dances in the evening. I was further ahead just staying home, practising all day and playing evenings. My dad used to say that I loved to work at nothing all day. That line appears in "Takin' Care of Business," and every musician knows what I'm talking about.

Much later, when we leased two brand-new Buick station wagons so that the band could travel, my dad was incredulous. "How are you going to pay for them? You aren't making enough! You're going to get stuck with these and you'll be coming to me for money." He just didn't understand that a musician or a band could make a living at what they did.

Garry Peterson faced the same obstacles with his parents, the difference being that his dad, Ferdie, had been a musician and knew firsthand the pitfalls of that life. Ferdie, who had a day gig as a mechanic at Air Canada, insisted that Garry get a university education and become a dentist. They used to have terrible fights over that. Garry completed one year of university before packing it in. I sincerely doubt that he's ever regretted not becoming a dentist.

I figured that the only way to get my parents off my back was to stay in school. So I enrolled at MIT, the Manitoba Institute of Technology (now known as Red River Community College), which was way out near the airport in northwest Winnipeg. I studied business administration; being in a band, it seemed like a good idea to learn how to handle finances. I signed up to take business law, banking, insurance, accounting, and economics. It seemed pretty easy and practical enough. I had no interest whatsoever in any kind of manual labour job because I didn't want to risk damaging my hands. But even though I was fairly diligent about going to classes, all I wanted to do was play music. I was the only guy at MIT with a photo of the Beatles in my locker. At least it kept my parents at bay, and I did learn some valuable skills that I applied in my bands, even though I never actually finished the program. In June 1965, just days before I was to write my final exams and graduate, I dropped out. "Shakin' All Over" was a hit record in the States, and Paul Cantor and Scepter Records were inviting us to come to New York to tour and record. It was the big time calling and I wasn't about to miss that call.

After we came back from our disastrous U.K. trip in the spring of 1967, I needed to make more money than I was earning in the band. I had a wife by then and had to support her. I grew up in an era where wives didn't work: they stayed home and ran the household so that when hubby came home the house was clean and dinner was on the table. Lorayne had done some modelling, but I didn't want other guys ogling her. And although being a full-time musician made it difficult to find a house to rent, we'd managed to find a great little bungalow at 160 Luxton Avenue in the North End for $75 a month. When I went to meet the owner, he asked me what I did for a living and I said I was a musician. He responded, "Yeah, okay, but what's your real job?" I told him I played in a band. As it turned out, he played in a Romanian band with his brothers, so I got the house.

I could manage the monthly rent, but the Guess Who was so far in the hole that I had to take on three guitar students each week after school to earn extra money. They paid me $15 an hour, which was a lot of money back then. I just recycled Lenny Breau stuff for them, but that money bought our groceries. One of my students was Rob Matheson, who later co-wrote a couple of Guess Who songs. He gave me some poems he'd written; I put them to music and they became "When You Touch Me" and "Lightfoot." Then we got the CBC television show, and after that things were better. I also started writing for and producing local bands, which, while it didn't bring in any big money, nonetheless offered valuable experience and lessons in how to produce and write for others. It was also good for me because it connected me with other players who were struggling to make it. I felt like I was giving something back, since I had some experience they didn't have. I wrote, produced, and played on Sugar and Spice's debut single "Not to Return," and recently got an email from their bass player, John MacInnes, who's now a Queen's Council lawyer in Calgary and listens to *Vinyl Tap* all the time. I've also heard from the Murphy sisters, who sang on the record.

On the one hand, it's tougher nowadays to make a living as a musician: gigs are harder to find, the pay is generally low, and instrument and equipment costs have escalated significantly. And it still takes both luck and perseverance to make it. On the other hand, musicians in Canada today can access a number of financial support programs set up by provincial and federal governments to help them make records or tour. As well, many recording artists are marketing their own music independently and don't need to court a major label, who'll take most of the money anyway. The reality is that you don't have to become a megastar to make a living from music. You just need to be creative, clever, adaptable, and resourceful as well as talented. I know plenty of working musicians who make a decent living doing what they love without having to be huge stars. It's all about doing what you love.

Most of your contemporaries, and
even some of your band members,
indulged in alcohol and drugs.
Did you ever feel the temptation?

Promo shot of Randy taken
on Salt Spring Island, 2008.

I have a predilection for addiction. In other words, if I get into something, it becomes an obsession with me. I didn't just casually collect Gretsch guitars, I obsessively bought some 380 of them. Same thing with sweets. I'm like that potato chip commercial where they say, "You can't have just one." It's part of my genetic makeup. Thankfully I never became a drinker, smoker, or drug user because given my inclinations, I would have gone into each with gusto to the point of addiction and beyond. If I'd gotten into drugs I'd most likely be dead by now. But knowing this about myself and my internal chemistry isn't why I chose to abstain from these vices, nor was it my Mormon faith. That came later and fit the lifestyle choices I'd already made.

When Burton Cummings joined the Guess Who, he wasn't smoking at home in front of his mother, and if he was drinking it wasn't out in the open because the drinking age was still twenty-one. When he drank, it was late at night at someone's house. My father had assured Burton's mother that I was a decent boy who didn't smoke or drink. Burton and I did drink together early on, but that was over by the time we began writing together in 1967. During our brief drinking period, though, Burton and I used to drink until we fell down. I remember a friend, Jack Skelly, having to pick me up in a hotel hallway and carry me back to my room because I'd drunk so much that I'd passed out in the hall. I was pretty much a non-drinker until Burton joined. After that, we'd have competitions to see who could stand up the longest. He usually beat me. We really used to get into it.

My drinking career ended abruptly one night at a party at Jim Kale's house in Norwood. It was early June 1966 and Chad Allan was leaving the band, so we were having a farewell party. I got paralytically drunk, so drunk in fact that I drove over my own foot. Try to figure that one out. I don't recall whose car I was moving so that someone else could get their car out of Jim's driveway, but it was one of those old two-door cars where the doors are really long. I sort of perched myself half in the car and half out, with my butt partly on the seat and one foot on the ground. It was apparently slippery. There I was with this big car door ajar, and at that moment the door blew all the way open in the wind. I was hanging out of the car as I put it in reverse. When I did so, the wind pulled me farther out of the car and my foot slipped. The vehicle rolled backwards and my left foot went under the front wheel. I immediately put on the brake and yelled for help. My father came running out of the house, reached in, and put the car into forward. It lurched ahead and he then put it in park. He looked at me, drunk and pathetic, having just run over my own foot, and said, "I'm ashamed to call you my son." I was devastated. That was the last night I ever drank.

My smoking was equally short-lived. I still can't understand why I even attempted it because I don't like being around smoke. Neither of my parents smoked. The other guys in the Guess Who all smoked, and I found I wanted to be around it less and less. One of the hazards of playing in a rock group was playing in smoky clubs, and I hated it. We'd get on airplanes, and back then people would smoke in them, and I'd be trapped. It didn't matter where I sat, the smoke would be all over me. I couldn't stand it. However, as a student at community college in the early 60s, I fancied myself a pretty sophisticated young man indeed. Being such a cool dude, I thought I should be smoking a pipe. So I bought one, along with a little pouch and some tobacco. I remember sitting in my dad's living room chair feeling rather chic and mature as I filled my pipe with apricot cherry–flavoured tobacco, leaned back, and lit up. I was puffing away confidently when my mother yelled from the kitchen, "Something's on fire!" As I got up from my chair to reassure her that it was just her sophisticated eldest son, I fell face first onto the floor. I was so dizzy I wanted to throw up. I vowed to never smoke again.

Performing onstage before hundreds or even thousands of people is an incredible adrenaline rush. For however long you're up there, you feel like the king of the world. For many musicians that adrenaline rush is addictive, and that's why so many rock stars take drugs: to feel the ultimate high of highs when they're not onstage. You get to the point of craving it. I was fortunate to have avoided all that. I saw firsthand what drugs did to Lenny Breau. They robbed him of his talent, his career, and ultimately his life. For drug addicts, the number one priority, from the time they wake up in the morning until they go to bed at night, is to score drugs to get them through the day. I saw that with Lenny.

I remember Dion and the Belmonts sitting at the back of our tour bus in 1965, using tweezers to pull tobacco out of their cigarettes and then stuffing in white powder before lighting them up. They were getting blitzed out of their minds. But if a cop ever bothered looking at them, he'd just think they were smoking a regular cigarette. I was scared of all that stuff—I'd heard the heroin stories about Gene Krupa and Frankie Lymon. Another time I sat beside Dion on the bus. I was enamoured of the living legend who'd had so many hits like "Runaround Sue" and "The Wanderer," and there he was singing doo-wop songs with the Belmonts. He was wearing jeans and cowboy boots and had his legs up, singing away, and I'm beside him gaga over all this when he suddenly stops, looks at his boots, and says, "Wow, whose feet are those?! Look at those boots! Whose boots are those?!" I'm thinking, "They're yours, for god's sake! They're at the end of your legs!" He was just blotto. We'd all bought cowboy boots at some store somewhere and he didn't recognize his boots or his own feet.

In the late 60s, the Guess Who all used alcohol and drugs, but I was never tempted. I saw what it did to them and didn't like it. I saw them lose control, and I didn't want to lose control. Jim Kale became belligerent when he drank. I once saw him, three sheets to the wind, get his face kicked in when he mouthed off to the wrong guy. As he was going down he was still mouthing off. You couldn't do anything to stop him. That kind of stuff scared me. Jim would go to this dark place—he'd be banging on your hotel room door in the middle of the night, drunk and screaming at you. I knew I couldn't do that and get up the next morning and go to the bank to deposit the gig money from the night before. I had responsibilities, not just for myself and my family but for the band. We had people depending on us. While the other guys were tripping out on drugs I was counting up the money, bundling it, paying the bills, mailing home the receipts to our accountant, and depositing the rest. Since I'd studied business, I liked that role. I wasn't interested in being blitzed out. Taking care of the business occupied my mind rather than chasing the high with sex, drugs, and booze. However, in doing so I became the person to rebel against. To the other guys, I was Mr. Straight, the parent, the narc. I remember Burton telling me, "You're nothing but a fucking narc. Leave us alone." They'd be in the hotel room next to mine, partying all night long, and I'd have to put up with it and try to get some sleep.

It drove a wedge between us that festered until it all hit the fan on May 16, 1970, when I found myself out of the Guess Who. Drugs were de rigueur in the music business by then, and in the 70s, it only got worse with cocaine. It was an accepted thing, and to not do drugs meant you were regarded with suspicion, not trusted or allowed into the inner circle. You were branded an outsider. Everyone—from the musicians and crew to the promoters, managers, record company reps, radio deejays, and even the music media—was using drugs in one form or another. It was almost inescapable, and taking a non-drug stance was tantamount to a betrayal of the very business itself. There was a widespread misconception that drugs enhanced your creativity, but a lot of what I saw or heard from drug-addled minds wasn't very creative or listenable unless you, too, were in a mind-altering state.

In the July 1970 issue of *Rolling Stone* magazine, an article on my leaving the Guess Who declared that I'd never make it in this business straight. I was the anomaly; drugs were the norm. I was branded a loser, an outsider because I didn't do drugs. Even Burton said in interviews that I'd never be successful being straight. That gave me something to prove, so when I did succeed and ultimately surpass the Guess Who, it felt good. BTO's "Hey You" reflects that feeling of being on top again and showing all the naysayers, including and especially those in the Guess Who, that I was not to be written off. I succeeded on my own terms and without drugs. In a 1974 interview in *Rolling Stone*, Burton said, "I hate the guy. I'm afraid I couldn't give a damn if Randy Bachman was dead tomorrow." That was very hurtful. But I was just following my own path.

The risk to the group of one of us getting busted was serious. Having a drug bust meant we couldn't cross the border. I knew that some guys in the band were bringing drugs in for personal use. They weren't thinking about the band. I had to fire my own brother Tim from BTO after giving him three chances to clean up his act. He was abusing drugs and putting us all in jeopardy by concealing them when we toured. It was a tough decision and I've agonized over it ever since, but I felt that for the future welfare of the band I had no choice but to cut him loose. It was hard on Tim at the time. I never had a problem with Fred having the odd beer away from the band because it never interfered with the music and never went to excess. But if it threatened our ability to carry on, then it was a serious issue and I'd have to put my foot down. Lots of people around me have a drink and it's okay. It wouldn't be my choice, but it's fine for many as long as it doesn't become excessive or a problem.

The U.K.'s Thin Lizzy opened for BTO on several tours, and we kind of got to know them. They were a great rockin' band, with twin lead guitars and the powerful voice of Phil Lynott. "The Boys Are Back in Town" is still a great song. But their reputation for hard rock was matched by their excessive drug and alcohol use. Phil later died from complications related to years of heroin abuse, and guitarist Scott Gorham was a heroin addict until cleaning up in the 1990s. One-time Lizzy guitarist Gary Moore passed away after decades of alcohol abuse.

BTO had a no-alcohol or -drugs policy backstage, and this gave us something of a negative reputation in the business: radio and record people wanted to party with the band, only unlike all the other bands on the road, we didn't go in for that. I think it caused a bit of resentment and a backlash against us, but so be it. My attitude has always been, "If you want to goof around with drugs do it somewhere else. Don't waste my time." The other factor was that I never wanted to disgrace my parents or my own family. I didn't want my father to ever again be ashamed to call me his son, nor did I ever want my children to witness their dad high or involved in a public scandal.

During rehearsals for the Guess Who's highly anticipated 2000 Running Back Thru Canada tour, Jim Kale promised he would clean himself up. A lot of money, not to mention the reputation of the band, was on the line. There'd been so much publicity and expectation surrounding this tour that to fail just wasn't in the cards. We were like the return of the conquering Canadian heroes. Nonetheless, when Jim showed up at rehearsals he was barely able to stand. He had to sit slouched over. At one point he said, "Randy, cover for me." He was falling asleep. He did have health issues, but they were compounded by his substance abuse. He was a liability. So we called a meeting, and with tears in my eyes I told him that while I dearly wanted him onstage with us, we just couldn't risk it. He had to go. The next day, we brought in Jim's original replacement in the band back in 1972, Bill Wallace. With Bill the energy level of the entire rehearsal room went up a thousand percent. Jim's problems had been dragging everyone down. He retained his portion of the tour proceeds as per the contracts, and he paid Wallace out of his end. But Wallace saved our asses on that tour.

In the past, when Neil Young and I would get together, he respected that I was straight and never tried to force the issue, and I in turn accepted that drugs and alcohol were a part of his routine and who he was. When you read his autobiography, *Waging Heavy Peace,* he led a Keith Richards kind of life for a while, but now seems to be looking to make amends for some of the wreckage he left behind. He lost several close friends as a result of overdoses. He really is a different person now, and our relationship has changed because of it. We had dinner together recently and it was a whole new Neil. I told him that sitting with him was so nice now because we hadn't been able to do that before; there'd always been too many distractions.

I asked him what made him give up alcohol and drugs after all these years. He told me that he hadn't gone through any rehab program; his rehab was his own mind, his ability to just stop. He said that when he'd had his aneurysm back in 2005 his doctors insisted he have an MRI, magnetic resonance imaging, where your brain is scanned. The results revealed all the damage done by decades of drug use. It was an eye-opener for him to see all those dark areas in his brain. Also, his dad had suffered from Alzheimer's disease, and Neil didn't want to risk his own chances of succumbing to it. So he called his team together and told them that he couldn't be around this stuff, drugs and booze, anymore. They had to respect that and to have a totally clean environment around him. Some of his crew chose to leave. Backstage with Neil nowadays is like being at one of my shows: no booze and good healthy food. And no toking or toots before the show by anyone in his entourage.

I missed out on opportunities to meet some of my contemporaries because drugs were involved. I have no regrets about my choice not to be around cigarettes, alcohol, or drugs. I know I can't be, and I also know both the risks and the outcomes. It's not a religious thing by any means. It's a lifestyle decision I made and continue to adhere to.

You've been an integral part of the
Canadian music scene going back to
the early 60s. What are your thoughts
on the evolution of Canadian music and
the state of the music industry today?

Randy at the 2011 Juno Awards live show at the
Air Canada Centre in Toronto, March 27, 2011.

The media often refer to me as the elder statesman of Canadian rock 'n' roll. That's just because I've been around so long. But in that time, some six decades, I've witnessed a lot of changes in the Canadian music scene. Back when I first started out in the early 60s, Canadian music was very regionalized, with no national star system. Bands like Jack London and the Sparrows in Toronto and the Collectors in Vancouver all enjoyed hits in their respective areas, but those records never travelled any farther. The Ugly Ducklings, for example, would pack halls in and around southern Ontario, but when they came to Winnipeg they could barely fill a small club like the Pink Panther. With "Shakin' All Over" in 1965, the Guess Who became the first Canadian rock 'n' roll band to break out of those regional barriers and have a hit right across the country.

The big thing about "Shakin' All Over" was that no one knew who we were; all it said on the record label was "Guess Who?". That was the greatest scam perpetrated on the Canadian music scene at the time. It fostered all sorts of rumours about who it might be on the record, and because it had such a British sound to it, a story spread that it was guys from the Stones, the Beatles, and other bands, who for contractual reasons couldn't use their own names. So that "Guess Who" label piqued the curiosity of radio-station music programmers, who gave this mysterious record a spin. Once they heard the song there was no denying it. That record had magic and a British sound just when all things British were in demand. It was goosebumps when you heard it. It still has that quality today, a feel-good record that you want to crank up. Getting Canadian radio to give a Canadian record a chance back then was no cake walk. It took a brilliant promotional move on the part of George Struth and George Keen at Quality to make it a hit.

Up to that point, Quality Records existed to license American records from the several labels they had agreements with and release them in Canada. There were no national Canadian labels at the time, just regional ones. It was all American or British labels or their subsidiaries. But Quality had distribution rights across Canada, so we wanted to be on their label. No big American labels were signing Canadian bands at the time.

We were inexperienced prairie boys who had no comprehension whatsoever of the opportunities a hit record offered, and no ability to capitalize on a hit. Our manager, Bob Burns, was small-time, and in any case it would have been difficult to take advantage of our success: there wasn't any national promotion, no Canadian fan magazines, and few opportunities to appear on national television. So, with a Canadian hit and an undeniably appealing record, Quality licensed "Shakin' All Over" to New York–based Scepter Records. Again, we were clueless about how to make the next move. I'd go to Kresge's downtown because I knew the woman at the record counter and she'd let me look at the latest issue of *Billboard* magazine to check out the Hot 100 singles each week. At that point it was, "Oh, we're #22 this week. Cool. Time to go to class." It wasn't until we received a phone call from Paul Cantor in New York that we realized both the magnitude of the record and the potential to tour. Paul tracked us down by getting hold of Quality Records in Toronto. He had to go in search of us, and I'm forever grateful that he did.

By the mid 60s, we were Canada's #1 band, but what did that mean? Not much. The Guess Who's history, at least when I was in the band, is really eight years of losing money, two years of breaking even, and one year of making good money. It was all about a survival instinct: maybe if we just keep going something will happen for us. And it was pretty much the same for our contemporaries. If you wanted a shot at the big time, the only choice you had was to pack your bags and head south. That road south was well-worn by Canadians seeking greener pastures in the United States. The list of those who left is long and impressive, and includes the likes of Neil Young, Joni Mitchell, Paul Anka, Blood, Sweat and Tears' David Clayton-Thomas, Zal Yanovsky from the Lovin' Spoonful, the Diamonds, Denny Doherty of the Mamas and Papas, and on and on.

There were a lot of great records by Canadian artists back in the 60s, and I recall them fondly. The Beau-Marks' "Clap Your Hands" had to be one of the stupidest songs ever, but it was also one of the catchiest, and that's why it became a hit. In 1960, everyone was singing that silly song. Bobby Curtola's success prompted me to believe that if a guy with a modicum of talent from Port Arthur, Ontario, could make it, then Chad

Allan and the Reflections from Winnipeg, a city ten times that size, could make it, too. We backed Bobby on some Winnipeg dates and across western Canada, all the way to Edmonton for Klondike Days and to Calgary for the Stampede, because it was an opportunity for us to travel and promote our records. We had "Shy Guy" out at the time. At the Stampede we played the Teen Tent with Bobby, sponsored by Coca-Cola. That was our first encounter with screaming girls, who came to see Bobby every night. It was our taste of the rock 'n' roll limelight. The brains behind Bobby Curtola, brothers Dyer and Basil Hurdon, were smart businessmen for their time. They had their own record label, Tartan Records, wrote the songs and published them, owned the masters, and had a young, good-looking front man to go out and promote them live. They had it made. Bobby Curtola was a decent singer and performer and a nice guy who came along when Canadian teenagers were looking for their very own Elvis or Cliff Richard. He filled that void, and he was very successful at it.

Then there was the Ronnie Hawkins school of rock 'n' roll in Toronto. Rompin' Ronnie had moved north from Arkansas on the advice of Conway Twitty, who assured Ronnie that the pickins were better in Canada, not to mention all the fresh-faced Canadian girls. His brand of rockabilly/rhythm 'n' blues came to dominate southern Ontario. Some great players came out of his bands, like Robbie Robertson and the other guys in the Band as well as Domenic Troiano and Robbie Lane and the Disciples.

Burton and I always admired Gordon Lightfoot. He was a real down-home, down-to-earth kind of guy who was always nice to us, never snooty, no star trip or ego, and still to this day a very nice guy. And because Gordon both wrote and sang great songs, he was Canada's own Bob Dylan. Leonard Cohen wasn't nearly as good in the early days; his songs weren't that great and he wasn't a singer, he was a poet with a guitar. Gordon, meanwhile, enjoyed several hits. I remember that after Neil Young got me in to see Mo Ostin at Reprise Records with the first Brave Belt album, I ran into Gordon at breakfast in Los Angeles's Continental Hyatt House. We sat together and talked. He'd just left United Artists to sign with Warner Brothers, and told me that one of the conditions of his signing was that he had to accept their producer, Lenny Waronker, rather than who he wanted or had used on his previous albums. He asked if I'd had to give up production when I signed with Reprise. I told him I wouldn't do that. Gordon made it big; Brave Belt didn't. Back then I hadn't realized how the game was played in L.A.: the labels decided who produced you because they were shelling out the money. Sometimes it worked and sometimes it didn't. I'd been so shafted in the Guess Who that I didn't want to sign away anything. Maybe it was ego, but it was also self-preservation. I just didn't want to give away my effort and creativity, as I'd done in the Guess Who, to someone who hadn't contributed to them and yet reaped their rewards.

Despite the limitations of the Canadian music industry, some great records came from Canadian artists. Crowbar's "Oh What a Feeling" has only one chord in the whole song, but what a fantastic tune. The Stampeders' "Carry Me" was another terrific record. Rich Dodson deserves more recognition than he receives as a songwriter. All the Stampeders' songs were great, and "Sweet City Woman" became a huge worldwide hit for them.

"Brainwashed" by David Clayton Thomas and the Boss Men—
what an amazing piano solo on that. Bobby Taylor and the
Vancouvers' "Does Your Mama Know About Me" was another
fantastic song, recorded at Motown in Detroit. That's Tommy
Chong, later of Cheech and Chong, on guitar on that record,
along with Floyd Sneed, who went on to play drums for Three
Dog Night. "Signs" by the Five Man Electrical Band, who used
to be the Staccatos, is still a terrific song that I wish I'd written.
Les Emmerson wrote some classic songs with that band. The
Ugly Ducklings played raunchy R&B music, and were Canada's
very own Rolling Stones or Pretty Things with their really long
hair and funky clothes. April Wine made super records, produced
by my friend Ralph Murphy. "Charlena" by Richie Knights and
the Mid-Knights from 1963 is a great R&B song that features
George Semkiw, who later engineered several BTO albums for
me, on guitar. I loved all these artists because they were just like
me, trying to make it in the big music world. We'd hear about
some of these bands, and maybe Doc Steen or PJ the DJ might
play them, but we really had our own prairie records that were
played on radio in Winnipeg, especially local bands. Lots of
local bands had big records in Winnipeg, including the Jury, the
Shondels, the Luvin' Kind, and the Deverons.

Once we started travelling eastward, we discovered that
the Toronto music scene was quite different from Winnipeg's.
Known as the Boss Sound, it was far more R&B and soul influenced. That may have been because there was a strong black
community in Toronto. When we first started coming down to
Toronto to play or record they had all these big R&B horn bands
with a guy out front trying to be like James Brown—bands like

Grant Smith and the Power, and Shawn and Jay Jackson and the Majestics. These boogaloo bands, as we used to call them, would make fun of us from Winnipeg. We used to reply that we had wheatfield soul. So when it came time to name our first RCA album, that was it. To heck with those guys. And we ended up having the biggest hit of any of them with "These Eyes," while no one beyond Toronto ever heard of Grant Smith and the Power (sorry, Grant).

In January 1971, the federal government introduced Canadian content rules, or CanCon, which mandated that radio stations play a minimum of 30 percent Canadian content (now 35 percent) between six a.m. and twelve p.m. CanCon was defined as fulfilling at least two of four criteria: the music was composed by a Canadian; the music was principally performed by a Canadian artist; the recording was wholly done in Canada; or the lyrics were written by a Canadian. This is known as the MAPL system: Music, Artist, Production, and Lyrics. Radio stations across the country protested vehemently, claiming that their rights were being infringed upon and their profits put in jeopardy. They even took to Parliament Hill in an effort to halt the CRTC (Canadian Radio-television Telecommunications Commission) from implementing these draconian measures. But they were unsuccessful, and CanCon came into effect.

The results of fostering a strong Canadian music industry by giving it a helping hand were felt soon after—as Canadian artists, using success in Canada as a launching pad, were able to notch up commercial successes outside our borders. Income from Canadian songwriting abroad rose from $200,000 in

1969 to $1.3 million in 1974 and to over $6 million by 1987. And it's way beyond that now. The Guess Who didn't benefit from Canadian content regulations because we'd earned our success—the big success with "These Eyes" and everything that followed—in the U.S. first. But BTO certainly benefited from CanCon. I've always said that CanCon was a good thing, and needed at that time. If you want to make radio stations play Canadian records, then legislate it so that they have no choice, because up to that point, Canadian radio wasn't playing much Canadian-made music.

Before CanCon, a survey of radio stations across the country revealed that they were playing an average 5 percent Canadian content. And while CanCon was only 30 percent when it came in, other countries had similar laws that were much higher than ours. Germany, for example, had something like 70 percent; that's why they had so many German bands covering British and American records there. The BBC had 50 percent. CanCon virtually built a Canadian music industry and gave Canadian musicians, singers, and songwriters a chance. We couldn't compete against the Beatles or the Stones or the Beach Boys on the radio before CanCon. Now we had a leg up. It gave Canadians hope and an opportunity.

But it wasn't just all about flag waving. The wider economic benefits were significant. It's the ripple effect: force Canadian radio to play 30 percent Canadian content, and they have to find that content. Initially they played a lot of Anne Murray, Gordon Lightfoot, and Guess Who records, but the demand was there for Canadian recordings. Record labels sprang up to sign artists who now had a chance to receive airplay. Recording studios were built to record these Canadian artists. Songwriters wrote songs. Music publishing, promotion, management, booking agencies, touring companies, concert promotion, concert gear—all this stuff rose up. It's a simple case of demand and supply. And what stays in Canada? The artists and the profits. CanCon brought Canadian music from a barely million-dollar business to a billion-dollar one. In the end it was the right thing to do, and still is. You can actually make a living as a musician, singer, or songwriter in Canada without having to forsake your homeland.

Bryan Adams has been very critical of CanCon in recent years. However, by the time he spoke up about it, he didn't need it. But he sure needed it when he was starting out. He was just repeating what manager Bruce Allen, the self-styled "mouth that roared," was saying. The two guys who've benefited the most from CanCon, Bryan and Bruce, are the ones putting it down. The bottom line is that there wouldn't be a Canadian music industry today without CanCon. Trooper, April Wine, Rush, Bryan Adams, Loverboy, Corey Hart, Glass Tiger—they're all products of the initial wave of CanCon artists.

Besides CanCon, we also need to revise the tax system that still chases artists out of the country. I talked to Prime Minister Stephen Harper about this when he had me over for lunch at 24 Sussex Drive a couple of years ago. Being a musician himself, he was keen to meet me, and I was flattered to be invited. Imagine if Celine Dion, Avril Lavigne, Shania Twain, Alanis Morissette, Justin Bieber, Bryan Adams, and Neil Young all came back to live in Canada because our tax system was attracting instead of repelling them. As it is, they come back to get their Governor General's Awards or their Junos, and many musicians come back for the free health care—then they leave and pay their taxes elsewhere. Stephen Harper's reply was, "Put it down in writing and give it to me." That's the last I heard about it. The government funds programs like FACTOR and Video Fact and legislates that Canadian content be played on radio, but when artists do make it they're taxed right out of the country and go reside somewhere else. It doesn't make sense. And look at all the people who work for these big artists, people who'd be paying taxes here as well if they came back.

I had this whole plan for revising taxes written out back in 1999 for Prime Minister Chrétien when we were in Winnipeg playing the Pan Am Games' closing ceremonies. After our performance I was in the lobby of the Delta Hotel when in walked Chrétien with his RCMP secret service guards around him. We'd never met before and I'm not sure he recognized me. To him, I was probably just another potential vote. He nodded to me and I nodded back at him. Then I went to reach into my vest pocket to pull out my letter about reforming the tax system for artists, a letter I'd been holding on to in the hope of an opportunity to present it to him somehow. But as I did so my arm suddenly got chicken-winged behind me, with two RCMP guards moving in while two others pushed Chrétien out of the way and into the elevator. I said to the RCMP guys, "What just happened here? I have a letter in an envelope to give to Mr. Chrétien." One of them replied that they hadn't known, and that they couldn't take any chances when someone in proximity to the prime minister puts his hand in his pocket. It could be a gun. Someone had hit him with a pie recently, so they were being extra careful. Like I've got a pie in my vest pocket? So he never got my letter.

Despite the benefits accrued by CanCon over the years, the Canadian music industry today, like the music industry in the rest of the world, is in a shambles. The whole hierarchy is gone, and the record labels that wielded so much power in the past are in steep decline. They're dinosaurs trying to find a place in the new digital-download landscape. They're not developing talent anymore; it's pretty much a DIY mentality now, where young artists starting out have to market themselves and their music out of their own basements. Recording nowadays is also very much DIY, with digital recording technology and programs like Pro Tools available to anyone. I can only hope that artists today will reap the rewards more directly than they would being chattel to a record label that takes the majority of the money.

I'm still tied to the Guess Who royalty rate we signed in 1969 because when the band renegotiated their contract with RCA in the early 70s, they didn't grandfather me into the deal. And we're still getting the same mechanical rate on record sales: two cents. Mechanical rates have since gone up, to eight and later to twelve cents, but we're stuck with two. And of that, Garry, Jim, and I are getting one-sixteenth of a cent per sale on "American Woman" while Burton gets all the publishing money (more about that later).

The explosion of CDs in the 90s that killed vinyl off presented a huge boon to record labels: they had all these tracks already recorded and could license them to compilations or re-release them at virtually zero cost. The demand from classic and oldies radio formatting meant that what was old was new again, with a whole new lease on life. CDs cost maybe sixty-nine cents to make, and with no recording or promotional charges, the record labels made huge profits for basically doing nothing. Added to this was the fact that most of the recording artists were already under existing contracts way back in the files that paid royalty rates from thirty or forty years ago. It was a windfall of staggering proportions for the music industry. They didn't have to seek out and take a chance investing millions in a new artist who might fail; they had surefire winners already signed. So the record labels took advantage by ripping us off with all these bad contracts that everybody signed back in those days when very few artists had decent contracts.

Then along comes some computer geek who invents Napster, and suddenly we're being ripped off again for our songs by free file sharing. Then Steve Jobs comes up with iTunes, selling our songs as individual tracks, no B-sides and no albums. But the record labels still have their hands in the till, making money off our music. None of the contracts that I or anyone else signed back then had the word "digital" in them. It wasn't even in anyone's vocabulary. But the record labels simply extended their existing contracts to include a means of music sales that no one at the time had conceived. New contracts with existing artists should have been negotiated for digital rights, but the labels weren't about to kill the golden goose or share the milk from the cash cow.

Digital downloading, not the Napster style of stealing music, does put more money and control in the hands of the artists, however. It reduces or eliminates the record labels' traditional role as sole provider or gatekeeper of music sales, thereby in many respects cutting out the middleman. But the artists have to flex their muscles to get it.

It's actually written in the copyright law that after a certain amount of time, an artist's master recordings and a songwriter's songs will revert to the artist and songwriter, respectively. So the Guess Who's recordings will ultimately revert to us. This kind of thing will force a lot of band members, or their heirs, to speak to one another again in order to renegotiate how their music will be distributed and how the money will be split from that point on. Once the tidal wave of master-recording-rights reversion starts—and songs are no longer owned by record labels or controlled by iTunes—then digital music providers will have to negotiate with the artists themselves, including the Deep Purples, the David Bowies, and us. It's going to have a profound impact on the whole music business. As it is, record labels get 90 to 98 percent of the profits, but after that it'll be the artists getting a fair shake and the bulk of those profits. The beneficiaries will no longer be Universal Music. It's going to be a new revolution and will change the dynamic of the business.

Soon, iTunes will be getting notices to take an artist's music down until a new agreement is signed between that artist and iTunes, or whatever digital provider. It'll mean more money for the artists, who've been shafted for years by the robber baron record labels. It'll require some research, too, as many of the companies that existed back then have been swallowed up by bigger conglomerates or have simply disappeared altogether. But the contracts are somewhere, and someone is controlling them. Intellectual property lawyers will have a field day tracking this stuff down. Still, it's up to the artists to initiate all this because the record companies and conglomerates aren't going to do it without a fight. For everyone who got screwed, this is their chance to get unscrewed.

I'm currently involved in getting several of my masters back through revisionary rights. I'm getting back *Axe, Survivor, Ironhorse,* and *Union* so that I can put them out myself. And at some point the Guess Who masters will be reverted. With Brave Belt, we put the original corporation, Brave Belt Ltd., back together and applied to get the masters back. It was Fred, Robbie, and I, but Robbie didn't show up at the meeting. He was duly notified of it but chose not to attend. We never expected him to. So Fred and I outvoted him. Each of us still gets our royalties, but I have the masters back, meaning that no one else can release them. Chad Allan was never in the corporation. When I started working with him in the fall of 1970 it was a Chad Allan solo album, but as it evolved, with more and more of my participation, it became two separate deals with Warner Brothers, his and Brave Belt's. When Chad left the Guess Who, he signed everything over to Quality Records.

Decades later, when I bought what was labelled the Selkirk Tapes, I thought I was buying a live tape of us playing the Selkirk mental institution many years ago. I kept telling my lawyer that the vendor wanted way too much money for a simple live tape. But when I finally got the box of stuff it said "Selkirk Communications" on it, which was the parent company that owned Quality Records. So I ended up owning the masters for all the Guess Who–related recordings from Quality Records and Reo, their subsidiary. When I paid out royalties I also included Chad, even though I didn't have to legally, because he needed the money. I just felt that if it wasn't for him, I wouldn't have been in the band.

Radio, too, is in a troubled state. It's been fragmented into all these different demographics, and now it's narrowcasting to what are considered target or niche markets. Advertising revenues are down because listenership is declining. Satellite radio offers a far better selection of genres without the need for commercial revenue.

I grew up at a time when radio was vital and exciting. Deejays programmed their own shows and chose which records they played. Radio playlists covered a wide musical palette. I remember that on radio, and this went right up into the early 1980s, every deejay shift would play a couple of dusty discs— golden oldies or rusty relics—maybe once an hour. But by the latter 80s, radio programmers started noticing that those dusty discs were getting more requests than the newer stuff being played. In other words, a significant percentage of the listenership was responding more to those "classic" tracks. So some keen-eared programmer decided to format an entire station to classic rock or oldies, and it just proliferated everywhere. It was the baby boomers who had the numbers, and therefore the economic clout, to have radio play the songs of their generation. And, of course, businesses recognized the purchasing power this generation still held and jumped on board with commercials.

I don't understand why, instead of playing the same thirty or forty songs over and over, classic-rock radio doesn't expand its programming to include a recording artist's new track back to back with his or her classic track. Every artist they play—whether it's Deep Purple, Van Halen, Pat Benatar, Heart, the Doobie Brothers, John Fogerty, Aerosmith, Blue Oyster Cult, Yes, the Eagles, or Bachman and Turner—has released newer material since those hits. We're the guys who still know how to make that music. Why not do a "Then and Now" format or show? Play a BTO classic then right after play a new Bachman and Turner cut. That was then, this is now. Radio can't survive by endlessly playing the same forty-year-old tracks, especially when these bands are still out there touring and recording. Our *Bachman & Turner* album has all the hallmarks of the classic BTO sound updated with new songs for the new millennium. We're not recording New Age hippie junk.

I've talked to several radio programmers about this format concept. Promote these artists and their new recordings, and these artists will come to your radio station or play your Christmas charity show. No one is promoting our new music; we're having to do it ourselves. BTO songs from the 70s are played on the radio constantly, everywhere around the world. The irony is that we're still writing and recording, and yet no one will play our new tracks. Radio is cobwebbing itself to death. It isn't open to new recordings by classic-rock acts. Create a new classic-rock format and these bands will be kissing your feet and doing whatever you want.

I'm disappointed that the *Bachman & Turner* album was only a blip on the radar and didn't resonate more, because it had some really strong songs and great production. We went for an authentic BTO sound by using older amps and guitars. But radio being what it is today, the album just didn't get a chance. It's frustrating when you feel you still have it in you and still have something to say but all they're playing is your older tracks. A lot of bands of our vintage feel the same way. No one wants to be merely a nostalgia act. They're all still writing, recording, and creating. Fred asked me recently if I wanted to record another album together, but my feeling is, "Why bother if we're not going to get any radio play?" Don't get me wrong—it's great to be able to have new music for our fans, and we sell lots of the albums on the road and from my website. But it's frustrating to put in all that work—and I put in a ton of work getting that *Bachman & Turner* album in shape—only to feel that it's not even being given a chance. I told Fred that maybe we should release a double-sided single, me and my song on one side and him and his on the other, and see what happens. Let people download it and enjoy it. Or if we do a song for a movie, then there might be interest for an album.

Classic Rock magazine out of the U.K. did this cool thing where they took four of our classic BTO songs and four of our new *Bachman & Turner* tracks and called it *Forged in Rock*. It was a great idea and was well received. That kind of concept can work—using your best-known songs to help introduce your new recordings. But if the music industry and radio aren't going to change, then what's the point? Even CanCon can't change that. It remains a vicious circle.

There are so many ways to make radio interesting again, but getting the people in charge to change is like trying to get the Pope to accept abortion. They just don't want to do it, and that's really sad because they're digging themselves into a hole and narrowing their listenership instead of broadening it. I've kept my own radio show format loose, which allows me to play just about anything from any era or genre. That's one of the reasons I love doing *Vinyl Tap:* I'm not confined or limited by a narrow definition.

With downloaded music sales surpassing
CD sales, and with all the changes in how music
is made and distributed, are music fans today
missing out on anything? How has the way
we experience music changed?

The Guess Who with manager Bob Burns and
CKRC's Doc Steen (centre) holding silver discs
for "Shakin' All Over," spring 1965.

Nowadays, kids don't get the tactile sensation of holding an album, looking at the cover art and the photographs, reading the liner notes and recording details. It's a sterile process, downloading individual tracks. Young people today don't buy albums, they digitally download songs. In the past, you paid attention to the entire package: the songs, the sequencing, the cover art, the back cover. Kids get nothing of that context today. They sample songs and download the ones that appeal to them. So they might pick a song off our *Bachman & Turner* album along with the new Black-Eyed Peas, Taylor Swift, and Franz Ferdinand songs. Sequencing used to be very important. You had to have a strong track to open the album and you ended that side with a track that enticed the listener to turn the album over and listen to the remainder of the tracks. You wanted the sequencing to have a flow to it and to make some musical sense and statement. CDs changed that because there was no flip side.

Think about the tracks on the Beatles' *Sgt. Pepper's Lonely Hearts Club Band,* for example. There's a definite structure to the ordering of the tracks on side one and side two. Taken as a whole (and it should be a given that there's an overall concept), the album has a flow that fits perfectly. It opens with the welcome and introduction to Sgt. Pepper's Band, which segues into the introduction of singer Billy Shears and "With a Little Help from My Friends." Ending side one with "Being for the Benefit of Mr. Kite" is the perfect set closer that encourages you, as if you needed it, to want to flip the record over for more. And, of course, concluding the album with "Good Morning, Good Morning" and the rooster crowing, which leads into the reprise of "Sgt. Pepper's Lonely Hearts Club Band" with a segue into "A Day in the Life" and its crashing piano chord at the end that seems to go on forever, is unrivalled. Obviously, the songs weren't recorded in that order, but the band took the time to consider the perfect sequencing to enhance the overall listening experience. When you take those songs I've just mentioned out of that context and download them as individual tracks, it's not the same listening experience at all. Untethered from the sequencing, they become merely random songs.

Today, kids see music as far more disposable. It's instant gratification by downloading an individual track. Easy come, easy go. Two days later they've moved on. When I used to buy an album or a single I'd listen to it for days on end, and would come back to it even after I'd bought other records. Before I bought it I might have stared at it at the record shop and imagined what sounds were inside it. I still have all my old singles and albums. They're actual things to me, not just a digital sound bite made up of a million 1's and 0's.

Think of your favourite vinyl albums, and what immediately comes to mind are the covers. Album-cover art, whether a photograph or a cleverly conceived painting or graphic, was a key component in creating and marketing an album. I was often inspired to buy a record just because its cover artwork was so compelling. Albums like King Crimson's debut with that gaping mouth, Cream's *Disreali Gears* with its psychedelic collage, Derek and the Dominoes' *Layla* with the haunting-looking painting, Nirvana's *Nevermind* with the baby swimming for the dollar bill, or the Doors' *Morrison Hotel* where the band peers out from the hotel window, just to name a few—that's art. Would *Sgt. Pepper's Lonely Hearts Club Band* be the same without that iconic cover image of dozens of well-known personalities? When we recorded albums in the Guess Who and BTO, careful consideration was always given to what would be on the cover, front and back. It enhanced the appeal of an album. All that's lost now with digital downloading. I used to pore over liner notes like they were some religious artifacts, taking in all the information I could glean about the artist or the recording I held in my hand. Kids get none of that today unless they Google the artist.

Even digital sound is inferior. There's no depth, definition, or fidelity. It's all upfront with no bottom end. Listen to a BTO record on vinyl or on tape. Compared to a CD, there's so much "bigness" from the tape or vinyl. A CD sounds like it's coming from a tiny little speaker. As I said earlier, you can't push CD to get distortion. There's no bigness on CD. Yet sound quality isn't important to the downloading generation because they're listening to the music on iPods or similar devices that flatten out the sound.

The album as we used to know it is dying out. Only boomers like me are buying them because we still want that tactile experience. Kids aren't buying albums much anymore. I'll admit that I buy individual tracks from iTunes for *Vinyl Tap,* but I'm buying tracks I already have on vinyl because I need a clean version to play on air, not the scratchy old vinyl. I used to play vinyl when I first started doing the show, but it was risky; it might skip or pop or sound like someone frying bacon in the background.

Back in the day when 45 singles were still released and were the measure of an artist's success before albums overtook them by the latter 60s, the B-side or flip side of a single was never taken for granted as a throwaway. When you had to save your money for two weeks to buy that single, that's all you had, so playing the B-side was just as important as the A-side. In fact it was often more important: you'd heard the A-side on the radio, that's why you went out and bought the single, but the B-side was a bonus, generally a track you'd never heard before, a hidden gem. Back then you shared your records with your friends. After school we'd go to someone's house and bring over our latest 45s and play them. We'd spend hours just playing 45s and listening to them until our mothers would holler out the front door or phone looking for us to come home for dinner. If I bought Dale Hawkins's "Suzie Q," I'd call my friends to tell them what I had, and we'd get together to listen and share it. We didn't have tape recorders then to record our friends' records. We'd just listen to them and basically memorize them, so that if someone asked me, "Have you heard the B-side of the newest Gene Vincent 45?," I'd be able to recall it from memory. Often the B-side was where you really got to know the artist, because he or she might have actually written that side, whereas the A-side might have been written by a professional songwriter—like someone from New York's Brill Building, a legendary office block on Broadway that housed dozens of songwriters, including Goffin and King, Mann and Weil, Barry and Greenwich, Neil Sedaka, and Neil Diamond, who toiled away in tiny offices writing hits for artists to record.

Releasing a single was always a crapshoot at the best of times. No one ever knew if they had a hit on their hands. There are so many factors at play, not just the strength of the song or the quality of the recording, so why limit your chances with a throwaway B-side? There are plenty of examples of artists who scored a hit with a B-side. Why would you waste that opportunity?

It was a really big deal for recording artists when they had their single flipped over and the B-side became a hit. It was a compliment to their talent. "Laughing" was starting to descend from the charts when some deejay flipped it over and started playing the B-side, "Undun," and that became a hit on its own, pushing that single to over a million in sales. We never regarded "Undun" as a throwaway. RCA wanted another soft, ballady kind of song for a follow-up single to "These Eyes," so we gave them "Laughing." But instead of putting some aimless blues jam or a previous album cut on the B-side, we chose a newly recorded track equally as compelling as "Laughing," if not more so. It was a smart move and a validation that B-sides should never be taken for granted. We had the same thing happen with "No Sugar Tonight" on the B-side of "American Woman." It, too, became a hit on its own after "American Woman" had started to drift from the top of the charts.

We put "It's My Pride" on the flip side of "His Girl." While the A-side was a soft ballad written by Toronto songwriter Johnny Cowell, the B-side was a revolutionary sound for us. I talked Jim Kale into playing the fuzz bass solo on that track, and Garry Peterson played his jingle sticks. (His dad, Ferdie, a well-known drummer in town, had invented these things he called jingle sticks: metal pipes with Plexiglas at both ends filled with ball bearings that rattled around.)

Some of my favourite records were B-sides. The first time I heard Eric Clapton's guitar playing was on the B-side of the Yardbirds' "For Your Love." The track, "Got to Hurry," was a basic blues instrumental, but Clapton was wailing on bluesy guitar with his distinctive style and sound. It was a revelation. And every Cliff Richard and the Shadows B-side was as good as the A-side. Same with the Beatles: each of their B-sides was a hidden treasure if you hadn't yet bought the album; they could have been A-side hits themselves. Imagine being that good. Songs like "I'll Get You," "There's a Place," "This Boy," "We Can Work It Out," and "Rain" were all B-sides. Amazing. In fact, the Beatles did have several double-sided hits. "I'm Down," the B-side to "Help," was like the ultimate Little Richard song sung by the ultimate Little Richard fan, Paul McCartney.

"This Boy," the Canadian-released B-side of "All My Loving," was phenomenal. The blend of their voices was so smooth and gave them a very distinctive sound. We used to do that song in the Reflections, and it always brought the house down. But nailing those harmonies took a lot of practice. The Beatles crafted a unique harmony style and sound with the three voices that blended so well together. It's almost a Four Freshmen vocal thing on "This Boy," with John on the bottom, George in the middle, and Paul on the top. They learned a lot about harmony vocals from girl groups like the Shirelles, the Cookies, and the Marvelettes. The Beatles radicalized harmony singing. "This Boy" had an almost baroque harmony style.

Every Beatles single was different from the last one; that's what made them so incredible. I remember being on the road and hearing a deejay announce that at two p.m. that day they'd be debuting the new Beatles single. At the designated time, we pulled over, stopped the car, and listened in to hear the new single. It was a momentous occasion when a new Beatles or Stones single was released.

The first record I ever bought was a 78 by Elvis Presley with "Hound Dog" on one side and "Don't Be Cruel" on the other. "Hound Dog" was this great in-your-face R&B rocker, while "Don't Be Cruel" had that rockabilly swing plus the Jordanaires doing doo-wop vocals in the background. Quite the contrast, which added to the appeal of the record. You were getting two sides of Elvis's sound. And Scotty Moore's guitar playing on both sides was outstanding. To this day, I still don't know what chord he played in "Hound Dog" during the second solo. What an amazing recording. I met Scotty Moore once; he was a very humble guy. And he virtually created that Elvis sound.

The Beach Boys' B-sides were as good as their A-sides, too. The gorgeous "Don't Worry Baby" was the B-side of "I Get Around." Actually, "I Get Around" was the song I learned to sing falsetto on when we performed it in Chad Allan and the Reflections. I did the high part in "Don't Worry Baby," too.

Those songs were my first experience in stepping forward to the microphone. I wasn't comfortable with my normal singing, especially compared to Chad Allan, who had this wonderfully smooth Buddy Holly voice. I never had aspirations to sing lead, something that happened purely by happenstance, but it wasn't easy when you've got guys like Burton Cummings and Fred Turner singing beside you. I was content to be the Claptonesque kind of guy, laying down the cool licks and riffs, having a little moment when I got to play a solo before stepping back and leaving the front of the stage to the singer.

What's interesting about the Beach Boys' recordings is that the first verse is generally just the lead voice. Then on the second verse the oohs and aahs come in, laying the groundwork behind the lead vocal. And then on the bridge and the final verses it's full out with the multiple voices and harmonies. The Beatles also built the harmonies, verse by verse, as the song developed: listen to "Paperback Writer," for example. The Eagles did that, too. The Everly Brothers, on the other hand, would come right in at the start of every song full tilt, the two voices coming right at you together. But what harmonies they had.

The Rolling Stones' B-sides often explored a whole other side to the band. Brian Jones was the icing on the cake for them. He could play any instrument he picked up or someone shoved in front of him. He really gave the Stones a wider depth of styles and sounds—harpsichord, recorder, marimbas, sitar, mellotron.

There are so many great B-sides. "Tales of Brave Ulysses" was the B-side to "Strange Brew" and changed the guitar world with Eric Clapton playing a Vox wah-wah pedal. It was the first recording of a wah wah, and it was a revelation. I loved it instantly and couldn't wait to get a wah-wah pedal myself. "Butchie's Tune" by the Lovin' Spoonful was the B-side of their megahit "Summer in the City" and featured some exceptional country picking by guitarist Zal Yanovsky from Toronto. Zal integrated Nashville piano player Floyd Cramer's signature trills into his guitar picking, and that style would go on to influence Neil Young and Stephen Stills in the Buffalo Springfield (and by extension influence me on tracks like "No Time" and "Minstrel Boy"). The Shadows' "36-24-36," the flip side of their instrumental hit "Kon Tiki," was one of the first songs to give the bass player, in this case Jet Harris, a solo. That was very bold for its time. We picked up on the flip side of the Hollies' hit "I'm Alive" and recorded "You Know He Did" on our *It's Time* album. One of Neil Young's most endearing and enduring songs, "Sugar Mountain," was an unreleased gem of a B-side to "Cinnamon Girl." I could go on and on.

When I started going on the road, I stopped buying 45s because I had nothing to play them on; I'd catch up on my record-buying when I got home. I have what a friend once described as a "phonographic" memory. If I hear something, I can play it. So I started to rely more on the radio than on buying 45s.

I keep hearing that vinyl is making a comeback. Sales of new recordings released on vinyl are on the rise, but that's likely the result of dedicated audiophiles who recognize the deficiencies in digital sound or boomers still holding on to their turntables. I fear that digital downloading is here to stay for the time being—until someone comes along with another technological innovation that, like digital downloads, offers convenience over quality.

For many of us, radio offered our initial introduction to the music we came to love. And vinyl, whether LPs or 45s, was our first experience of possessing that music for ourselves. Both have undergone tremendous changes in recent years. Who can predict how music will be disseminated in the future?

In your first *Vinyl Tap Stories* book
you talked about your love of Gretsch guitars
and how you came to own the largest collection
of Gretsch models in the world.
What other guitars have special value for you?

Randy with one of his rare Todt guitars.

In *Vinyl Tap Stories,* I talked about how I acquired my coveted 1959 Gibson Les Paul Standard. I was at a Guess Who gig in a church basement in Nanaimo, B.C., in late 1968 when a young man approached me offering to trade his Les Paul for my Mosrite guitar. He didn't like the Les Paul. That guitar is currently on display at the Rock and Roll Hall of Fame and Museum in Cleveland, and I'm delighted to have it there. After I left the Guess Who in 1970, I stopped using that guitar, other than on occasion in the recording studio, because it was so heavy. Playing it every night was a killer for my left shoulder. In Brave Belt and later BTO, I wasn't playing it unless I was sitting down. By then I was using my Legend guitar, my old Fender Stratocaster that I kept customizing.

I acquired that guitar around 1967, and over the next several years I virtually rebuilt it from the ground up. During the Guess Who I'd replaced the single-coil Fender pickup nearest the neck with a Rickenbacker pickup. I later replaced the Rickenbacker with a Gibson humbucker pickup and a Fender Telecaster pickup at the bridge—which made for a nice contrast between the trebly Telecaster and the chunky humbucker—and left the middle Strat pickup intact. That Legend became my all-purpose, Swiss Army knife guitar. I added a giant whammy bar that Gar Gillies had made me; it hung way back from the guitar so that I could get all these great feedback sounds. In smashing it around (for a short while we copied the Who and pretended to smash our gear at the end of the night), I broke the nut where the neck joins the headstock. That nut is a piece of plastic or metal with notches in it for each string to go from the neck to the tuning pegs on the headstock. I got one of my mother's knitting needles, broke it off, filed some notches in it with a nail file, and hammered it into the body to make a new nut. Later, when I was in my country-rock phase, I tried putting a stringbender on it. Clarence White from the latter-day Byrds had invented this device, built into his Telecaster, that allowed him to get the sound of a pedal-steel-guitar bend by using an actual steel-guitar rod put through the body of the guitar and attached to the upper strap peg. If you pulled the guitar down by the strap slightly, the B string would raise a tone that sounded like a pedal-steel guitar. I chiselled out the back on my Strat to reposition the springs so that if I pushed on the guitar I could get that same pedal-steel-guitar rise on the B string. But after chiselling it out I discovered that I couldn't saw the block, or the body. The hole remained in the back, though, so I put the Titano organ logo sticker on it, a large T with the eagle, that I got from Chad Allan.

The weird triangular headstock on my Legend guitar was the result of the original owner's transforming the Strat from a standard six-string to a bizarre nine-string model. He added octave strings for the three high strings so that it would sound something like a twelve-string guitar. In doing so, he added three more tuning pegs on the bottom side of the headstock. I used to stab the head and neck of the guitar into a phoney Garnet cabinet during our Who phase, and one time part of the headstock broke off. So I left it as a triangle. It was originally a black Strat, but Russell Gillies and I stripped it down to the wood and then varnished it. That poor guitar went through the ringer, but it had a great sound; I played it for the rhythm guitar on "American Woman." Like my original Gretsch 6120, my Legend Strat was later stolen. There's a guy doing a book called *Lost Strats*, and he's found photos of me from Brave Belt playing that guitar.

Between my Gretsch and the '59 Les Paul, I played a brown triple-pickup Rickenbacker 360 six-string model. That was a mistake. When I ordered it from Lowe's Music on Kennedy Street in Winnipeg, I thought I was ordering one like George Harrison's in *A Hard Day's Night* with the two pointed cutaways. But the new catalogue had come out with the same model number but a slightly different body style with the rounded horns, only I didn't know that. When the guitar arrived, it wasn't what I wanted, but by then it was too late. I loved the neck but the sound was too trebly and too clean. I wanted a dirtier, deeper sound, and the Rickenbacker's was even cleaner than a Fender's. I played that Rickenbacker on "Tossin' and Turnin'." Duncan Wilson from the Mongrels later bought it.

For a short period in 1969, I played a black Gibson Les Paul Custom model. Because of increased demand for vintage 50s Les Pauls, Gibson started remaking them in the latter 60s, and it was one of these reissues that Russell Gillies ordered for me. I played it for a few months, including when the Guess Who did a big show at the Rainbow Stage in Winnipeg that summer. Les Paul Customs, or SG Customs, are known as fretless wonders because the frets are smaller and slimmer, meaning that your fingers glide over the neck, barely feeling the frets. Les Paul created the fretboard so that he could do all his fast runs and licks on it instead of stumbling on every fret. It was a fantastic guitar to play, but I couldn't get sustain from it because it didn't have normal frets. To get sustain you need slightly higher frets and heavier strings. I didn't know at the time that I could have gotten thicker frets for it. Instead I told Russell to sell it. I loved the look of that guitar, the ebony colour, but I couldn't get my "American Woman" sound out of it.

Years later with BTO, we played the same venue in Westchester, New York, where in 1970 we'd met Bob Sabellico, who temporarily replaced me in the Guess Who during my gall-bladder problems. The day after our BTO gig, I went to a place called Bill's Music to check out what they had, as I often did on the road. On the wall were two vintage black Les Paul Customs. One had two black plastic P90 pickups on it and the other had two gold humbuckers. Both were 1959s. What was rare about them, besides the date, was that they were two-pickup models. When Gibson was making the original black Les Paul Customs they made them as three-pickup models. These guitars had only two as factory stock, no alterations. So I asked the owner if they were for sale, and he told me they belonged to the Rolling Stones' Keith Richards. One of Keith's roadies had brought them in for repair a year or so earlier but had never returned for them, and Bill was still owed $125 each for the repairs. So I told him I'd like to buy both guitars.

There's a thing known as a mechanics lien, which works like this: if you haven't been paid after ninety days (in some states it's longer) for your repair work, you can send a registered letter to the owner identifying the work or object repaired, in this case the guitars by serial number, and stating that you're owed X amount for the work now completed. You also state that if payment isn't received in, say, 150 days, you'll sell the item in question in order to recoup the outstanding money owed. Bill said he'd do this. When I called him back a few months later, he told me he had the receipt for the registered letter being received by the Stones' office but no response to his request. I gave him some more time, and when I called again he still hadn't received any response from Keith Richards or the Rolling Stones. "Will you sell me the guitars?" Bill replied, "Sure." "What do you want for them?" and he said "$750." I didn't know if that meant together or each and didn't care. I told him I'd do the deal and gave him an address to send the guitars to. In a moment of generosity that I later came to regret, I told Blair Thornton of BTO about these guitars and asked him if he wanted one. He took the model with the P90s and I took the one with the humbuckers. We played both these guitars on *Four Wheel Drive* and *Head On*. I could have had them both. Blair's still got his.

That guitar became my solo guitar on those albums because it had such a brighter sound than my Les Paul Standard. But it was heavy, even more so than my '59 Standard, so I don't play it onstage. When I took it apart, I found something stuffed alongside the pickup to stop it from vibrating. It was a matchbook from the Bag o' Nails pub in London, where all the rock elite used to hang out. On the matchbook are the initials "KR," so

I know it's authentic. I still have that guitar. Ironically, over the years I've acquired a number of 1959 Gibsons; they're different models, but that was a wonderful year for Gibson guitars and a real renaissance period for the company. I've got eleven or twelve of them.

For a while in the 80s, I played Kramer solid-body guitars. I was always looking for the next new thing that other guys were playing. Eddie Van Halen turned me on to Kramer guitars when BTO toured with them. He got me a few and I liked them for a while, but I always went back to the meat 'n' potatoes guitars, the Les Pauls and Strats. They're your basic rock 'n' roll guitars.

When Bachman-Cummings played the Molson Amphitheatre in Toronto a couple of years ago, just before the sound check I received a call on my cell phone from someone named Tina. She introduced herself by listing what companies she used to be marketing manager for, and then she told me she was now the marketing manager in Toronto for Gibson Guitars. "I'm the Gibson girl," she said cheerfully. The company was opening a Gibson headquarters in Toronto where you could come down, hang out, and try out their latest models. And if you had a gig in town you could call them up in advance, tell them what you'd like to use, and they'd bring it to you so that you wouldn't have to travel with your guitar. They have similar headquarters in Nashville, London, and Los Angeles. After the gig, the guitars go back to the showroom. Many of the big names in the guitar world have done this, so these guitars have been played by the best.

After her introduction, Tina asked me why I wasn't playing my 1959 Gibson Les Paul guitar, the "American Woman" guitar.

I told her that it's like fifteen pounds of solid mahogany, and it's hard to hold for an entire set. It's too much weight on my shoulder. She replied, "What if I could get you a 1957 replica-model gold-top Les Paul that's been chambered out?" In other words, the guitar body has been hollowed out, rendering it much lighter, half the weight of the full Les Pauls. It's about the same weight as a Fender Strat. "Would you play it?" So I asked her to bring it down and let me try it. It was an endorsement guitar, and they'd give it to me if I liked it.

So I was doing the sound check at Molson's and it was getting close to five o'clock, when the IATSE stage-union crew have to stop work for a mandatory break. At about five minutes to five, Tina came running in, quickly introduced herself, and handed me this gold-top Les Paul. The 1957 models were the first gold tops to have humbucker pickups on them instead of the plastic P90s. I plugged it in and started playing, and it was the "American Woman" guitar! Burton stopped what he was doing and yelled out, "Where has that guitar been this whole tour?" I used it that night. I didn't even change the strings. I was just smokin' with that guitar all night long.

Afterwards, I told Tina that if we were going to have a rela-tionship, Gibson and I, then if I'm onstage and I break a string on the Les Paul, someone's going to be handing me a Fender or a Yamaha. Therefore I needed a spare chambered-out Les Paul. That was no problem for her; she got me another 1957 gold-top reissue. Tina later got me two sunburst Les Pauls like my original 1959. I've got four of them now, and they're all under eight pounds. So I'm very happy with Gibson and my association with them. I had a friend of mine add a Bigsby tailpiece to the

'59 replicas. He'd invented a way to float the tailpiece without drilling holes into the body.

I went to the annual NAMM (National Association of Music Merchants) show in Nashville to appear at the Gibson display. For doing that they built me a custom-made Gibson Super 4000 model. Only two were ever made—one is with the Chet Atkins estate and the other is in the Country Music Hall of Fame museum—but they made one more for me. It took them a year, and they'd send me photos of the guitar as they built it. I don't play it often because it's so rare and gorgeous. Gibson is looking into making a limited-edition replica of my 1959 "American Woman" Les Paul guitar. I'm very excited about the prospect, having a guitar made in honour of my sound.

I started collecting Gretsch guitars, every and all models, in the latter 70s after my beloved orange Gretsch Chet Atkins 6120 model was stolen from my car in Toronto. In seeking to find it, which I never did, I started buying Gretsches. By the time I stopped I had some 380 guitars. It was nuts because I couldn't play them all, but it was like an obsession with me. Among the collection were some ultra-rare models where only a couple were made. I was acknowledged as possessing the largest Gretsch guitar collection in the world. But what was I going to do with them? At some point, I realized that I couldn't keep them all.

Selling my collection turned out to be a smart financial move: I quadrupled my money. When I started collecting Gretsch guitars, nobody wanted them. They weren't hip. They were from the 50s and 60s, and in the latter 70s up to the 90s, everyone wanted old Gibsons or Fenders. Gretsch guitars were generally big and often very ostentatious looking. So I was able to get them dirt cheap. Then the Travelling Wilburys came along, and they were all playing these cool-looking Gretsch guitars. For MTV, everyone was looking for different kinds of guitars with unique colours and shapes, so they were turning to Gretsch Sparkle Glo models or green or orange Nashvilles, that sort of thing. As a result, the value started to increase. Now Gretsch guitars are ultra-cool and worth a lot, especially the vintage ones, which I had in the hundreds. It was the right time to sell. Fred Gretsch Jr. and I dickered back and forth until we came to an agreement on a price for the lot. They plan to house my collection in the Gretsch guitar museum.

But I haven't stopped collecting guitars—I'm just collecting different makes and models now. Several years ago I saw a video by Swedish pop duo Roxette from the 80s. The guitar player, Per Gessle, was playing this strange-looking Hofner guitar. He's pictured on their debut album with one. I'd never seen anything like it, and I thought to myself, "Man, I'd kill to get a cool-looking guitar like that one." I was familiar with Hofner guitars from the 60s; Paul McCartney played a Hofner violin bass that he made famous as the Beatle bass. They were sort of mid-priced German guitars—in Europe, if you couldn't afford to get an imported Fender or Gibson, you got a Hofner. But I soon discovered that there were also Hopfner, Hopf, and Hoyer. My friend Henry Gross, who wrote and recorded the song "Shannon," is a big guitar collector, so I asked him about these German guitars. He directed me to a website, and all the guitars there are simply gorgeous, the most beautiful guitars I've ever seen. They're handmade models and feature unique charac-teristics, whether in the inlays on the neck, the binding around the body, or the shape of the F holes. I absolutely fell in love with those postwar guitars.

They're all arch-top guitars. Apparently there was a renaissance in arch tops in Europe after World War II, in the wake of Django Reinhardt's popularity as a recording artist. Craftsmen in Germany, Poland, and Czechoslovakia who used to handcraft violins and cellos for symphonies turned instead to making arch tops to meet the increasing demand for what were called "hot jazz" guitars. Nothing was amplified at the time, so they constructed these arch tops with F holes and an arched top, as opposed to the standard sound hole in the middle, to make them very trebly; that way, they could cut through the sound of the other instruments in the band or orchestra. It wasn't a mellow sound at all. This arch-top renaissance lasted until the late 1950s, when Gibson and Epiphone recognized the market and started mass-producing for European demand.

Many of these craftsmen were in Iron Curtain countries under communist regimes where they weren't allowed to make guitars. That's why a lot of the guitars don't have a name on the headstock: the maker could have been arrested if he were found out. The craftsmen would acquire the wood and the other parts surreptitiously, perhaps on the black market, make the guitar and sell it, then use the money to feed their families and buy the materials to make another guitar. The craftsmanship is astonishing. They carved the tops by hand and assembled the guitars piece by piece. By varying the style and size of the F holes, for example, they could get a distinctive sound. The builders would also use unique materials and create distinctive designs in the inlays. They're kind of ugly beautiful, each one different from the other. No two are the same. They made these guitars in a barn or in their little shop at the back of their house, that kind of thing. Most of them have Schaller tuning heads and hardware because that's a German company.

If you look inside one of the F holes, you can sometimes see the initials of the craftsman who made it written lightly in pencil. That's the only way they could brand their guitars without being discovered. One of the master craftsmen was Herbert Todt, who lived in East Germany and would make one guitar a year. I got my first Todt guitar for Christmas one year. I have ten of them now and they're incredible; each one is unique.

I started collecting German and Eastern European guitars around the time I was preparing to sell my Gretsch collection. No one wanted these handcrafted models because they don't look cool like today's guitars. They're your grandfather's guitar. So they were being sold at garage sales, junk stores, antique shops. It was the same thing with Gretsch guitars when I started buying them. When the Berlin Wall came down and Germany reunified in 1990, no one wanted anything made in East Germany. It was all deemed to be inferior, whether true or not. My daughter Bannatyne studied German in school, and so I asked her to trawl the internet and translate the info about the guitars for me. Banna then became my broker as I started acquiring these guitars. She'd contact the person selling it, get all the details, negotiate the price, and arrange for it to be shipped over here or have people she knew or had hired arrange to pick up the guitar and ship it. The prices were cheap. I bought them unplayed. Some of them need work because they haven't been looked after over the years, but all of them are stunning.

I discovered a book on German arch tops, called *Hoyers, Hopfners and Hopfs*, which is a history of these guitar models. It's quite a fascinating read. Besides Todt, Lang was another hand-crafted German make. In the book is the name of the premier North American collector of these guitars, and it turned out he lives in Toronto. I managed to find his phone number, so I left him a message saying that I was interested in collecting these guitars. He called me back a few hours later, and we agreed to meet at his house—and when I got there, he had 110 of these German guitars. As a result of our meeting he agreed to help me acquire more guitars. I now have 150 models, all bought one at a time and all from Germany, purchased through German eBay. I have them all photographed and catalogued.

I've also started collecting Harmony guitars. A lot of guitar players I knew back in the late 50s and early 60s played Harmony guitars because they were inexpensive but still good quality. I bought my first single cutaway Harmony Rocket after learning that it was the guitar model the Kinks' Dave Davies played when he recorded "You Really Got Me." I plugged it into a little amp, and there was that Kinks sound. I used several Harmony guitar models through tiny amps when we were recording the *Bachman & Turner* album. They have a real vintage sound. Keith Richards played a Harmony Rocket in the early days of the Stones; you can see it in dozens of photos. A lot of us older players are going back to these inexpensive early models. Neil Young played an old Hagstrom guitar that he found in a guitar store on his *Chrome Dreams* album. It's got a plastic body, but he liked it enough to actually play it onstage once for an encore of "Mr. Soul."

Every guitar is different, even two that are exactly the same make and model. As with a car, a pillow, or a jacket, sometimes something just speaks to you; it resonates within and you want it. Of course, it's great to have all the elements in a guitar: craftsmanship, beauty and appearance, tone, playability, a voice—and a oneness with you. It doesn't matter if it costs $100 or $10,000; the price is irrelevant. It's an emotional-connection thing. That's why losing a guitar or having one stolen can be a traumatic experience. The guitar is the only instrument that you wrap your arms around, hold to your chest, feel its vibrations, and vibrate with. You can take it with you anywhere you go, and it can make you feel good any time you're feeling down. A guitar is the "world's" instrument. Put ten different language–speaking people in the same room, each with a guitar, and watch what happens. They can all communicate through the music.

When you started out as a musician,
all you needed was a guitar and an amplifier.
Today, though, guitarists need a host
of gadgets and gizmos. How did your music
change with the evolution of guitar
effects and sound enhancements?

The Guess Who

Randy with his Garnet BTO amp, Herzog, and
wah-wah pedal at the Guess Who concert at
Winnipeg's Rainbow Stage, summer 1969.

When I got my first electric guitar, my Silvertone from the Simpson-Sears catalogue, I didn't know that you needed to have an amplifier, too. I just thought an electric guitar was something you plugged into the wall like a toaster or a television. So when I started playing with Garry Peterson and classmate Perry Wauksvik in the Embers in junior high, I used to use the school's Caliphone system for an amplifier. It had a turntable and speakers and a microphone input, plus another input that I could plug my guitar into. I had to phone ahead to schools or community centres and ask if they had one of these things before we could play there. They used them for record hops, square dances, and calling bingo numbers—an all-purpose portable PA. My first professional amp experience was plugging into Mickey Brown's big Harmony amplifier, which had reverb in it. That was with Mickey Brown and the Velvetones. It didn't give me the Shadows sound, but it was cool. We used to plug my guitar, his guitar, and a microphone into this one amp.

The first guitar sound effect I can remember on an amplifier was tremolo. Tremolo and vibrato are often confused as being the same thing. The misunderstanding arose when Fender introduced their series of guitar amplifiers in the late 50s through to the late 60s and mislabelled their tremolo effect as vibrato. Even the popular Fender Tremolux amplifier identified the effect as vibrato. It's believed that Leo Fender used the term "vibrato" instead of "tremolo" so that people wouldn't confuse it with Gibson's use of "tremolo." Simply stated, tremolo occurs when the sound seems to be going off and on, varying its volume.

If you listen to the Buffalo Springfield's 1967 hit "For What It's Worth" ("There's somethin' happenin' here..."), Neil Young is playing his lead lines using a very slow-speed tremolo on a Fender Twin amplifier. It has that off-on sound. Link Wray's classic guitar instrumental "Rumble" also uses tremolo on the guitar sound. Bo Diddley often used this effect on his recordings, and it was especially notable when he played his chord solos up high on the neck. John Fogerty used tremolo, too, but it was particularly effective on "Born on the Bayou." The guitars on Tommy James and the Shondells' "Crimson and Clover" are using tremolo. I used tremolo on "Use Your Imagination," an Artie Wayne song that the Guess Who recorded in New York in 1965. A lot of people thought I was using a tremolo effect on "Clock on the Wall" back in 1967, but all I was doing was varying the volume pod on my Fender Telecaster guitar with my little finger to make a sort of tremolo sound. Tremolo isn't used much anymore. Most Fender guitar amplifiers back in the 60s came with it built in, but you can get an effects pedal that will do the same these days.

Vibrato, on the other hand, varies the pitch of a note up or down. There are two ways to employ a vibrato effect. Finger vibrato is created when you move your finger slightly on the fret of a string, thereby wavering the pitch of the note up or back to what it was. You're bending the string and raising the pitch. All guitar players do this. But this method only allows you to go up because you can't go below your finger. The other way to achieve vibrato on a guitar is by using a vibrato arm, which allows you to go down and up. Although nowadays called whammy or wang bars (and sometimes mistakenly called tremolo arms), they're technically known as vibrato arms because it's like the vibrato in your voice when you vary the pitch of the note slightly.

Bigsby was the first company to manufacture vibrato-arm tailpieces for guitars beginning in 1948. They were, and still are, large metal devices attached to the back body of a guitar where the strings begin, with a spring-mounted movable arm that allows you to alter the pitch. Chet Atkins popularized them on Gretsch guitars in the 50s. The first whammy bar I had was a Bigsby vibrato tailpiece on my Gretsch 6120. I used that on "Shakin' All Over," at the point where the band stops and I hit that E minor chord, varying the pitch off the sustained chord. That gave the song a distinctive sound—but the secret to that sound wasn't just my using the vibrato arm, which the original Johnny Kidd and the Pirates recording didn't use. Simultaneous with my hitting that E minor chord, Jim Kale slides up an octave on his bass. It's hard to hear because of the way we recorded it through one amp and one microphone—we lost the bottom end—but it's an integral part of that signature chord. A lot of people don't know or realize that it's Jim's bass slide at the same moment that gives that part such a distinctive sound. It's not just my vibrato arm; Jim and I together give that part oomph. Jim also uses finger vibrato on the note. No one does that bass part when they play that song.

There are plenty of examples of my vibrato arm in early Guess Who recordings, including "Made in England," "I'd Rather Be Alone," "When Friends Fall Out," and "Minstrel Boy." I'm using it at the end of every line in the signature riff in "No Time" just to add a little shimmer to each note. You can also hear it on my solos in "Takin' Care of Business," where I recorded it on my Gretsch with the Bigsby. The "American Woman" lead guitar sound is me using my Bigsby vibrato at the end of each of the lead lines.

Those lead lines, by the way, are also double-tracked to give them more strength. Everybody thinks it's just one guitar. After doing that CBC show for two years, Burton and I got so good at double-tracking that I'd double all my lead lines and he'd double all his vocals. That gave the sound a thickness. By then I had my 1959 Gibson Les Paul Standard with a factory-installed Bigsby tailpiece on it. I doubled my lead line on "No Time"; you can hear it when I take off on one of those lines and play a solo. I used my Fender Legend Stratocaster on the *Canned Wheat* version of "No Time," but I'm playing my '59 Les Paul on the *American Woman* version. The second version has a thicker, heavier tone to it.

Neil Young still uses a Bigsby vibrato on both his big Gretsch hollow bodies and his 1953 Gibson Les Paul, which he calls Old Black. It's actually a gold-top model that was painted black before he got it from Jimmy Messina in 1969. Neil uses vibrato to give his notes a shimmer. He's a master at that. Listen to "Cowgirl in the Sand" and you'll hear it to great effect. For many years I didn't use a Bigsby because it can be a real pain to change strings.

The name "whammy bar" originates from guitarist Lonnie Mack and his 1964 album, *The Wham of That Memphis Man.* Lonnie had a Bigsby tailpiece mounted on a Gibson Flying V guitar with a little piece of metal holding it in the open space between the two wings of the V. He was able to get some cool sounds from that whammy bar.

Bigsby vibratos tend to be wound pretty tightly, meaning you get a limited varying pitch, not the dive-bomb sounds of the note dropping a full octave or more. To get that effect you needed a different kind of vibrato arm, one that initially came with the higher-end Fender guitar models: Stratocasters, Jazzmasters, and Jaguars. With the Bigsby, the strings went over the bridge or saddle and into the tailpiece itself so that you could waver the pitch. But Leo Fender put in a spring unit where the strings went through the body, which allowed you to get a vibrato effect by pulling on the string-mounted arm. That arm was actually more like a stick, a bar, or a thin pipe, with springs mounted underneath the bridge where you didn't see them. Because the bridge floated, or raised and lowered with the bar, you could get more variance in the pitch. You could also change the tautness of the springs by tightening or loosening the arm where it screwed into the vibrato piece. That allowed you to achieve different vibrato styles.

When I switched from my Gretsch with its Bigsby tailpiece to a Stratocaster in 1967, it had a tighter vibrato arm, and to do the Shadows sound you needed it tight. It wasn't about creating swoops or dives but just giving a note a slight flutter, as Hank Marvin would do. That was part of his distinctive sound. Jimi Hendrix loosened the springs on his Strat, meaning he could get more variance in the pitch of the note, especially if he was sustaining it. He was the first to get that dive-bomb effect from his loose Fender vibrato arm. So, whereas Neil Young keeps his arm tightly sprung to give his notes a slight flutter at the end of a line, chord, or riff, Jimi kept his loose so that he could make all these sonic excursions with a sustained note or controlled feedback. Same gadget or effect, just used differently.

I broke many of those Fender vibrato arms when I'd remove some strings to get that distinctive Hendrix *whoo whoo* sound. Eventually the old bar wouldn't fit anymore, and Russell Gillies had to drill a hole in the body of the guitar to attach a new one. The hole had to be rethreaded, so I asked a guy named Doug who did welding for Garnet Amplifiers to make me a little vibrato arm out the front and a big one out the back that was like solid wrought iron and would never break. That one was phenomenal. At the same time I got a six-inch railway spike and put it into the end of the body of the guitar, where you hook your strap on, and sharpened it to a point. I'd stick it in the stage and let it feedback indefinitely while we walked off, leaving that thing squealing and howling. Of course, it left a hole in the stage.

Kids nowadays still use whammy bars, but they use them to do dive bombs, dropping the note down a whole two octaves. They don't use it like Hank Marvin did, or Neil or Chet Atkins.

Reverb, short for reverberation, was the next amplifier effect I remember becoming popular. Reverb was kind of like a slight echo delay, giving your guitar a depth, as if you were playing it in a bathroom or onstage in an empty arena. It was definitely a bigger sound, thicker, as if you were hearing it a mile away. Many surf guitar players—Dick Dale, the Surfaris, the Chantays, the Ventures—used reverb a lot as part of that surf-guitar sound. In the early days, to get an authentic reverb you'd put your amp in a bathroom, put a mic just outside, and then record that sound. The bathroom's metal and porcelain fixtures gave the sound from the amplifier a depth and distance. Or you got a giant empty oil drum and at one end you put a speaker and at the other end a microphone. I've been in studios in the South where they had this giant metal container, like an old oil furnace tank, and they filled it not to the top but maybe halfway with water or sand. You could vary the depth of the reverb by raising or lowering the amount of water or sand in the tank. That's how you adjusted how much reverb you wanted. Duane Eddy did that and created a gigantic reverb sound on all his recordings, beginning with "Rebel Rouser."

Echo chambers were sometimes built under recording studios to give the recorded sound more "wet," or depth. You'd send the sound to the room and place a microphone there to record the reverb-drenched result. Neil Young found these old Indian caves under his property near Redwood City, California. In one he has a JBL speaker at one end and a microphone at the other. If you listen to a song like "Unknown Legend" from his *Harvest Moon* album, that deep echo/reverb comes from the echo chamber under his driveway. If you stand in his archives building across the road from his Broken Arrow studio while he's recording, you can actually hear the echo chamber beneath you.

Slapback echo was perfected by Sam Phillips on early Elvis Presley Sun recordings. Those tracks are wet rather than dry. As I described earlier, we got the same effect accidentally while recording "Shakin' All Over" at the television station in Winnipeg when the tape operator forgot to unpatch the playback speakers so that both heads on the machine, record and play, were activated. This created a very slight delay that enhanced the depth of the sound. That's why that recording has such a terrific sound to it.

Some recording studios had what was known as a plate reverb, which involved an aluminum plate enclosed in its own room. For example, in Abbey Road Studios where the Beatles recorded, they had a six-hundred-pound plate mounted on a wall in a room. Phil Spector and the Beach Boys both relied on plate reverb to get that unique depth to their sound. You had different points on the plate where you could get more or less reverb, or delay, and you could vary the amount, using a one-second or a one-and-a-half-second delay, that kind of thing. There'd be little contact microphones, or pickups, at these different points on the plate; you'd play the dry recorded sound into the room, and the microphones would record it as it resonated off the plate. I had one of those in my barn studio in Lynden, Washington, in the latter 70s. We hung it on the wall in a specially built room and put Fibreglas around it and then Gyproc so you wouldn't hear the outside noises like birds chirping. Speaking of which, if you listen to the Beatles' *Love* album done as the soundtrack to the Cirque du Soleil show in Las Vegas, you can hear birds chirping in the background of "Because" as the three Beatles are singing a cappella. Giles Martin told me that birds nested in the outside walls of Abbey Road Studios, and they were there chirping when the original recording was made for the *Abbey Road* album.

Fender amplifiers were the first to come up with a spring reverb at the bottom of the back of the amp. The innovation behind this method lay in capitalizing on the fact that sound travels down a wire to a speaker: so why not get a spring, which is wire anyway, and attach the sound to that? It will come out the other end with reverb. You controlled the amount of reverb you wanted with a dial on the amp. The trouble, though, was that if you accidentally kicked or bumped these amps the springs would bang together and make a huge explosive noise. There were guys who incorporated that into their own sound. Chris Isaak's "Wicked Game," for example, has a reverb-drenched lead guitar on it, plus vibrato. And Fender spring-mounted reverb was the quintessential sound of surf guitar. Listen to "Baja" by the Astronauts for that classic Fender reverb sound.

Before they made amps with reverb built into them, Fender made a separate reverb unit that you could plug into and from that into your amp. Those had a tube in them to boost the signal. Neil Young uses one to get more distortion because it's like a pre-amp. That's the sound he gets at the start of "Woodstock."

When I joined the Silvertones in 1962, I met piano player Bob Ashley, who had a Kortung tape recorder. I could get the Hank Marvin Shadows guitar sound with that. Hank first had a Meazzi Echomatic unit and later a Binson Echorec unit, both of which were manufactured in the U.K. You couldn't get them over here, although a few years later you could buy an Echoplex unit. Tape echo works by recording sound on a magnetic tape, which is then played back. The tape speed, or distance between heads, determines the delay. Ashley's tape recorder allowed me to create my own homemade echo effect. That became my sound, and it set me apart from the rest of the guitar players in town. If you turned both the play and record tape heads out you could get an echo. As Neil Young says in his autobiography, it was that sound that made him come to see me playing in the first place. Everyone else had a dry sound, but mine was wet. I could also turn it up and get that spacey *whamp whamp whamp* electronic sound at the start of "Telstar," then turn it down and play the solo alongside Ashley on organ. I used to rent Ashley's tape recorder for $5 a night. Finally I said, "I've been paying enough for it, can I buy it from you?," and he said okay. It had a little pause button that I could get distortion from. This was before anyone in town had a fuzz-tone pedal. You couldn't play Hank Marvin's style or Shadows songs without echo, and I had that with Bob's tape recorder. I coveted that tape recorder!

A lot of the old blues players back in the 50s used to get a distorted guitar sound by playing through small tube amplifiers that they'd run on 10, full up. Listen to Jackie Brenston and His Delta Cats' recording of "Rocket 88" from 1951, reputed to be the very first rock 'n' roll record, and you can hear Ike Turner's distorted Fender Stratocaster. Chuck Berry's guitar sound on his 1955 debut single, "Maybelline," is distorted. Listen to Link Wray's "Rumble" and hear the distortion on his guitar. Robbie Robertson, still a teenager at the time, played with a distorted guitar sound on early Ronnie Hawkins recordings. One of the best examples of amplifier distortion is on Dave Davies's driving guitar riff on the Kinks' 1964 hit "You Really Got Me." He was simply overloading a little amplifier. While many recording artists and producers sought to avoid distortion, rock guitarists wanted it.

In the summer of 1965, Keith Richards used a Gibson Maestro Fuzz Tone pedal on the Rolling Stones' megahit "Satisfaction." I remember watching them on *The Ed Sullivan Show* and seeing him step on a little box on the floor that his guitar was plugged into. That was a fuzz tone, which provided distortion that was controllable and could be turned off and on. It was transistorized and worked like a tiny pre-amp, boosting the signal from the guitar to the amplifier. Keith's Maestro was the first fuzz tone I ever saw. After that Sullivan show, fuzz tones became almost compulsory for every lead guitar player. Jeff Beck played one on "Heart Full of Soul" and "I'm a Man." In fact, you can actually hear him turning on his fuzz tone just before the call-and-response bit in that song. The Maestro Fuzz Tone had been around for a few years, but it didn't start to sell until Keith Richards and "Satisfaction." I bought one and used it often—guitar sounds were turning harder and the fuzz tone gave you a grittier sound, both for rhythm chording and for biting leads. You can hear my Maestro fuzz pedal on the Guess Who's "Believe Me" in 1966, the hardest, most distorted sound we'd ever recorded to that point. Not long after that, Gar Gillies built a fuzz tone into his Garnet guitar amps. It was called the Stinger and had a pull-out switch to activate it.

In BTO, I had a Muff pedal and a Big Muff Pi. That was my lead guitar sound in that band. These pedals had a very distinctive sound. I used two of them live, one for a nice rhythm crunch sound and the other for lead.

The first time I heard a wah-wah, or Cry Baby, pedal was on Cream's "Tales of Brave Ulysses" in 1967. I was in New York later and bought one at Manny's Music when they first went on sale to the public. The first wah-wah effect came from a trumpet player named Clyde McCoy, who used the plunger on his trumpet on "Sugar Blues." In 1967, a technician working at Lowry Organs was experimenting with the volume pedal on an organ, and instead of using a volume control he adapted it for a tone control; it had that *wah wah wah* sound, which is what you get when you simply move the tone control on your guitar from 1 to 10 and back fast, varying the tone from treble to bass to treble. That became the Vox Clyde McCoy Wah-Wah Pedal. Later they became known as Cry Baby Pedals. Clapton used one on "White Room" as well, but it was Jimi Hendrix ("Voodoo Child," for example) and Jeff Beck ("Morning Dew") who really took wah-wah pedals to great heights and helped popularize them. I used one on "Heygoode Hardy" in 1967 on *A Wild Pair*, on "Guess Who Blues," and later on "Friends of Mine" on the *Wheatfield Soul* album, so I was in there right at the beginning. In fact, I did a whole *Vinyl Tap* episode on the wah-wah pedal. If you're still not sure what one sounds like, just listen to the guitar on Isaac Hayes's "Shaft." Can you dig it?

I remember when the great British drummer Simon Phillips was hired to play with Stanley Clarke on an album being recorded at my barn studio in Lynden, Washington. Simon showed up with his kit, and of course he had a trap case with his snare and all his hardware. He opened up his case, and inside were four wah-wah pedals that belonged to Jeff Beck; Simon had been touring and recording with Jeff. Some of these had been modified, so that instead of going *wah wah* they went *aaw aaw*. Jeff would do amazing things with his wah wah on tracks like "I Ain't Superstitious," including getting that *aaw aaw* backwards *wah wah* effect. Later, I ran into Jeff in London when he was playing at the Royal Albert Hall. I was backstage after the show, and told him I had his wah wahs—they all had the initials JB on them, and one said *Aaw Aaw* on it while the others said *Wah Wah*. Jeff's eyes lit up and he exclaimed, "Really?!" I asked him if he wanted them back and he said yes. He figured he wouldn't use them but would like to have them anyway. They were a mix of Vox Wah Wahs, Cry Babys, and the Clyde McCoy models, and they'd all been rewired.

Once the Guess Who started touring in 1965, I acquired a Fender Bandmaster amplifier with two channels and forty watts of sound. It was loud for community clubs and town halls, but I had to really push it to the limits when we played bigger venues on package tours across the United States. I used to take my Fender amp for repair to Gar Gillies, who owned Cam's Electrical Appliances on Sargent Avenue. He was an electronics genius as well as a well-known jazz musician, and his son Russell was our road manager. Gar would replace the blown-out tubes and repair any burned-out circuitry. He started to boost the power of my Fender by adding additional tubes, but it still wasn't enough, so Gar made the first Garnet amplifier for me. He'd already made us a PA system that included these giant driver horns. He later made Garnet amps for the rest of the guys in the band, and when other bands saw us using these cool big amps, they wanted them too. That's how the Garnet Amplifier Company began.

Eventually Gar stopped selling and repairing electrical appliances and went exclusively into amplifier making. Garnet was the sound of Winnipeg rock in the 60s. Everyone used them.

Nowadays, original Garnet amps are very collectible and go for big bucks on the internet. There are serious Garnet collectors out there. I know of one guy in Winnipeg who has an entire basement filled with Garnets in various models. Gar made the largest line of Garnet amps for us and named them BTOs: Big Time Operators. They had a hundred watts and stood almost six feet high with their speaker cabinets. This was several years before Bachman-Turner Overdrive.

In 1967, after our return from the U.K. and having heard Hendrix and Cream with Eric Clapton, I asked Gar to build me a pre-amp that would give me that U.K. rock sound. It had to be more powerful than a simple fuzz tone. So Gar built the Herzog, and that, plugged into a Garnet BTO amp, became my sound. The Herzog is the sound of "American Woman." I'd go to Gar's shop on weekends and work with him to get the sound I wanted. We'd have these things howling as we tinkered with them, and went through several prototypes before finding the correct specifications. I wish I had those early Herzog prototypes today. Once Gar started manufacturing and selling them, I gave the original one—it was in a metal box—to my brother Tim and I took one of the newer ones in the black leather covering.

I don't use a Herzog onstage anymore, but I still have several of them. Gar called me a few years before he died to tell me he was scaling down his shop, but that while clearing out and moving to a smaller space to work (he never stopped working on amplifiers and became renowned as a tube amp expert) he'd found a box of original Herzog parts. He offered to make me a few. I asked him to make as many as he could and to send them to me; I'd send him a cheque for what I thought was a fair price. He was able to make a dozen or so, either from those parts or by modifying them with other parts if he was missing something. I've given one to Neil Young, Lenny Kravitz, Steve Cropper, Bob Rock, and a Nashville studio-musician friend of mine. In putting them together Gar substituted parts he was missing or tweaked things differently so they didn't all sound the same. My amplifier tech checked them all out, and every single one had a slightly different sound. I don't want to take them on the road with me, though, because I don't want to risk damaging or losing them. Besides, I can get 99 percent of my original sound without the Herzog.

I recently played with Gordie Johnson of Big Sugar and the Watchmen at the Yorkville Amplifier Company's anniversary event in Toronto. Playing with Gordie is like playing with John Entwhistle. He's so loud. I had this small Yorkville/Traynor amp, and as I was carrying it onstage Gordie said, "You'll never be heard." He was right. Gordie had this huge rig, with two Herzogs through an Ampeg SVT and these giant cabinets, and I couldn't hear a thing but him.

Gar's heyday was the Herzog and the Garnet Session Man amplifier that he modelled after the Fender Twin. They were very versatile amps with great sound; I used two of them in Brave Belt. Gar made me a little eight-watt amplifier he called the Banshee. That's what I'm using on my leads in "Takin' Care of Business," with me sitting directly in front of this tiny Garnet amp playing my Gretsch 6120 double-tracked. You can hear me using my Bigsby at the end of the solos.

I stopped using Garnets after moving to Vancouver because I couldn't get them serviced out there. No one knew how to fix them, and sending them back to Winnipeg just wasn't feasible. Now, back in '65 when the Guess Who played on the Kingsmen's "Louie Louie" tour, Norm Sundholm, the Kingsmen's bass player, told us he was leaving the group at the end of the tour to start an amplifier company with his brother Conrad in Portland, Oregon. They'd already been building amps in their garage, and Norm was using one on that tour. When BTO played Portland early on in our career I met Norm again, and he said he'd send me their Model T Sunn amp head. Sunn amps were generally very clean sounding, but this model had a bit more bite to it, a tougher sound. So BTO started using Sunn amplifiers. The Who used them and later on Hendrix did, too. I tried a Marshall stack once and didn't like the sound—it was too toppy, too trebly. The Sunn Model T had five inputs, so if I plugged into the middle input then patched input 1 into 2 and 4 into 5, I could get a nice distortion sound that worked really well with my two Big Muff Pis on the floor. We took the grill cloth off our giant Sunn amps and had nice wooden cabinets with a Canadian flag in the middle. I gave those amps to the National Archives in Ottawa; at the time, I figured I wouldn't need big amps again.

Transistor amps are pretty much the norm these days, but you can still get a tube sound with effects pedals. Transistor amps were shunned when they first came out in the latter 60s because they didn't give you the warmth of a tube sound. However, they proved to be more durable and reliable.

A favourite amp for the studio won't be the same as the amp for gigs because you just can't travel on airlines with amps anymore. It's too costly. This started the whole backline business everywhere, with bands requesting specific gear at gigs from a backline company. The standard amp I request for backline is a Fender Blues Deluxe or a Hot Rod Blues Deluxe. That's the workhorse amp, unless you're a heavy metal guy who needs a wall of Marshalls. I rely on that for a clean sound with a slight reverb. For every other sound I rely on my pedal board, designed especially for me by Colin James's guitar tech. That's where I get my sound. When I have to fly to a gig, I simply bring a guitar and my pedal board.

Nowadays you can get all the sounds you can imagine digit-ally. All the effects pedals are digital, and there are so many more of them. You can pick and choose from a variety of very specific sounds, like late 60s British blues rock, mid 60s fuzz tone, Hendrix Marshall sound, and even my Randy Bachman "American Woman" tone. SansAmp created a rack mount that includes about fifty different digital sounds, featuring distinctive ones like clean Fender, dirty Fender, clean Vox, 60s Vox—and when I got to #48 it was my "American Woman" sound. It even had that noisy tube sound that you got back then, plus the sound of my Les Paul plugged into a Herzog then into a Garnet ampli-fier. It blew me away. Unfortunately, when they tried making a pedal version for me, it didn't work out because it was housed in a small box and kept shorting out. It would have been too costly to fix the problem.

Besides my Big Muff Pi, I use two Roland Boss Blues pedals, which have been modified by this guy I found on the internet who does that kind of thing. So I get my "American Woman" sound spectacularly now. When I put them both on, it's my 60s sound again.

Neil Young's pedal board is this big orange thing with about six switches that he built himself, so he's the only person who can repair it. He gets an incredible distortion sound, several different distorted sounds in fact, but he doesn't use a distortion pedal. When he steps on a switch it just raises or lowers the volume control on his little tweed 1950s model Fender Deluxe amp. He works the volume and tone controls on this old amp to get that tube distortion that sounds so awesome. He mics the amp and gets the gigantic distorted sound in arenas, but onstage it's just this little amp. He's very particular about the parts he uses in that old amp. His equipment techs treat it like rocket science.

Neil doesn't like to hear his guitar in a monitor. He only wants to hear his authentic guitar sound onstage from the amp alone. When I saw him playing in London a few years ago, I was backstage before the show when his longtime guitar tech, Larry Cragg, carried a skateboard out onto the stage as they were setting up. He was also carrying a clothesline, like the one your mother had in the backyard. Right in front of the drums he strung the clothesline and stapled it to the skateboard, and on that he placed Neil's little Fender amp. So whenever Neil moved around on the stage, Larry was behind the amp line, pulling the clothesline and making that little amp move forwards or backwards on the skateboard, following Neil. If Neil went over to the drummer during a song, Larry pulled the amp back. If Neil stepped to the front of the stage to solo, the amp moved up behind him so that he could hear it. Later, I asked Larry about it and he said, "Well, we thought it would work and when we tried it, it did, so we've stuck with it." I thought that was hilarious, and just so Neil.

When I look back over all the incredible innovations that have shaped guitar sounds, it's quite a journey. Digital technology will continue that journey, making new and interesting sounds available to young players, and to old ones like me. The fact that today anyone can have just about any sound or style at their fingertips, or foot tips, is astounding.

You've rarely spoken about the period right after you left BTO. You launched a solo career and made recordings with the groups Ironhorse and Union. What stands out for you from this period?

Tom Sparks and Randy in
action with Ironhorse, 1979.

A lot of people don't know about that period in the latter 70s to early 80s and the music I was recording and releasing. It's kind of a lost period for me because I didn't have the gigantic hits. But it was definitely a time for trying some new things, stepping out of my comfort zone after BTO.

On the last BTO album, *Freeways*, I'd tried to make our sound a bit more contemporary by using horns and strings and different tempos. We couldn't keep chugging away on the same hard rock template; we needed to progress. Unfortunately, though, our manager, Bruce Allen, and the other guys in the band didn't agree. As a result of these musical differences, along with the fact that our gruelling, non-stop touring schedule was burning us out, I left the band. The album suffered disappointing sales, but that didn't deter me from wanting to change my game up. When I left the band, I had a pile of songs I wanted to record, songs that didn't necessarily fit the BTO mould. I finally had the opportunity to slow down a bit and take stock of the last seven or eight years. As I looked at my life I thought I had it all: beautiful wife, wonderful children, great family life, gorgeous house all paid for, money securely invested forever—everything I wanted was at my fingertips. Life seemed perfect.

Things are never perfect, though. Burton Cummings and I hadn't talked in seven years. He'd slung a lot of mud at me during that time, but when he played a solo concert in Vancouver in 1977, he stopped in the middle of the show and in front of five or six thousand people he apologized for the bad things he'd said about me over the years. He dedicated the next part of the show to my wife and me, and then started out with about twelve bars of Barbra Streisand's "The Way We Were" before segueing into "These Eyes," "Laughing," "Undun," "No Time," and "American Woman." Everyone else was up on their feet going nuts. I sat there in tears.

Backstage, we hugged and posed together for photographers. Having disbanded the Guess Who in 1975 to launch his own solo career, Burton was riding high with "Stand Tall," his million-selling debut single. His first solo album included a cocktail jazz version of "You Ain't Seen Nothing Yet." Burton invited me to appear on his first CBC television special, and to guest on his second solo album, *My Own Way to Rock*. He was recording with legendary producer-to-the-stars Richard Perry at Studio 55 on Melrose Avenue in Hollywood. Richard Perry is like a god in the recording business, having produced Streisand, Carly Simon, Diana Ross, and Ringo Starr, among a long list of other notables.

So I went down to L.A., and when I visited the studio, there were the Pointer Sisters, Tom Scott, and the guys from Toto, who'd just recorded an album there. I played on several tracks on Burton's album and liked the vibe of the studio. So I decided to record a solo album there. With all those great players and singers, it was like a ready-made backing band. I was able to book guys like Jeff Porcaro and Tom Scott, along with Burton's bass player Ian Gardiner, originally from Winnipeg. Burton played on the album as well.

I arrived with thirty-three songs—all this stuff from BTO that I wanted to record on two or three albums. So we started recording, and I discovered that all these players smoked marijuana. They'd do a couple of recording takes, then disappear to toke up and come back blottoed. I had them booked for two weeks solid at double scale, so I had to sit them down and tell them that I needed them to do all the tracks straight. "I'll pay you for the full two weeks even if we finish early." They agreed, and we punched out the tracks in less than two weeks. I chose eight for *Survivor,* which I'd conceived as a concept album or a stage play, with little story links on the album sleeve between each song. It was semi-autobiographical: sixteen years of Canadian dreams and playing in a band, riding the highs and lows, concluding with the song "Survivor." I'd written the songs after meeting a playwright in New York who wanted to mount a Broadway production. There was a storyline, character development, and different life transitions throughout. It had a sense of wholeness to it, as opposed to random songs geared for the pop charts. The playwright passed away before we could develop the stage production, but I still had what I thought was a strong solo album. I felt pleased with it, not as a commercial entity to compete with BTO on the charts, but as a new direction for me. It was something I felt I really needed to do at that moment in my career. It was definitely out of my comfort zone going to L.A. and working with all these big names.

I appeared on NBC's *The Midnight Special* in 1978 with saxophone player Tom Scott guesting with me. I played "Is the Night Too Cold for Dancin'?," which was the lead-off single from the *Survivor* album. Everything looked rosy—but then two weeks later Freddy Hein, the head of Polydor and the guy who'd signed and championed me, called to tell me he'd been replaced. The way it works in the music business is that whoever takes over at the top has his or her own priorities and doesn't want to inherit a predecessor's projects. Suddenly, *Survivor* went from being the label's top priority to being on the outs. So I went to the Scotti brothers, Tony and Ben, and asked if they could promote the album. They'd done Donny Osmond and Foreigner, and had just had a huge hit with Sammy Davis Jr. and "The Candy Man." If they could promote that song, they could promote anything. They listened to the album and told me it was great but that it was over. The album had been out barely a month, but Polydor had put the word out that they weren't supporting it. Ironically, after I'd called my album *Survivor,* the guy from the Ides of March came out with a band called Survivor and scored a hit with "Eye of the Tiger." The Scotti brothers were behind that song. *Survivor* hit the discounted-record bins almost as fast as BTO's first album without me did.

Nonetheless, I'm still very proud of that album, and I think it deserves to be re-evaluated by releasing again. It's about my rise from a humble start in Winnipeg to the big time. It was misunderstood and never received the attention it deserved. I'd still like to see it as a play someday. I want to get the rights back, and hope to release it with all the bonus tracks we recorded at Studio 55.

The Scotti brothers told me to go back to the drawing board and do another album, but to make it a band album. I wasn't really looking to form another band and go out under a band name again, but they convinced me that that was where my strength lay. So I signed with their Scotti Brothers label, distributed by WEA (Warner Elektra Asylum), and came up with a name for my new band: Ironhorse. BTO's former road manager, John Austin, stayed on with me as my home studio engineer at Barn Studios in Lynden. He had a friend from Seattle, Tom Sparks, who wrote and sang. John introduced me to Tom; we hit it off and decided to build the band around our songwriting. I returned to Studio 55 in Hollywood to record the first Ironhorse album, working again with engineer Howard Steele. Having Tom also contributing songs was kind of like a BTO thing, where Fred would contribute a couple of songs per album for variety. Tom had three songs on that first Ironhorse album. The other two players in the band were studio guys, so it was basically Tom Sparks and me.

Tony and Ben Scotti told me they wanted another stuttering song like "You Ain't Seen Nothing Yet," so that became "Sweet Lui-Louise," which went to #1 for sixteen weeks in Italy, of all places. It managed to reach #16 on the Billboard charts in North America, which was an impressive start. We went over to Italy and toured; the video of us on Italian TV is hilarious (you can find it on YouTube). Tom Sparks was a great musician and songwriter. "Stateline Blues" received considerable airplay.

"Old Fashioned" was dedicated to Eric Clapton. I don't know whether he ever heard it. Overall, *Ironhorse* had more of a BTO feel to it, with solid rock riffs. It was a bit of a return to a familiar form.

The album and single were garnering a lot of airplay in Los Angeles. Carl Wilson heard it, along with the buzz around the band, and called to ask if we'd like to open for the Beach Boys' big 1979 North American tour. That was a huge break for us. Without hesitation, I said yes. It was a thrill to be with the Beach Boys—they were one of my favourite bands, and I loved every one of their records. The first gig went fine. The second was a sellout in Philadelphia at the Spectrum. I went to the sound check and had just returned to my hotel room when the phone rang and my world fell apart. My wife, Lorayne, was calling to inform me that she wanted a divorce. Here I'd thought I had a perfect life, but it all came crashing down on me without any warning signs that I could see.

Without going into all the details, my impending divorce and custody battle became the focus of my life, overriding music and the band. I was devastated. Lorayne and I agreed to take some time away from each other, so I carried on with the Beach Boys tour throughout that summer, all the while holding out hope of a reconciliation that, in the end, never happened. Every night after Ironhorse's set, I'd quickly change my clothes and then stand in the wings and sing to myself all my old parts in "I Get Around" and "California Girls" that I used to sing in Chad Allan and the Reflections. Despite being preoccupied with my domestic dilemma, I had a wonderful time on that tour, and got to know Carl Wilson well. Later, we even wrote some songs together, including "Keepin' the Summer Alive" and "What's Your Hurry Darlin'."

The first Ironhorse album had been successful enough to warrant recording a follow-up album. While in BTO, I'd also been producing the Canadian band Trooper, so when their keyboard player and second lead singer Frank Ludwig left the band, I brought him into Ironhorse and he became my Stevie Winwood, with that husky voice playing keyboards. Tom Sparks had bowed out, so it was basically a whole new band on that second album. I wrote some songs with Frank, and I had "What's Your Hurry Darlin'" from Carl Wilson and me. We recorded the album at my studio in Lynden. Looking back, the turmoil surrounding me informed the songs and the overall mood of that album, which I titled *Everything Is Grey*. I got away from the heavy guitar riffing, and with Frank on keyboards I was able to use synthesizers for a more melodic 80s sound. I was definitely distracted, but still, I tried to focus on the music. There's no doubting what songs like "What's Your Hurry Darlin'" and "I'm Hurting Inside" are about. The latter is one of my greatest songs. It's my Roy Orbison hurting song, like "Crying" or "It's Over." I've never been one to write personal songs, but it does come out unconsciously and I guess it did in that song.

Everything Is Grey was my therapeutic divorce album. My therapy was to keep working. Overall, the album has an appealing pop sound that's belied by its morose lyrical theme. "What's Your Hurry Darlin'" should have been a big hit. It was a great song and still is. A lot of people know that song, but don't know that it's me on it because Frank Ludwig is singing lead. It also doesn't sound like anything else in my song canon. In the photo of me on the back of the album cover I'd lost a ton of weight and shaved off my beard, all because of the stress of the divorce. I ate nothing but fruit for several months and cried about fifty pounds of tears. I'd get up and go running every day, wearing a bandana and crying as I ran. No one knew it, though; they thought I was just sweating. Emotionally it was a very difficult time, and my slimming down was a result of that. When Carl and I wrote that song, he was in the process of getting a divorce from his wife, Gina, and I was going through my divorce with Lorayne. So when we met up at Caribou Studios in Colorado, we wrote a bunch of songs that, unconsciously or maybe consciously, reflected our shared situations. You tend to write from what's affecting you or what's going on in your life, and I guess that stuff just came out.

With the ongoing custody battle over the kids, I couldn't tour to promote the album—I needed to be close to home and close to the kids so that it didn't look as if I'd abandoned them. I think it's a strong album, but that really hurt its chances. In the middle of all this, I got a call from Carl asking me to come down and produce the next Beach Boys album, including our song "Keepin' the Summer Alive." But I had to turn him down; I was afraid that if I left, Lorayne might grab the kids and take them to a Mormon compound in Utah. So there went my chance to produce the Beach Boys. We'd written "Keepin' the Summer Alive" perfectly for them, but the version they recorded and released was nothing like how that song should have been. Bruce Johnston of the Beach Boys told me years later that they'd initially recorded it with the drums way up in the mix, thundering along and driving the song the way I had envisioned it, but Brian Wilson didn't like that version and brought that powerful-sounding beat down. We later did the song on the Union album *On Strike* and it sounded great.

There were even more problems. At the time of the album's release, Scotti Brothers Records was part of a wider investigation into corruption in the music industry, so they closed down. We were left in the lurch, and it killed any chances for the album in the States. That was unfortunate because there were several songs on that album that could have been hits. I'd like to get the rights back to those two Ironhorse albums and re-release them with bonus tracks.

Fred Turner and I had kept in touch after I left BTO and remained cordial. He was the married guy with a family and Robbie and Blair were still the young single guys, so Fred would call me up for advice from time to time. When BTO finally broke up after two mediocre albums and no hits, I was doing Ironhorse, but it wasn't happening for any of us. So one day in speaking with Fred I asked him if he had any songs. Portrait Records was starting up again after a hiatus in the latter 70s, and they had offered me a deal. It was a happening label, with Cyndi Lauper, Sade, Aldo Nova, and Heart. Burton Cummings had also been on the label until they dropped him. Lennie Petze was heading up Portrait Records now and he wanted Fred in the band. Ironhorse bass player Ron Foos had left to join Paul Revere and the Raiders, so it was a perfect opportunity for Fred to come on board on bass. We went into my studio in Lynden and recorded the *On Strike* album with Frank Ludwig and drummer Chris Leighton. Fred had the songs "On Strike" and "All Night Long," Frank and I had written a couple more songs, and we had "Keepin' the Summer Alive." We had some great material and felt good about the recording sessions. "Texas Cannonball," Fred's "On Strike," and "Stay Away from the Honky Tonks" were strong songs, and my song "Mainstreet USA" had hit written all over it. Fred's gravel-truck voice steamrolling over several of the tracks gave the album a beefier edge that was reminiscent of BTO but in a more contemporary context. Once again, though, I turned in a solid album that I couldn't tour to support.

A mistake I made in recording the *On Strike* album was that my studio had 604E monitors, which are too toppy, too much treble. I sent the finished tracks to Lennie Petze, who liked the songs but asked if I'd let him send the tracks to a new young mixer on the East Coast named Bob Clearmountain. Lennie was convinced that if Bob mixed the tracks we'd have three or four hits on the album. I said no, it was my baby and I wanted to see it through. He asked me again if Bob could mix just a couple of tracks for radio, and again I refused. That was a mistake. I asked if I could sit in on the mix, and Lennie replied that Bob only worked alone. For $2500 per track, we could have had Bob mix them and we would have had a hit. I regret that—there were some good songs on that album. So in the end, Union was a great band that never got off the ground because of my divorce and my stubbornness about the mixing. Bob Clearmountain went on to become one of the top producers and mixers in the business, working with Bruce Springsteen, Bon Jovi, even the Rolling Stones. I hope to get that album back, too, and release it with all the outtakes. "Rough Ride" is a fabulous track from those outtakes.

When the album came out in 1981, the baseball strike was on, so Portrait Records figured they'd get lots of attention with the *On Strike* title. The first single, "Mainstreet USA," was sent directly to radio and received strong phone-in response at several key stations, including in New York. Everyone was excited about the single and the album. Then a week later the record went flat. Turned out that the independent promo men, who were usually hired to work a record and turn it into a hit, were miffed that they'd been bypassed and were now trying to bury the album unless we funded them. As a result of this little power play, the album lost its momentum. Payola, or the practice of pay-for-play, was still going on in the record business at that time—despite a congressional investigation back in 1959 that allegedly halted the practice—and we refused to play ball. Nonetheless, we started gearing up to do a tour. We had dates booked. We did a handful of gigs around Vancouver and Seattle, and then my lawyer informed me that if I went out on the road I'd lose the custody battle over my kids. So that ended Union.

Survivor, the two Ironhorse albums, and the Union album all had their moments, but not a lot of them. They kind of got lost in what was happening musically—dance music, New Wave, techno-pop—and the fact that I was limited in my ability to tour and promote them. There are some great songs like "Everything Is Grey," and "Mainstreet USA" should have been a huge hit.

While I'm on the subject of forgotten albums in my catalogue, it's worth talking about my so-called solo debut album, *Axe*.

That was never intended to be a solo album, just a little side project I recorded over a free weekend in March 1970 when the Guess Who had some time off. It was Garry Peterson and I at RCA's Chicago studio, with engineer Brian Christian and a couple of friends, Wes Dakus and Domenic Troiano, sitting in. Unfortunately the timing of its release, coming after I had very publicly left the Guess Who, obscured the reality of what it was intended to be.

When the Guess Who signed with RCA, they weren't the label to go to for rock bands. The happening labels at the time were Warner Brothers, Reprise, Elektra, Atlantic. Nobody was going to RCA. Jefferson Airplane was their big rock act. But what RCA did was go inside their bands and ask guys to do an album. They did that with Jorma Kaukonen and Jack Cassidy from Jefferson Airplane, who recorded a bunch of bluesy jam albums as Hot Tuna while still in the Airplane. So Don Birkhimer at RCA came to Burton and me to ask if we'd do an album of our songs stripped down to just piano, guitar, and voice, just as we'd first conceived them in Burton's living room on Bannerman Avenue. It was to be called something like *Cummings & Bachman Do Bachman & Cummings*. We were very flattered, and of course said sure. At the same time Don also approached me and said, "Since you like Chet Atkins, Lenny Breau, and Hank Marvin so much, would you do a guitar instrumental album like Harvey Mandel?" (Harvey had done a couple of guitar albums, *Cristo Redentor* and *Games Guitars Play*, that had been well received.) Because I already had a fan base from the Guess Who, they thought it would sell. It was never intended to be a big Claptonesque thing, just a few guitars noodling. I had a bunch of songs already, I played bass and guitars, and it allowed me to produce myself. I think it pissed Burton off because they asked for a solo album from me and not from him. He'd been pitching an album with his buddies, musical comedy duo and self-styled "toilet rockers" Maclean and Maclean, but they rejected it.

The Guess Who had a weekend off in mid March. Lorayne and the kids were away visiting her parents, so rather than go home to an empty house, I used the three days, March 16 to 18, to book RCA's Mid-America studios in Chicago, where we'd recorded *American Woman*. I also booked engineer Brian Christian, who'd worked with the band. Garry Peterson joined me. We went in on Friday evening, set up, I wrote down a rough song list and arrangements on a sheet of paper, and Garry and I recorded the bed tracks alone. That was the first time I was producing myself, telling the engineer what to do, and working on the arrangements. It was marvellous. We did the basic songs, and the next day I added bass and some of the guitar parts. I'd called the Mandalas' Domenic Troiano on short notice, and he flew in from Los Angeles on Sunday. Wes Dakus also arrived from Edmonton, and we overdubbed guitar and pedal steel. Troiano and I did some nice guitar interplay together. That night I mixed it and it was done, quick and easy.

There's no singing on the album and no rock or pop songs, just dumb little guitar things I used to fool around with in a dressing room or on a bus. I wasn't out to be Jeff Beck or Jimmy Page. There are no raging solos; it's just me doing my noodling. So it wasn't very demanding—it's kind of like dinner-hour music you put on in the background. I had no time to think of anything more. Most important, I had absolutely no idea at the time that I'd be leaving the Guess Who or that this would be viewed as my first solo album. I was all set to get together with Burton the following week and finish writing the songs for the next Guess Who album.

The following month, the whole band was back at that same Chicago studio to cut the tracks that became *The Way They Were* album, released after the band broke up. We'd planned to return to the studio in late May to complete the overdubs on those tracks, but that, of course, never happened.

The photo on the back of the *Axe* album is a very cool shot of me with my Gretsch 6120, my Fender Legend, and my '59 Les Paul on the floor beside me. Those are the three Bachman guitars. Behind me is a Garnet Lil' Rock with a Herzog on top of it. There are some personal indulgences on the album, such as my naming a song for my son Tally. "Zarahemla" was a name from the Book of Mormon (I'd converted to Mormonism in 1966 when I married Lorayne, who was Mormon), while "Not to Return" had been written for Sugar and Spice back in Winnipeg.

The album didn't sell, but it has become something of a cult favourite that a few people dig. Over the years, I've had people come up to me in the strangest of places and tell me how much they liked *Axe*. Guitar legend Roy Buchanan once told me it was one of his favourite albums because it's not fifty thousand notes a minute. It's laid-back and relaxed. He'd put that album on and play over it, using the songs as grooves to solo with. Steve Vai said he liked it, too. There are some tasty moments on it, I admit.

Still, *Axe* bombed because everyone thought it was my solo debut. There was the Guess Who with "Hand Me Down World" and the *Share the Land* album, and then there was me, the guy who'd apparently left the band to go solo, with my quirky little instrumentals. And it wasn't that way at all.

In hindsight, this period was a turbulent one for me, an ongoing search for the right combination of musicians and the right formula. Often, it isn't just a question of having the right song; turning a record into a hit involves many other, behind-the-scenes factors. It's not just about talent. During these years, my personal life kept me from pursuing my goals. Still, I have no regrets about the commercial failure of the recordings from this time. The songs were there, but I wasn't able to give them the focus and push they needed. My family was my priority, and I'll never regret that.

Chad Allan was the original singer in
the Guess Who, and in Brave Belt, too.
However, he left both bands before they
hit it big. Whatever became of
Chad Allan and others like Bob Ashley?

The Guess Who (Chad Allan and the Expressions), circa 1965; left to right: Bob Ashley, Randy Bachman, Chad Allan, Jim Kale, and Garry Peterson.

Over the decades, I've discovered that many people are under the mistaken impression that Burton Cummings was the only lead singer in the Guess Who, and that it's his voice on our first hit single in 1965, "Shakin' All Over." But Burton joined almost a year after we recorded that song. The original lead singer in the Guess Who was Chad Allan. He's the one who formed what would become the Guess Who back in 1962. He left the band in mid 1966 but hooked up with me again in 1970 to form Brave Belt. He left that band, too, a year later.

As a result, Chad (Allan Kowbel) has earned the reputation as the Pete Best of Canada. Like Pete with the Beatles before Ringo replaced him, Chad missed the ship when it finally sailed in. I owe him a big debt of gratitude, though. It was Chad who brought me into his band and encouraged me to play lead guitar. He gave me the opportunity to become Hank Marvin to his Cliff Richard—to have a role, a role I wanted. And when the Beatles came along he allowed me to be George Harrison. Chad put the original Guess Who lineup together. He was a kingpin in the early Winnipeg music scene and became a kingmaker for the guys who became stars because of him. He was a catalyst in both bands, the Guess Who and Brave Belt. But the fact is that I was a can of gasoline waiting for the match to light it. And when that match came, Chad was already gone. His leaving the Guess Who led Burton Cummings and me to develop our songwriting collaboration. And when he left Brave Belt, it allowed me to take the reins and ultimately steer the ship in the right direction.

I had a drive and a passion back in the early 60s, but I never saw that in Chad. I always seemed to be the temporary leader of the bands Chad and I were in together. If something went wrong or didn't go his way, he'd be gone. He just wasn't reliable. He didn't have that 100 percent commitment to the long haul and the further vision. He'd walk away, unlike me, who just stayed and kept knocking at the door until I finally knocked it down. Chad had two chances, both with me, and he blew them. I believe that, deep down, he was afraid of success.

What a lot of people either forget or don't know is that Burton joined the Guess Who by replacing Bob Ashley, our keyboard player, not Chad Allan. We needed a keyboard player, not a lead singer. Still, I knew that Chad's commitment was waning.

In fact, he'd once ducked out on the band in Wisconsin, going home to see his girlfriend and leaving us high and dry to play the gig without our singer. When Chad ditched us that night, at first we didn't know he'd left. The next morning, I called his room and there was no answer. I went and knocked on the door; again no answer. So I got the hotel manager to open the door and I saw that his bed hadn't been slept in. Turned out he'd had someone from the hotel drive him to the airport in the middle of the night and had flown home. We were all set to go to the gig and he'd gone. So I phoned his home, and to my surprise he answered. He said he didn't want to do the gig; he was very matter-of-fact about it. That was disappointing to me—up till then we'd been "all for one and one for all." We played that night without him. Bob Ashley, who didn't like performing before audiences, had left the band just prior to that gig (Chad was covering his piano parts until we found a replacement), meaning we had to do the gig as a trio: Garry Peterson, Jim Kale, and me. How we got through it I don't know. We certainly weren't a power trio like Cream or the Jimi Hendrix Experience. I think we played a lot of instrumentals; none of us were lead singers then.

So when Burton replaced Ashley, not only did we get a great keyboard player, but he could sing, too—and I knew that he was our little insurance policy in case Chad ever bailed on us again.

For about six months in 1966 we had both Chad and Burton in the band and, oh my god, we were like the best band anywhere. We could literally do anything—any tunes, any style. We could be the Beach Boys and the Kinks all rolled into one. That lineup recorded the *It's Time* album that spring. It was an incredibly exciting musical period, but in the back of our minds we knew Chad's commitment was soft. He didn't like Burton, and hadn't been part of the decision to bring him in. He resented Burton's voice and thought Burton was looking to take over the band and push him out. But with the two of them it was like the Beatles. Chad was our more pop-oriented Paul McCartney voice while Burton was our John Lennon shrieker with attitude.

I begged Chad to stay, but he wouldn't. He couldn't stand sharing the limelight or losing his name in the group: it wasn't

Chad Allan and the Guess Who. Chad was insecure and felt threatened. He felt that Burton stole some of his limelight, but that wasn't the case. At the time, Burton idolized Chad.

Bob Ashley was a very talented piano player, but he hated being in the public eye. He and Jim Kale both lived on Clonard Avenue in St. Vital and worked at the Wheat Board. That's where they met my brother Gary. It was Gary who told them about me, and as a result I was invited to audition for Allan's Silvertones, Chad's band, which Bob and Jim played in. Bob could do all that Floyd Cramer piano-trill stuff superbly.

Bob's mother, Simone, spoke French and helped me get through French class in high school. She became my French tutor. She also gave me a rhyming dictionary that I've used in every songwriting session since the early 60s. I still have it. And, as I described earlier, it was Bob's tape recorder that gave me my Shadows sound.

In the early days of the Reflections, Bob was the star instrumentalist in the band; he played more solos than I did. When he got a little Hohner organ, it expanded the sound and range of the group: we could do "Telstar" and songs like that. Bob also had perfect pitch, which for him was both a blessing and a curse because it used to drive him crazy when I'd bend a note. To him, it was like scratching fingernails on a blackboard.

There we were in the summer of 1965 on the road in the U.S., our dream come true, backing the Crystals and the Shirelles. We were such a versatile band that we could play anything. But these girl-group chicks would tease Bob about being so shy. They'd do it onstage, and he hated that. He also had this thing about being watched. Before we'd go onstage he'd ask me, "How many people are here tonight?" and I'd tell him, "About five hundred." He'd get all panicky and say, "That's a thousand eyes staring at me!" He was very self-conscious. What kind of person counts the eyes looking at him?

After he left the band at the end of December 1965, Bob played a bit around Winnipeg before disappearing from the public eye for decades. No one knew his whereabouts. Turned out he'd been in Toronto and was still playing, albeit out of the public eye and the pop music world. He's been involved in accompanying musical theatre productions and symphony work.

Last year, right out of the blue, I heard from Bob via my radio show. I hadn't seen him since 1966. He came down to see me playing at a jazz gig in Toronto. He looked exactly the same as he did when we played together in the Reflections—same hair, same glasses, same physique, hadn't gained an ounce. We had a great visit and went to dinner at the Hard Rock Café.

Chad Allan pursued a low-key music career after leaving the Guess Who. He completed university and played lounges around Winnipeg with the Sticks and Strings. He also hosted CBC-TV's *Let's Go* with us as the house band. After I left the Guess Who in the spring of 1970, I did some television work at CBC, and that's when I reconnected with him. He was recording a solo album and invited me to play on it.

But once I came on board, the project evolved into the first Brave Belt album. I kind of hijacked his solo album and made it a band effort, my band effort, even though I didn't really have a band until we started recording. And Brave Belt wasn't what

Chad had intended his solo album to be; he came and told me as much after we'd recorded all the tracks.

Still, I was excited about the prospect of turning Brave Belt into my own little Buffalo Springfield, and I'd brought the album to the point where I was ready to sell it to a record label as a band. When we signed with Reprise Records, I put Fred Turner's name on the contract because I knew the band needed another player and someone with a voice that contrasted with Chad's mellower vocal style. Some of the material that was more reflective of Chad's lighter vision was left off the album, songs like "West Coast Girl" and "Hands and Faces." Mo Ostin allowed Chad to release "West Coast Girl" as a single that no one played, unfortunately. It was a great song, with Bob McMullien orchestrating. We kept the band-sounding tracks for the album while the other songs, with the cellos and all that, Chad released as a couple of singles. That sound was his dream, but mine was to get a band together and get something played on the radio.

Sometimes you have to compromise for a greater goal; you contribute to the whole. Chad didn't want to do that. That's just the way he was. I was more into creating something not merely for my own satisfaction or creative outlet but for wider acceptance by the public. I wanted validation that this was something good and not just something I could sit in my basement and listen to and appreciate. That's why Brave Belt was already falling apart just as we were launching the band. Chad never bought into the band vision. He never lost the solo album mindset.

Only Chad Allan knows the true reasons why he left Brave Belt. I only knew the excuses he gave me at the time—why he wouldn't come to Thunder Bay for a two-night gig, leaving us once again high and dry. That weekend became the turning point for us: it was through the crucible of losing a key band member that we managed to find the magic formula for the band. We virtually became Bachman-Turner Overdrive that weekend in everything but name. Could we have made it with Chad? I don't know.

Chad made some bad decisions, and it cost him. I knew they were bad at the time. I knew he wanted to make music, but he only wanted to make local music. He didn't have the vision, the dream, or the determination to look beyond Winnipeg. The *Winnipeg Free Press* did a feature story on Chad's whereabouts a couple of years ago, and I thought it was a bit mean-spirited. He plays seniors homes now, accompanying himself on accordion, and he can't sing much anymore. I know that because several years back I brought him up onstage to sing "Shakin' All Over" at a gig in Vancouver and he could barely get through the first line. I had to sing the rest, and afterwards he left the stage right away, embarrassed. The newspaper article juxtaposed his current situation with that of Burton Cummings and me, and that wasn't fair. We all make our choices in life and live with them. It's not been easy for Chad, living with regret and being reminded of it every time he turns on the radio and hears a Guess Who or BTO song. But there can be no denying that without Chad Allan, Burton Cummings and I may not have had the successful careers we've enjoyed. He was the catalyst for our success, whether he realized it or not. Back in the day, Chad Allan was a big star on the local scene, and no one should forget that.

Next year, 2015, marks the fiftieth anniversary of "Shakin' All Over." I'd love to do the ultimate Guess Who reunion with everyone who played in the band over its ten years—from Chad Allan and Bob Ashley to Greg Leskiw, Bill Wallace, and Don McDougall—and to celebrate that song and the group's history chronologically, bringing guys onstage as the history transpired. We've lost Bruce Decker, Kurt Winter, and Domenic Troiano, but even so, that would be a wonderful event.

You've said that the Guess Who could have been the next Beatles, and Bachman-Turner Overdrive was very successful when you left. Could you have stayed with the Guess Who or BTO instead of leaving both when you did?

Randy in Phase One Studio, Toronto, with BTO, 1974.

When you've spent as much time in the music industry as I have, it's easy to look back and wonder "what if?" It's a difficult thing to know, but in both cases, the Guess Who and BTO, I think the simple answer here is "yes." If the Guess Who had had a decent manager, things might have turned out differently. When you go into the corporate jungles of Toronto or New York, the people you're dealing with know all the tricks, whereas the people who managed the Guess Who were prairie guys like us who didn't know the ropes. To be fair, it was a whole new ballgame that none of us, managers or band, was prepared for. We needed someone who could steer us in the right direction, provide good advice, and not only make the right decisions but also have the strength of character and level of respect to get us all onside for those decisions.

When the problems between me and the other guys in the band came to a head in May 1970, a strong manager would have called us all together and said, "Look, Randy has serious health issues with his gallbladder he needs to get immediate attention for, and he'll need a suitable time to recuperate. Let's take six months off the road and everybody clean up and get their act together. We'll release one of the tracks we have in the can already as a follow-up single. Then we'll reconvene in the fall and do the American Woman tour with everyone firing on all four cylinders." But instead, after our triumphant show at the Fillmore East on May 16 where I played my heart out after the confrontation with the guys, it was a case of Burton and Jim Kale saying, "Screw you! You're out of the band." I understand that Garry Peterson went to Burton and Jim and tried to get them to change their minds, but they wouldn't listen.

It turned ugly on the flight home when Burton and Jim berated me loudly and drunkenly. The plane had to make an emergency stop because of the ruckus they caused. One of them even threatened to shoot up my house with a rifle. While there were certainly lifestyle differences that had driven a wedge between me and the others, my being a teetotalling Mormon, those differences had been there for several years already and were not insurmountable. But tempers were raised, and no attempt was made to clear the air and let cooler heads prevail. The assumption by the other guys in the band, that I was sabotaging them, was completely erroneous. However, in that emotionally charged moment of confrontation, there was no way to explain things. Instead of trying to settle things between the two factions in the band, me on one side and Burton and Jim on the other, everyone positioned themselves for after the fallout. They couldn't see that by letting the fracture in the group burst open, they were killing a great thing. The die was cast.

The reality is that after the break, the band never had hits as big as the ones the original four-piece lineup had enjoyed, and the Guess Who's reputation rests on those hits. Everyone was looking out for themselves and not looking at the bigger picture. We had the next album pretty much all written, with songs like "Palmyra" and "The Answer." We could have finished it in the studio with a few overdubs and put it out while we cooled off and collected ourselves. There was no reason why we couldn't have stayed together.

I learned many important lessons from my experiences with the Guess Who that I applied to Bachman-Turner Overdrive. I wasn't in control of the Guess Who, but in BTO, I was captain of the ship—until the crew decided to mutiny. We were on a treadmill and needed to stop and reassess our sound and approach. We put out albums too soon and too fast, and as a result the quality started to decline. But from Mercury Records it was always, "We need the next album!" Rush, rush, rush. Keep milking the cash cow before it inevitably runs dry. There was no long-term plan. Fred Turner wasn't as creative because he was burned out. He needed a rest to recharge his batteries. Robbie and Blair were demanding an equal share of the songwriting, but they were inexperienced and their material wasn't up to an acceptable standard to be included on our albums. If you listen to the two BTO albums they did after I left, neither was a writer. So when I tried rejigging the band's formula by adding new textures and instruments to our sound on *Freeways*, the others turned against me.

We needed to slow down, to take some individual time off from each other and from the rigours of the road and recording. We certainly didn't need the money. As I explained earlier, we'd taken some $10 million and plugged it into guaranteed annual annuities. We could have regrouped in six months or longer and seen what we had to contribute. But, as in the Guess Who, we didn't have strong enough management or support from the record company to ease up. They rushed out a greatest hits album even before *Freeways* was released, assuming we were already on the inevitable downward swing. The reality is that no recording artist can stand still and hope to gain new fans while retaining the old ones. You have to evolve; otherwise, you're stuck in a rut that you can't get out of. BTO needed to retool the engine. But no one would admit that and take the necessary steps. Could I have stayed with BTO? Yes, if we'd been able to take some time off, then come back together refreshed and rejuvenated. I was still creative and had some thirty songs waiting. Some of those went to my next project, *Survivor*.

Both the Guess Who and Bachman-Turner Overdrive are regarded as Canadian music royalty, and rightly so. Both bands have been honoured by just about every institution in Canada. But do I think either band will ever be inducted into Cleveland's Rock and Roll Hall of Fame? When you look at the Mount Rushmore of Canadian rock music, both the Guess Who and BTO are up there, but it doesn't matter to the Hall of Fame. It's a very political body. Despite their collective list of hits, both bands are regarded as lightweight in the U.S. Lesser artists than us have been inducted. Even Leonard Cohen is inducted, and he's hardly regarded as rock 'n' roll. But it is what it is. It's all about what someone considers "cool," and I guess we just weren't cool enough. My '59 Les Paul "American Woman" guitar is on display in the Cleveland Rock Hall museum and I'm deeply honoured, but the Rock Hall is separate from the Hall

of Fame induction, with a completely different board of direc-
tors. I remain hopeful that someday one or both of these bands
will finally be recognized by the Rock and Roll Hall of Fame.
Neil Young has been inducted twice, as a member of Buffalo
Springfield and as a solo artist, and Rush finally received the
nod. You never know.

Your relationship with Burton Cummings
has been a roller coaster.
Will you ever work with him again?

Randy and Burton Cummings reconcile following
Cummings's Vancouver concert, 1977.

This is probably the question I'm asked most often. There's plenty that Burton and I could still do. We could do a jazz album together—we both love that Mose Allison/Georgie Fame jazz style—or a stage play, anything. The sky is still the limit. However, none of this could happen unless he makes things right. Most Guess Who fans and Canadians in general know nothing about the issue that divides Burton and me. Only a few people know the truth. Burton and I share a wonderful songwriting legacy that will outlive us both. I still want to celebrate the songs, but I'm not going to do so with him unless he rights the wrong between us.

I had a really great relationship with Burton in the early years. I took him under my wing when he was still a teenager, nurtured his songwriting talent, and cultivated that collaboration. But people still ask me if I'll ever write with Burton Cummings again, and I say no. That's why we did that *Jukebox* album of cover songs in 2007 when we were Bachman-Cummings: we weren't going to record any new songs together.

That's just the way it is, and that's the way it will be as long as the song publishing issue remains unsettled.

The term "song publishing" dates back to the early twentieth century, when the primary source of income from songwriting was sales of sheet music, hence the word "publishing." The total income from a song, the royalty, was split 50/50 between the songwriter and the music publisher. But by the 50s, airplay and record sales began overtaking sheet-music sales. Nevertheless, the arrangement remained. A publisher's job was to hustle the song to recording artists in order to get it recorded and start earning money. The legendary Brill Building in New York housed not only dozens of songwriters but also the offices of the song publishing companies. The songwriters were signed to these publishing companies, which paid them a salary to crank out songs that they'd then pitch to recording artists. Some of the greatest songs of the late 50s to early pre-Beatles 60s came from these Brill Building writers, who toiled away in tiny cubicles with a piano.

Song pluggers regularly pitched the songs they represented to artists who didn't write their own material, such as Frank Sinatra, Dean Martin, and Elvis Presley. Elvis's manager, Colonel Parker, began the practice of taking a slice of the publishing for himself, because getting a song cut by the King meant potentially a lot of money for the songwriter. That practice continues. Just ask René Angelil, who manages Celine Dion. If you want to have your song recorded by Ms. Dion you have to give her a piece of the publishing. It's not illegal. But artists like Buddy Holly, the Beach Boys' Brian Wilson, Bob Dylan, and ultimately the Beatles threw a monkey wrench into the old tried-and-true practice by writing their own songs. They no longer required the song pluggers' services; as self-contained sources of material for recording, they began to demand a piece of the publishing pie.

These individual songwriters set up separate publishing companies, but they were administered by established publishing companies for a percentage of the action. As a result, the role of publishing companies shifted slightly. They were still trying to hustle their songwriters' material—look at all the Lennon and McCartney and Dylan covers in the 60s—but they were also responsible for collecting royalties due from a number of revenue streams: performance income including radio, television, and film; synchronized licensing with film, television, or movies; print (sheet music); and mechanicals (record sales). Gradually, the norm became that an artist or band generated its own songs rather than relying on outside songwriters. That was the situation with Burton and me when Guess Who producer Jack Richardson offered us a production deal in 1968. We would provide the group's songs for recording.

In the 60s, many recording artists who wrote their own material were naive about publishing and routinely signed away their publishing rights without understanding just what they were giving up. This naïveté worked to the advantage of the song publishing companies, who knew the business and the income potential in the offing. The Beatles were babes in the woods when it came to knowledge of publishing and lost tens of millions, maybe even hundreds of millions, by not owning Northern Songs. Ultimately, that company was publicly traded on the stock exchange, and Michael Jackson ended up owning

the publishing on Lennon and McCartney's songwriting catalogue. Paul McCartney eventually learned the value of publishing
and now controls one of the largest publishing companies in the
world, MPL. It's long been rumoured that MPL controls the
rights to "Happy Birthday to You."

After doing *Let's Go,* the CBC-TV show, for a year, I set up
Friends of Mine Music Ltd. We'd been financially shafted by
the whole U.K. fiasco, and because I'd gone to business school,
I knew something about corporations and their advantages. So,
through Friends of Mine Music Ltd., Burton and I wrote the
chord charts for *Let's Go* songs each week and got paid a little
bit extra for doing that. And when we started writing our own
songs, they became Friends of Mine songs, administered through
BMI publishing at the time. But when we got the contract
with Jack Richardson and signed with his production company,
Nimbus 9, he told us that he needed a piece of the song publishing
in case we had what was known as a turntable hit: lots of radio
play but little sales. Burton and I didn't know at the time that you
got paid for your songs being played on the radio. It became a
problem for Jack because he'd mortgaged his house to take us to
New York to record the *Wheatfield Soul* album. He was investing
in us with no guarantee of a return, so he needed a bit of insurance. He needed to own our publishing.

Jack presented the publishing situation to us as a deal breaker.
If his company didn't get the publishing, they wouldn't sign us
to their production company. No "These Eyes," "Laughing,"
"Undun," "No Time," or "American Woman." I told Jack that
these songs, whether co-written by Burton and me or individually, were our babies, and so we should get them back once

he'd recovered his investment in the band. The deal between Burton and me was that we split our songwriting revenue 50/50 unless one of us wrote the entire song, in which case it was 100 percent. I didn't want anything of his and didn't think he should have anything of mine, like "A Wednesday in Your Garden" or "Undun." So, reluctantly, Burton and I acquiesced and gave Jack a full percentage, with the stipulation that this arrangement would remain in effect only until he earned some money, then it would be a lesser percentage until his investment was paid back. We would then get our publishing rights back. The plan was not in perpetuity, but merely to help Jack recoup his investment.

Through Nimbus 9, Jack took 100 percent of our publishing (which is 50 percent of what a song earns) and Burton and I got our writers' royalties. Friends of Mine Music Ltd. was given credit as a token but not paid any money. So when we started having hit singles, we'd see Nimbus earning big money, more than Burton and I did individually. Nimbus 9 also took half the record royalties as a production company. So, Nimbus was taking 75 percent of the total. I suggested to Jack that they must have earned their stake back by then. I received a letter back giving us 40 percent of their 50 percent on publishing, but only on the BMI performances; that meant on radio, not the mechanicals, which is on the sale of each record. At the time, the mechanical we got was two cents. It was better than nothing. I wanted it to increase a year later, but that never happened.

When I left the Guess Who, I thought I'd get my songs back, but Jack said no. There was something in our contract with Nimbus 9 that said that five years after your record contract ends you can get your songs back. The next thing that happened was that Jack had built a recording studio in Toronto but had gone bankrupt. So he was now selling Nimbus 9, which included our songs. I heard about it a few years later from Garry Peterson, who was playing again with Burton in a trio with bass player Ian Gardiner. It was at a Christmas party when he told me; Burton had never said anything. I figured, "Great. We can get our songs back."

What had happened, though, was that Jim "Jumbo" Martin, our road manager in the Guess Who, had been walking by Jack's studio in Toronto for old times' sake when one of the employees asked him if he'd like to buy Nimbus 9's publishing, namely the Guess Who song catalogue. Jumbo was working for Burton at the time and told him about it. Burton wasted no time in contacting his lawyer in L.A., who brokered the deal for Burton to acquire all the Guess Who songs, from "These Eyes" onward. All the songs, including the ones I wrote alone or with Burton, now came under the control of Shillelagh Music, Burton's publishing company. But at that point it was really a dead issue in terms of an income stream because this was still around 1980 and there was no classic rock radio, nostalgia movies, or CDs. It was just a bunch of golden oldies that might get played once in a while, but there was no lucrative market yet for these songs. The Guess Who album catalogue wasn't even in the stores anymore. All that changed a decade later.

The following year, I saw Burton at another Christmas party and asked him why I hadn't gotten my songs back. He said, "Oh, just call my lawyer and he'll take care of it." I called him the following week, and it was the first and only time a lawyer has ever told me to fuck off. He actually said that, and then he hung up on me. So I ended up getting my own lawyer and trying to sue to get my songs. But I lost. I should have gone after Burton for violating his fiduciary duty to me.

Burton was supposed to make it right when we got back together in 1987, but he didn't. Maybe I should have spoken up when we were inducted into the Canadian Music Hall of Fame that year and I had the chance at the microphone. Something like, "Here I stand with my one-time partner, and yet when songs like 'These Eyes' and 'Laughing' earn a dollar, I get 25 cents and he gets 75 cents. What happened?" But I didn't. The Juno producers were too worried about Burton going on the attack against Jim Kale for touring under the Guess Who name. That's another story. But I was later told by someone at the CBC that that was why we were so abruptly cut off and the broadcast went to a commercial. The director was fearful of a Cummings–Kale public spat. Truth be told, Burton did have a speech prepared vilifying what he called Kale's Klones.

During talks for the 2000 Guess Who reunion, I was cautioned by management not to muddy the waters by bringing up the publishing issue or the tour would be off. Burton would walk out. So I bit my lip and kept quiet. Since then, I've given Burton several opportunities to make things right. I've written him letters about it. But he's never wanted to discuss it. Think of all the money that's been generated by the Guess Who catalogue since that point. It's in the millions.

Every December 31, I'd send Burton a letter or an email wishing him a happy birthday. We used to celebrate New Year's Eve, which is also his birthday, by going out to a nice dinner in Winnipeg somewhere, Lorayne and I and Burton and his girlfriend, Jan. We'd work our asses off all year and then take that night off. We did this, the four of us, for three years before things got really crazy for the band. So in my happy birthday email I reminded him of those wonderful times when the four of us would get together. However, I added that I couldn't understand why he continued to avoid addressing the publishing issue. I told him that I couldn't work with him again unless that was fixed.

He was a kid when I invited him into the band. I was his big brother, picking him up for gigs and bringing him home as his mother insisted. I taught him about publishing and shared everything equally with him in our little publishing company. Then for him to grab the publishing rights and not tell anyone was hurtful. Imagine the money he made off Lenny Kravitz's "American Woman" cover. If he made it right, I'd play with him tomorrow. He says he's leaving all his money to the Humane Society, which is admirable, but not the point. I'm leaving mine to my grandkids. My songwriting is their legacy gift from me.

I used to wake up in the middle of the night sick to my stomach, thinking, "How could I have let this happen?" I've had lawyer after lawyer pursue it. Not long ago, some of my closest associates had an intervention-like meeting with me where they told me that I'm addicted to lawyers. I've had a half dozen or more lawyers try to fix this thing, but the only person who can fix it is Burton Cummings. They told me I had to write Burton a letter, so I did, just last year. It was an open, honest letter explaining how I felt—that he had poisoned the waters between us. In the letter, I said that I'd love to do other projects together, but under the current circumstances I couldn't work with him.

We went through the rock 'n' roll trenches together and built a musical monument for everyone in the world to appreciate. And we did it from Canada, which was significantly harder than for others who flocked to the States. But I told him I felt hurt every time he would announce "Undun" as one of the greatest songs to come from Canada or anywhere and that he was honoured to sing it, and then turn around and take the publishing income from that song. I was told by one of Burton's associates that the letter affected him deeply, but obviously not enough to rectify the situation. I can't turn the other cheek and smile anymore.

The bane of Burton's career is that he never achieved solo success in the United States. When we played in the States as Bachman-Cummings, people would be on their feet for the BTO tunes. They got a far better response than the Guess Who numbers, and nothing can follow "Takin' Care of Business." Burton couldn't play any of his solo songs, though, because they weren't hits in the States. That's why Fred Turner and I are able to play the U.S. and all over the world: BTO songs were huge worldwide hits, and it's our names, Bachman and Turner, on those songs. It doesn't matter who plays drums or rhythm guitar. We can go out without using Overdrive in the name. We were the Bachman and Turner of Bachman-Turner Overdrive, and people know they're getting the two guys who were the driving force of BTO, who wrote and sang those songs. What's even more gratifying is that, while everyone reacts to the hits, they also recognize the album tracks deep in our catalogue. When we play songs like "Not Fragile," "Sledgehammer," or "Rock Is My Life," they're all singing along. Fred will start the distinctive bass intro to "Not Fragile" and audiences go nuts everywhere: North

America, Europe, New Zealand. It's great. Fred and I get excited like little kids.

People may know the Guess Who name and its hits, but outside Canada they didn't and don't know the names of the guys in the original band. Even Burton Cummings's name isn't as well known as it should be beyond Canada. He's the voice of all the Guess Who hits, and people recognize that voice but don't necessarily know his name. His solo career in the United States didn't take off the way it was expected to after "Stand Tall" earned him a gold record. That's why he had to come back to Canada and focus on his career here.

Jim Kale and Garry Peterson can continue touring as the Guess Who in the States as long as they present a reasonable facsimile of our hits because the public doesn't know or care who's in the band. The nostalgia circuit, especially in the States, remains lucrative. It's baby boomers holding on to their glory days, and with that, their music. Mr. and Ms. Middle America want to go out for an evening to hear the songs they remember. It may be a state fair or a casino. They don't care whether it's the original members, as long as they hear the songs they know and love. But they're being sold a bill of goods, because although the marquee says Guess Who, it's a sham.

Still, this kind of thing goes on every night somewhere across North America. There are a hundred bands who are touring under a well-known name from the past, but who are made up of one or maybe two original members who've somehow acquired the rights to the name. The drummer from the Yardbirds tours under that name. For a long time, the original Animals drummer toured as the Animals. There's a Byrds band playing the casinos with none of the guys who played in its various lineups; those in the casino version weren't even born when "Mr. Tambourine Man" was a hit. The list goes on and on. Jim and Garry touring as the Guess Who is by no means an anomaly. Jim owns the name, and demand for a Guess Who band remains healthy on the nostalgia circuit. They don't play in Canada, though: up here, we know better.

Burton continues to be incensed about those two still touring under the Guess Who name. He never misses an opportunity to tear a strip off them, whether in concert, in the media, or on his Facebook page. It infuriates him further when promoters use our original recordings to hype an upcoming show by the ersatz Guess Who. I have mixed feelings. On the one hand, everyone has a right to earn a living. Jim was the one who invited me into the band in the first place, and I invited Garry into the band. Garry and I go back to our early teens at Edmund Partridge Junior High and our first bands together. On the other hand, the best thing that the Guess Who could do now is get off the road. It's a shame what they're doing, playing with guys who weren't even born at the time, doing our songs for people who don't know that these aren't the original band members. It's gone too far.

It does speak to the enduring legacy of those songs that people still come out to hear them, but I think those guys have toured them long enough. The mistake Burton and I made with the Guess Who when we got together in 2000 for the reunion tour was that we didn't buy the name back from Jim. He wanted a million bucks for the Guess Who name. Burton and I had the money, but at the time we had no idea we'd be doing that reunion thing for five years. We thought it would last a year. It was the same thinking on our parts back in the late 70s that allowed Jim to trademark the name for himself. Neither Burton nor I felt we'd ever need it, since we both had solo careers. During the Guess Who reunion period, we paid Jim a fee for the use of the name, then he resurrected it for his band once the reunion ended.

Beyond the music, the sad legacy of the Guess Who is the residue of bitterness and recrimination. What remains is a body of great music, and that's basically the stuff I wrote or co-wrote and played on. Those are the songs on which our legacy rests. But the sadness comes from everyone feeling as if they've been shafted. It's time someone rectified all this. Unfortunately, there's no Judge Judy for rock 'n' roll.

You have a very large family. Has being
a full-time working musician made it
difficult for you to maintain a close
relationship with your children?
And are you still close with your brothers?

Randy, Robbie, Mom, and Dad with the
platinum album *Not Fragile*, 1975.

I have seven children, a stepson, and twenty-six grandchildren. Keeping in touch isn't always easy, given that they're scattered around the continent. For most of my children, I was away on the road for much of their early lives and missed those important, day-by-day moments of their development. I was in and out of their lives. I missed so many birthdays. And after what became a very bitter divorce from Lorayne, I had to rebuild my relationship with them. It took time to heal some of those wounds.

Every Sunday, I sit down and write a mass email to all of them, kids and grandkids, keeping them up to date on what I'm doing and who I've seen in the family and asking what they're all up to. For the next few days, I get individual emails from them with photos and updates. I Skype them often, and they know they can call me any time. My youngest child, Callianne, is living eight blocks away from me now, and we meet once a week for dinner. She bakes really healthy things for me. The grandkids love me and I love them. Tal, my oldest, is pursuing his own music career (he scored a huge hit in 2000 with "She's So High"), and also works as my researcher on *Vinyl Tap*. And he's developed a whole new career direction as his alter ego, Ian Starglow, a fictional eccentric British rocker stranded in Victoria because of immigration issues. Tal is a master at accents and characters. Check out Ian Starglow on YouTube. It's hilarious. My daughter Lorelei and her husband, Jon, help me manage my website and merchandise.

At one time, all three of my brothers were involved in the music business with me. Timmy and Robbie were in Brave Belt and BTO, while Gary managed Brave Belt early on. Of the three, I'm closest with Gary—we're closer in age and spent more time together growing up. There's an eight- and ten-year gap between me and my youngest siblings, Timmy and Robbie. They were still just kids when I was already playing in bands, and they grew up with the Guess Who as part of their lives because it was such a part of mine. After leaving the Guess Who, I was blackballed in Winnipeg, so in order to find guys who'd work with me and respect my no smoking, no alcohol, no drugs policy, I turned to my family. Robbie had never played drums beyond our basement, but he was eager and available. Timmy joined later when Brave Belt needed four guys to fulfill our contracts after Chad Allan quit. Both went from no money to having piles of it, more than they could ever imagine. But it was because I'd brought them in that they enjoyed a windfall. Neither ever played in another band.

One of the hardest things I had to do was fire Timmy from BTO. After a couple of second chances, he continued to break the rules—namely, doing drugs—which was jeopardizing the entire band. It was strictly a business decision, and I had no choice but to make it for the overall good. Still, it was hard on Timmy, and I felt guilty for a long time, but we were on a speeding train and just had to keep going.

Tim returned to Winnipeg, where he became a concert promoter. I cautioned him that that's the riskiest part of the music business, especially in Canada with such harsh weather and vast distances. All you needed was a flat tire, a breakdown on the highway, a snowstorm, and you could lose your shirt. He knew that, having been in Brave Belt and BTO, but he insisted he knew what he was doing. A year later, he called me up and asked if I could lend him some money. He'd booked Supertramp for a cross-Canada tour. The band had broken first in Canada and was huge here, but a snowstorm tied them up somewhere on the road and a bunch of concert dates had to be cancelled. Deposits had already been paid, as well as advertising and promotion, so Tim needed $350,000 to stay afloat. I had six kids at the time and was building our dream home in Lynden, Washington. I said to him, "I told you not to go into this business and now you're asking me to be your partner?" He was trying to be a big shot with all these concerts, but he was in deep financial trouble. I wish I could have helped him more, but I simply couldn't. I did try to help him get his life in order, though.

Tim later moved to British Columbia to look after my dad when he was ill. We all appreciated his doing that. He was instrumental in getting BTO back together in the 80s, but after that he fell on hard times and suffered major health problems. He recently had a serious legal matter to deal with, an accusation that was ultimately disproved in court, but he didn't have the money to hire the legal support he needed. He called me, and this time I was glad I could send him the money to cover those legal bills.

Robbie and I have never reconciled, nor has he reconciled

with Timmy or Gary. Robbie never reconciled with my father, either. He's the outsider in the family. Robbie has these grandiose delusions about himself, and that self-entitled attitude where he figures the world owes him everything. I took him out of grade 11, got an old set of Garry Peterson's drums for him, and three years later he was a millionaire. He's never played with another band in his life. Without me, he might not have had the career he enjoyed. But Robbie feels that since he played drums on "Takin' Care of Business," he should have a piece of the publishing. That's not the way it works.

Robbie and I also had a long-standing legal dispute regarding the BTO name. When I left the band, I signed a legal document giving me the rights to the Bachman-Turner Overdrive name while Robbie and the others retained BTO. But there've been conflicts over that. When I created a stylized Bachman logo for my 1993 album, *Any Road,* he and the others sued me for infringement on the BTO wheel logo. That delayed the album's release while I had a revised logo designed. Then, when Fred Turner and I turned my solo album project into a Bachman and Turner album and went out on the road, Robbie and Blair issued an injunction against us using the name Overdrive. That didn't matter to us, but they claimed we were preventing them from earning a living. Ironically, neither of them was playing anymore. I know Robbie resents me and the fact that I've gone on to great success without him. It's got to be tough for a younger brother working with an older brother, and a successful one at that.

Why did it take so long for BTO to be inducted into the Canadian Music Hall of Fame? When CARAS (the Canadian Academy of Recording Arts and Sciences, which owns the

Juno name) indicated that they wanted to induct BTO into the Hall of Fame in 2003, the other guys in the group told them that they wouldn't appear onstage with me. They wanted the guy hired to replace me onstage with them instead, a guy who never wrote the hit songs or produced any of the albums but was fortunate enough to be named Randy. Seeking to avoid a public conflict, CARAS decided not to induct us after all. In the end, Tom Cochrane—who would have been inducted at some point anyway—got the nod that year. When Tom went up to receive his award, his first thank-you was to BTO. No one, except for us and the Hall of Fame committee, got the joke. Robbie toured for years playing my songs, the songs I wrote and produced and that made him rich, yet he denied I had anything to do with the success of the band. It's unfortunate that band politics delayed our induction into the Canadian Music Hall of Fame. It saddened me to be denied that honour in our home country, but I am so thrilled that BTO has at last taken its rightful place in the Hall and that the induction ceremony took place in our hometown of Winnipeg.

Gary and I remain close. He has our father's work ethic and has become a successful, well-respected real estate agent in Winnipeg. I was upset when he chose not to go with us as our manager when Brave Belt moved to Vancouver, but he had a wife and wanted to stay in Winnipeg. I see him every time I'm in Winnipeg; we have dinner together or I go out to his cottage.

Blood is thicker than water, but bad blood between siblings is never easily assuaged. Do I have regrets about some of what went down in the past between my brothers and me? Yes. But it is what it is.

You recently turned seventy, yet you
continue to record, tour, write and host
a radio show. Have the years affected your
health, and if so, how do you deal with it?

Randy still rockin' onstage with his
gold Les Paul guitar.

Reaching seventy was quite a milestone. But I'm not ready to hit the rocking chair with a good book. I continue to lead a busy life. I'm still around and rockin' because I didn't get distracted or succumb to all the temptations of the rock star life-style. Plus, I maintain a healthy and balanced regimen of diet and exercise.

My biggest problem is my knees, though. Fred Turner has the same problem—it's fairly common in guys who are still rocking past fifty. I could name a dozen examples, although it's not like we all get together and talk about our ailments. We're too busy rockin'. But it comes from standing so much. Rock isn't about sitting on a chair. I can do that with jazz or my storytelling shows. Fred and I carried a great deal of weight back in the day. We were big men; our girth matched our sound. And I carried that weight for many years, pushing 390 pounds before getting my gastric bypass. That's hard on your knees, your arches, and your ankles. Even when you lose the weight, those years of weardown are still there.

What I'm fighting now is knee-replacement surgery, trying

to avoid having it done. I get my knees injected with my own blood, in a procedure called prolotherapy. It's basically what Lance Armstrong was doing: you store your own blood, and your body makes more blood. Then you have your doctor shoot your blood into your muscles, meaning you get more blood and more oxygen. They do this a lot for athletes who have shoulder injuries and want to avoid having an operation. They inject it right into my knee joint, and that generates new cells—your immune system acts as your building block. The pain in your knees comes when your cartilage is gone, when bone is grinding on bone. So if you can replenish the little lining, the bubble wrap or cushion in there, you have no pain. I'd rather do that than take novocaine shots, which just numbs the pain. Then, right after I've had the injection, I go out walking or riding my bike. I've been to the best knee surgeons on the continent, and this works for me.

My knees don't hurt me now, but I do have to be careful. The ninety-day Every Song Tells a Story tour in spring 2013 was hard on my body because it was so rigorous. I had to book chiropractic visits every few days on the road to keep me in shape. Even the guys in my band who are half my age were dealing with health issues.

I've had rotator cuff surgery on my right shoulder from decades of holding a guitar. Three out of my four rotator cuffs were ripped and I was in a lot of pain. I had the surgery done between two Bachman-Cummings tours, with six weeks to recuperate. The doctors told me I'd need six months before I could play again. I couldn't sleep on that side or do anything with that arm, but I recovered in four weeks because I did this hyperbaric oxygen treatment four hours a day for those four weeks.

Hyperbaric oxygen therapy uses a pressure chamber to raise the oxygen to a level higher than atmospheric pressure by increasing the oxygen transport capacity of the blood. This results in a faster recovery of damaged organs and tissues. Six months later my doctor looked at my X-rays and said they looked like those of an entirely different person. I healed my shoulder in a tenth of the time as a result of that oxygen treatment.

When I decided to have gastric bypass surgery back in 2001, the procedure was still kind of secretive. Carnie Wilson, Brian Wilson's daughter, and Ann Wilson of Heart did it, but both had trouble maintaining the weight loss. TV personalities Star Jones and Al Roker both look amazing after having had the operation, and Chris Christie, the governor of New Jersey, recently had it done. It's a miracle for people like me who've spent a lifetime battling weight problems and trying every diet known to man. When I sat down with the doctor before the procedure, he said, "You have a rare opportunity to participate in your own miracle. How many people have the chance to do that? So are you going to participate in this miracle and then turn your back on it, or are you going to honour it? Are you going to get up every day and look down and see your feet, which you haven't seen in years?" When I got it done, I lost a pound a day, a total of 150 pounds. When I'd see my reflection, I'd barely recognize myself.

Rather than put the weight back on, I made a commitment to maintain a healthy diet and exercise routine, which I still adhere to every single day. I gained an entirely new lease on life and how I look at myself. In 2001, I wasn't large, I was gigantic. I didn't have a spare car tire around my waist, I had a tractor tire. If I'd kept on that way I have no doubt that I would have died back then. That's why I regard the operation as a life saver: having it done saved my life. But having the operation isn't all there is. You need to make a lifelong commitment to eating right and staying healthy, and not everyone sticks to it. I'm thirteen years on now and have no desire to turn my back on that commitment.

After I had the surgery, I didn't see the guys in the Guess Who reunion for maybe nine months. Then, I'd just checked into a hotel in Toronto when Garry Peterson called my room, saying he had some old photos of the Guess Who he wanted to show me. I told him my room number and to come on up. When I opened the door, Garry saw the new me and practically fell to his knees in shock. He hadn't seen me that slim since we were eighteen years old. I told him about the operation, and since he's still huge, I encouraged him to get it done. But he won't make the commitment to the lifestyle changes required.

Sure, it's a shortcut, but you have to follow certain requirements. For example, I can't absorb some kinds of iron in foods, so I have to take liquid iron supplements or vegetarian iron. I don't have to become a vegetarian, but I do have to watch the things I eat. Your whole body is one finely balanced organism. What people put their internal organs through, like eating the wrong foods and drinking excessive amounts of alcohol, is incredible. You're killing yourself slowly, not softly. I'm on a no-sugar and very low-carb diet; it's like the old Atkins Diet, but it's now called "wheat belly." Wheat nowadays is so modified that we can't absorb what's in it. Same with cow's milk. We just can't absorb it because it's so juiced up. Goat's milk is much better for you. I also avoid anything with aspartame because it's unnatural.

I have chiropractors in London, Los Angeles, Toronto,

Victoria, and Winnipeg, and they're all associated with terrific masseurs. They're my pit crew around the world. I'm like a vintage race car from the 40s who's racing cars that are much younger, so I need my pit crew to keep me on the track. I've been very fortunate to meet Mark Debrincat at On the Mark Physiotherapy in Winnipeg. He's got degrees in every facet of physiotherapy and works with all the Royal Winnipeg Ballet dancers as well as the Jets and Blue Bomber players. I go to him and he makes me feel like a million bucks. When I'm coming into Winnipeg, I'll call him in advance and he'll set me up with an appointment to do me from head to toe, three- or four-hour sessions. None of this slam, bam, cram wrestling stuff; he moves you around and finesses you so that you feel just great when you walk out. I love going to Winnipeg to see him.

Rather than spending my money on drugs or alcohol, I'm spending it on trying to live longer and continuing to enjoy what I do. In my apartment, I have a silk parachute suspended by chains from the ceiling. It looks like something Lady Gaga would use onstage, but it allows me to stretch my body without having to stand or sit. When my grandkids come over, they think it's great that Grandpa has a swing in his living room. I also ride my stationary bike each morning and my regular bike along the waterfront. And I visit a pool regularly. I got rid of my memory foam pillow—apparently the neurotoxins in it can affect your nervous system.

I want to live to be ninety-five or a hundred, but not in a wheelchair or on a respirator. I'm very conscious of what I eat and how I work out: you have to be if you want to live to a ripe old age and still be healthy enough to enjoy it. I've also been eliminating a lot of the stress in my life that was harmful to me. That's very important. I'm slowing down my schedule and trying to focus on one project a week rather than a half dozen. So I'll record four radio shows a day for two days straight, which will cover two months; the following week, I'll work with Fred (we're doing some casino gigs in the States); then the week after that, I'll work with a songwriter. It's all about pacing myself now.

Did I ever envision still rocking at seventy? No, but I've got to give credit to guys like Mick Jagger and Paul McCartney who are still out there doing it. There's a breed of us rock 'n' rollers who came out of the 1940s and that transition thing from Benny Goodman, Sinatra, and Tony Bennett into Elvis and then to the Beatles, Zeppelin, and Hendrix and all that. We're still playing, waiting for the next phone call to do the next gig. I'm booked into 2016 already.

I still get jazzed when famous people I look up to and admire know who I am. For example, when Steve Morse and Ian Gillan from Deep Purple came up to congratulate me after the Live 8 set, in the back of my mind I was thinking, "How do they know me?" I'm still the kid from West Kildonan with stars in his eyes. I once ran into Brian May from Queen at a guitar event in London, and he invited me to come to dinner. You tend to forget that these guys are like you. They worked hard at their craft, their instrument, voice, or songwriting, and they got lucky like you did. They caught a break and took it and weren't too stoned to seize the opportunity or fall into the traps that are everywhere. The music was always the focus. Same thing with meeting Paul Rodgers of Free and Bad Company and then having him tour with Fred and me, opening for us. I'm such a fan of these guys. I don't gush over them, but inside it's like I want to pinch myself. I felt like that meeting the guys in the Shadows: "They know who I am!" To look through my phone book or my BlackBerry and to see names like Eddie Van Halen, Ringo Starr, Neil Diamond, Neil Young, Jeff Beck, Bruce Welch—it's surreal. And I still love going to rock 'n' roll shows. I saw the Beach Boys' 50th Reunion Tour and got to go backstage to hang out with the guys, whom I've known for years. And when Bachman and Turner toured New Zealand with Pat Benatar and America, it was a thrill to meet them, hang out with them, and hear all those songs.

We're all trying to keep up with Mick Jagger. We all want to move like Jagger. It's not "hope I die before I get old"; it's hope I get to live for as long as I can. Imagine having to live down for the rest of your life a line you wrote when you were twenty. But the reality is that no one ever imagined us still rockin' into our late sixties. Jazz musicians did it and so did country musicians and classical players, but rock 'n' roll always had this live fast, die young ethos to it. We're rewriting the rule book. My job keeps me young. When I'm out there onstage with Fred, it's like a time-travel trip. I'm back to being that thirty-year-old guy again. I certainly don't feel seventy. I feel maybe fifty-eight or fifty-nine, so I think I'm very fortunate. I look forward to the last quarter of my life being productive and creative.

People ask me if I'll ever retire. Retire from what? To do what? I retired when I left MIT (the Manitoba Institute of Technology) in 1965. My job was going to school to keep my dad happy and off my case. People retire from jobs or careers either because they've had enough or they want to devote all their time to what has just been a hobby. I don't have hobbies and I love my job, so why would I retire? To go hang-gliding or bird watching, to garden or take ocean cruises? There was an old Mose Allison song, Georgie Fame recorded it, that Burton and I always like called "I Live the Life I Love and I Love the Life I Live." That sums me up. Same thing with Neil Young. When people ask him if he'll retire he always answers, "Why?"

I don't want people talking about me and saying, "Look what he's done"; I want them saying, "Look what he's doing now." That's my philosophy. I love playing with Fred Turner because it's another part of my life and career I get to revisit. And there's no baggage between us. It's all about the music. Fred recently told my manager, Gilles Paquin, that all he wants to do is play with me. I've also been doing gigs with the Sadies, who are half my age. While I don't necessarily agree with their lifestyle, playing with them is like Neil playing with Crazy Horse when they were in their prime. You never know where it's going to go, but you just get into it and follow it. Anything can happen. It's loose and fun with no expectations other than making some great music together. And I've got a tour booked next year playing with symphonies across North America. How cool is that? Who would have thought I'd still be so active at seventy?

How do you come up with the themes for
Randy Bachman's Vinyl Tap?
Do you think you'll keep doing the show?

Randy taping his *Vinyl Tap* radio show.

For the first couple of years of the show, the themes came from me or my producer, Tod Elvidge. But since then, people have been sending in ideas for themes. I'd say about a third to half the themes we do come via listeners (and as Dean Martin used to say, "Keep those cards and letters coming in, folks"). I get letters from listeners saying things like, "We're farmers and listen to your show. Can you do a show about farmer songs?" Sure. Then I'll research and find songs that fit that theme. I had a letter from an airline pilot who asked for a show about airplane songs. Well, other than Steve Miller's "Jet Airliner" or John Denver's "Leaving on a Jet Plane," there aren't a lot of airline songs, so instead I came up with a Trains and Boats and Planes theme show with songs from all three. I had a suggestion for songs that make people cry as well as songs that make people laugh. I've got devil and angel songs, summer songs, good and bad songs, yesterday and today songs.

I was on our tour bus a while back with my band, reading all these songs with the word "love" in the title for my Valentine's Day–themed show—songs like "And I Love Her, "Love the

One You're With," "What About Love," "Why Can't This Be Love." One of my crew guys said, "Those would be funny if you substituted the word 'lunch' for the word 'love.'" So it would be, "Here's Heart with their big hit 'What About Lunch'!" I can't wait to do that. "All You Need Is Lunch," "And I Lunch Her," "Whole Lotta Lunch."

By far the most popular show is still the cowbell show. That was fun getting a lot of cowbell songs together. To this day, I'll be walking down the street anywhere in Canada and someone will invariably yell out, "More cowbell!"

When Bachman and Turner toured New Zealand, people there told me they listen to my show. We get emails from as far away as South Korea, the jungles of Borneo, northern Alaska, Italy, Japan. Canadians are everywhere. Guys in jail are big listeners to the show, too. Talk about a captive audience. I did a prison theme once with songs like "Folsom Prison Blues," "Jailhouse Rock," and "Jailbreak." I told the guys listening from jail, "I'm sorry you're in there and I'm glad you're listening to my show, but what else have you got to do?" I've found I have an intimate relationship with my listeners. They seem to feel a bond with me even if they've never met me. On my last tour, instead of every second person saying, "I've been listening to your records since whenever," I was hearing every second person say, "I've been listening to *Vinyl Tap* since …" The show just seems to resonate with listeners.

One of the thrills of that last tour for me was discovering that I've connected with Canadians right across the country, whether in cities or small towns. The tour took me to places like Owen Sound, for example, where the Guess Who reunion and Bachman and Turner never went. These smaller places were great, and they loved having me perform in their community. I've been touring and recording for several decades, and of course I meet fans wherever I play, but this tour was a validation that *Vinyl Tap* has really become a part of people's lives. They look forward to tuning in each week and planning their schedules around the show. At every tour stop I heard, "We spend our weekends with you"; or, "We dance to your show every week"; or, "We get the whole family together, pull out the old records, and listen to your show"; or, "We have dinner every Friday night with you"; or, "We put the hockey game on mute, it's still on, and we listen to your show while watching the game." I get letters from people in remote communities living in log cabins saying how they save up their electricity to tune in every week, and then they talk about the show all week long until the next show. Everyone from eight to eighty tunes in. I had a letter from a woman who tunes into the show at eleven p.m. while she's in bed with her vibrator. Apparently she has a really good time getting off to my voice. Holy cow, that's a bit too much for me, but whatever rings her bell and brings my ratings up.

I have a rhythm to doing my shows now after so many years at it. It's easy and it's fun. When we tape them, a lot of what I say is off the cuff. It's not tightly scripted. I can't always remember what I said, so it's fun for me to listen to the show when it airs months later. My son Tal not only helps with research but also handles the mail from out in Victoria. The internet allows everyone involved with the show to be anywhere. We can even tape shows in my house—we don't all have to be together in one studio. The show still reminds me of listening to CKY or CKRC radio back in the 50s and 60s, where you'd hear a wide range of genres, styles, and sources. We play music from all over the world. That's what people enjoy, this array of music. It's a lot of work to put together, but it's a really wonderful format.

My first stint on CBC Radio was as a summer replacement. I was touring then, and so I could tape shows only at certain times. And because I didn't want to go into a CBC studio, I had to pay an engineer, and to buy some of the records I played. So that summer show cost me $600. Plus, it had only a modicum of listeners, because who listens to radio over the summer when you're out at the cottage? It really took off in the fall, though, when CBC ran reruns of the show. Everyone was back at work or at school and CBC had a labour strike on. That's when my listenership skyrocketed, because CBC had to air reruns of existing radio shows, and my show was new and exciting. I didn't get any more money for rerunning those ten shows, but halfway through the fall the radio ratings book came out and it was "Oh my god," the ratings were going through the roof and rising all the time. I was pulling in 10 percent more listeners than Danny Finkleman had been in that time slot. So they asked me to do the show on a more permanent basis for thirty-five weeks.

When I first tried taping that summer show, I was screaming and speed jive talking like Wolfman Jack or Hound Dog George Lorenz. But the CBC didn't want that kind of thing for their evening hours, some guy shrieking like Little Richard. It took me four or five attempts to find my groove. I had to find a place somewhere between the Wolfman and Richard Scott. Scott was an afternoon deejay in Winnipeg who had a show just for housewives where he'd purr into the microphone, "Hello, kitten. Time to light up and relax," and you'd actually hear him light up a cigarette on air and pour a drink. "The kids are at school and it's just you and me," he'd say, and then he'd play all these romantic songs. I used to hear him when I was home sick from school because my mother was one of those housewives who listened to him. Turns out that in real life he was a fat bald guy, but he created this sexy persona on air. So I found something in between yelling and cooing that worked. But I was drawing from the golden days of radio when deejays had personalities and were a big part of the local scene. I grew up listening to PJ the DJ, Dino Corrie, Daryl B, Ron "Keg" Legge, Doc Steen, Boyd Kozak. All these guys had personalities on air.

I've had female flight attendants come sit on the arm of my seat on a flight and ask me to say something. I'll reply, "Say what?" and they'll say, "We don't care. We just like the sound of your radio voice." So I'll slip into my Richard Scott voice: "Hello, kitten."

I get letters from kids who appreciate the musical history lesson they're getting and enjoy the opportunity to listen to recording artists they've never even heard of, people like Robert Johnson, for example. *Vinyl Tap* really crosses generations. It's the greatest job in the world for me because I get to talk about music and play what I want. Having a theme each week gives me a focus; otherwise, I'd be all over the place. And I can play recordings from the 1930s right up to today, any genre, any style. What a gig! CBC renewed me for another three years, and have basically told me I can do the show for as long as I want to or am able. I never get bored and it's never drudgery.

While my demographic is getting younger, occasionally I'll hear from a longtime listener who says something like, "How dare you play Lady Gaga alongside the great Tony Bennett!" I have a regular listener from Michigan who's a huge Duran Duran fan, and she'll email me after each show to say, "You could have played a Duran Duran song for that theme," and then she'll list the name of one of their songs that fit. But the bottom line is that the show is all about music, any and all kinds of music. I had a letter from a woman who wanted to hear the music of her teenage years, which was Cab Calloway and Bing Crosby. I don't want to limit the music I play or narrow it to particular tastes. It's all music. So I'll play Cab Calloway for her, and Duran Duran and Lady Gaga for the younger listeners, and if someone doesn't like that, too bad. That's their narrow definition of music, not mine. Lady Gaga struggled for several years and had an album turned down before she made it. She met a guy who invited her to write songs with him, so she rode the bus, in the rain, snow, whatever, each week for two years to write songs and develop her craft. She's no overnight sensation. She's sold a gazillion albums and she has something to say. Listen to a song like "Born This Way": it's written for anyone and everyone, doesn't matter what age, race, religion, or gender you might be. It's a celebration of who you are. If you don't like hearing that song on my show, wait a few minutes for the next one. It'll be something different.

I don't mind receiving critiques or corrections (I can't be right 100 percent of the time), but some of them are from wackos. I once did a theme about one-word songs and played James Brown's "Please Please Please." Someone wrote in complaining that that was a three-word song. Are you kidding me? Just because he sings "please" three times? Too Old to Die Young was a fun theme, but in between taping it and running it, one of the guys I covered passed away. It happens. Same thing happened with James Brown a few years back. We taped a show on him and his music, and then over Christmas 2006, before the show could air, he died. I got emails from people wondering where my mind was at, talking about James Brown in the present tense. I had to email replies to these people explaining that the show had been taped earlier.

At one point, CBC wanted me to take the show to television, like Jian Ghomeshi does with *Q*, but I don't do the shows in real time, so it couldn't work. Plus, I don't want a camera there. I don't want to have to do my hair or dress up. The way it is now, I can be sitting there in pyjamas and no one cares.

Some people have asked me, "When will you have Burton Cummings on the show?" That's not the concept of the show. I don't have guests. I'm on Salt Spring Island, so I could have Valdy on or Bill Henderson from Chilliwack. They live near me. But the reality is that I'm not an interviewer. Let Jian Ghomeshi or George Stroumboulopoulos do that kind of thing. My show is all about the music. I'm giving listeners a backstage pass to the music I've been around all my life and sharing my experiences.

I recently met the head of CORUS communications. They own about eight hundred radio stations. He told me how much he loves *Vinyl Tap* and that he told all his programmers across the continent to listen to my show, like a homework assignment, because I have a vitality that's lacking in radio these days. There's no enthusiasm or personality on commercial radio anymore. Radio exists for one thing: to play commercials. The music is secondary, and the deejays don't get to play what they want or pick the tracks for their shows. But listen to CBC Radio: guys like me, Jian Ghomeshi, George Stroumboulopoulos, Holger Petersen, we play what we want to play and we're enthusiastic about it. CBC Radio really owns the weekends. They have great music shows as well as comedy shows. Even young kids are starting to tune in. The CBC binds Canada together. This is a golden era of CBC Radio because it's intelligent radio. It's entertaining, informative, and fun. Everybody's abandoning commercial radio because of its cookie-cutter formatting. I'm thrilled and honoured to be a part of that renaissance.

Who'd have thought that in my later years I'd become a radio man? I've always shared my stories about whom I've met or what I've done, but to have people care about them and want to hear more is pretty amazing and very gratifying. It's that Sally Field thing: "You like me! You really like me!" And it's very easy to do because I can work around my busy schedule.

Randy Bachman's Vinyl Tap is really the continuing adventures of Randy Bachman: writing, recording, touring the world. Those experiences provide the show with fresh new perspectives. Chris Boyce at CBC Radio calls me the rock 'n' roll Stuart McLean. I kind of like that title. I love doing the show and look forward to many more years.

RANDY BACHMAN'S DISCOGRAPHY

Listeners have asked for a definitive list of all my recordings, so here's my discography. Keep in mind, though, that there are a dozen or more budget-label compilations of Guess Who and BTO hits on the market—too many to track down and include here.

SINGLES

GARY ANDREWS

1961   Come On Pretty Baby / Heartache and Disappointment (Rodeo 243)

CHAD ALLAN AND THE REFLECTIONS

1963   Tribute to Buddy Holly / Back and Forth (Canadian-American 802)

          Shy Guy / Baby's Got a Brand New Beau (Quality 1559)

1964   Stop Teasing Me / A Shot of Rhythm and Blues (Quality 1644)

BOB ASHLEY AND THE REFLECTIONS

1964   Made in England / Inside Out (Reo 8735)

THE GUESS WHO

1965   Till We Kissed / Shakin' All Over (Quality 1691)

Shakin' All Over / Till We Kissed (Scepter 1295 U.S.)

Tossin' and Turnin' / I Want You to Love Me (Quality 1724)

Hey Ho, What You Do to Me / Goodnight, Goodnight (Quality 1752; Scepter 12018 U.S.)

Hurting Each Other / Baby's Birthday (Quality 1778; Scepter 12118 U.S.)

1966   Believe Me / Baby Feelin' (Quality 1797; Scepter 12131 U.S.)

Clock on the Wall / One Day (Quality 1815; Scepter 12144 U.S.)

And She's Mine / All Right (Quality 1832; Amy 967 U.S.)

His Girl / It's My Pride (Quality 1863)

1967   His Girl / It's My Pride (Amy 976 U.S.; King 1044 U.K.)

Pretty Blue Eyes / Pretty Blue Eyes (Quality 1874)

This Time Long Ago / There's No Getting Away from You (Quality 1876; Fontana 1597 U.K.)

Flying on the Ground Is Wrong / If You Don't Want Me (Quality 1890)

This Time Long Ago / Flying on the Ground Is Wrong (Quality 1933)

Miss Felicity Grey / Flying on the Ground Is Wrong (Fontana TF 861 U.K.)

1968   Hurting Each Other / I'll Keep Coming Back (Quality 1974)

When Friends Fall Out / Guess Who Blues (Nimbus 9002)

Of a Dropping Pin / Mr. Nothin' (Nimbus 9004)

1969   These Eyes / Lightfoot (Nimbus 9005; RCA 0102 U.S.)

Maple Fudge / Of a Dropping Pin (Nimbus 9007)

Laughing / Undun (RCA 74-0195)

No Time / Proper Stranger (RCA 74-0300)

1970   American Woman / No Sugar Tonight (RCA74-0325)

1976   Silver Bird / Runnin' Down the Street (RCA PB-10716)

1984   Let's Watch the Sun Go Down / These Eyes (Ready SR 491)

BRAVE BELT

1971   Rock & Roll Band / Anyday Means Tomorrow (Reprise 1023)

Crazy Arms, Crazy Eyes / Holy Train (Reprise 1039)

1972   Never Comin' Home / Can You Feel It (Reprise 1061)

Dunrobin's Gone / Another Way Out (Reprise 1083)

Your Backyard / Is It Really Right? (Portrait 70011)

BACHMAN-TURNER OVERDRIVE (BTO)

1973   Gimme Your Money Please / Little Gandy Dancer (Mercury 73843)

Blue Collar / Hold Back the Water (Mercury 73417)

Stayed Awake All Night / Down and Out Man (Mercury 6052357 U.K.)

1974   Let It Ride / Tramp (Mercury 73457)

Takin' Care of Business / Stonegates (Mercury 73487)

You Ain't Seen Nothin' Yet / Free Wheelin' (Mercury 73622)

1975   Roll On Down the Highway/ Sledgehammer (Mercury 73656)

Hey You / Flat Broke Love (Mercury 73683)

Quick Change Artist / Roll On Down the Highway (Mercury 73710)

Down to the Line / She's a Devil or Away from Home (Mercury 73724)

1976   Take It Like a Man / Woncha Take Me for a While (Mercury 73766)

Lookin' Out for #1 / Find Out About Love (Mercury 73784)

Four Wheel Drive / Gimme Your Money Please (Mercury 73843)

1977   My Wheels Won't Turn / Freeways (Mercury 73903)

Shotgun Rider / Down Down (Mercury 73926)

1984 For the Weekend / Just Look at Me Now (Compleat CLT6)

My Sugaree / Service with a Smile (Compleat 137)

1986 Mississippi Queen / (Curb)

1989 Woolly Bully / (Curb)

IRONHORSE

1979 Sweet Lui-Louise / One and Only (Scotti Bros. 408)

Watch Me Fly / Sweet Lui-Louise (Scotti Bros. K11271 U.K.)

She's Got It / One and Only (Scotti Bros. 408)

1980 What's Your Hurry Darlin' / Try a Little Harder (Scotti Bros. 512)

Railroad Love / Symphony (Scotti Bros. 302)

UNION

1981 Mainstreet USA / Invitation (Portrait PRT A1458)

ALBUMS / CDs

THE GUESS WHO

1965 Shakin' All Over (Quality V1756)

Hey Ho (What You Do To Me) (Quality V1764)

Shakin' All Over (Scepter SPS-533 U.S.)

1966 It's Time (Quality V1788)

1967 A Wild Pair (Nimbus NNE 100)

1968	Wheatfield Soul (Nimbus NNS 102; RCA LSP 4141 U.S.)
	The Guess Who (Birchmount BM 525)
1969	Canned Wheat (RCA LSP 4266)
	Born in Canada (Wand WDS-691 U.S.)
	Super Golden Goodies (Quality SV-1827)
	The Guess Who (MGM SE-4645 U.S.)
1970	American Woman (RCA LSP 4266)
1971	The Best of the Guess Who (RCA LSPX 1104)
1976	The Way They Were (RCA APL1-1778)
1977	The Greatest Hits of the Guess Who (RCA AFL1-2253)
1984	Together Again (Ready LR 049)
1985	K-Tel Presents the Guess Who: 20 Original Hits (K-Tel NC-458)
1986	The Best of the Guess Who Live (RCA/Compleat Records Stereo 672012 R254270)
1988	Track Record: The Guess Who Collection (BMG KCD2-7115)
1997	The Guess Who: The Ultimate Collection (RCA 07063 67300-2)
	Shakin' All Over (Legend L-00010)
	Hey Ho (What You Do to Me) (Legend L-00011)
	It's Time (Legend L-00012)
1999	The Guess Who: Greatest Hits (RCA 07863 67774-2)

2000   American Woman (Original Masters—Buddha 74465
99734 2)

Canned Wheat (Original Masters—Buddha 74465 99763 2)

Running Back Thru Canada (BMG ViK 74328 811822-2)

2001   This Time Long Ago (Ranbach L00013)

The Guess Who: Shakin' All Over! (Sundazed SC 11113)

2002   The Best of the Guess Who (Camden BMG 74321 941602
U.K.)

2003   Platinum & Gold Collection (RCA/BMG Heritage 82876
52878 2)

The Guess Who Anthology (RCA B0000CDL7E)

2004   The Guess Who x 2: Artificial Paradise / Wheatfield Soul
(BMG 8287653014-2)

2005   Let's Go (Maximum MAX00072)

2007   Chad Allan and the Reflections: Early Roots (Regenerator
REGEN0701)

BRAVE BELT

1971   Brave Belt (Reprise RS-6447)

1972   Brave Belt II (Reprise MS-2057)

1975   Bachman-Turner-Bachman as Brave Belt (Reprise 2210)

2001   Brave Belt I / Brave Belt II (Bullseye BLR CD 4054)

BACHMAN-TURNER OVERDRIVE (BTO)

1973 Bachman-Turner Overdrive (Mercury SRM-1-673; Mercury 838 196-2 CD)

1974 Bachman-Turner Overdrive II (Mercury SRM-1-696; Mercury 822 504-2 CD)

Not Fragile (Mercury SRM 1-1004; Mercury 830 178-2 CD)

1975 Four Wheel Drive (Mercury SRM-1-1027; Mercury 830 970-2 CD)

1976 Head On (Mercury SRM-1-1067; Mercury 838-197-2 CD)

Best of BTO (So Far) (Mercury SRM 1-1101; Mercury/ Polygram 558234 CD)

1977 Freeways (Mercury SRM-1-3700; Mercury 838 199-2 CD)

Japan Tour (Mercury SRM-1-1143)

1984 Bachman-Turner Overdrive (Compleat CPL 1-1010; Sun 15072-7027-2 CD)

1986 Live-Live-Live (MCA/Curb D2-77328)

1987 Greatest Hits (Mercury/Polygram 30039)

1993 The Anthology (Mercury 314 514 902-2)

1994 Best of Live (Curb D2-776553)

1998 King Biscuit Flower Hour (BMG 280619)

2000 20th Century Masters: The Best of Bachman-Turner Overdrive: The Millennium Collection (Mercury 4809627)

2001 Universal Masters Collection (Universal/Mercury 4843621)

2003   The Collection (Polygram International 4442923)

Takin' Care of Business (Polygram Special Products 5381281)

2005   Gold (Mercury 005475)

2008   Definitive Collection (Mercury 7560383)

2012   40th Anniversary Deluxe Edition (Universal 5340188)

IRONHORSE

1979   Ironhorse (Scotti Bros. SB-7103)

1980   Everything Is Grey (Scotti Bros. XSB-7108)

UNION

1981   On Strike (Portrait BL 37368)

RANDY BACHMAN

1970   Axe (RCA LSP-4348)

1978   Survivor (Polydor PD-1-6141)

1992   Any Road (Guitar Recordings 9714-99406-2)

1994   Bachman "Plugged In": The Garage Tapes (RBSK 1006)

1996   Merge (Legend/True North TNSD 0117)

1998   The Randy Bachman Songbook (Ranbach RB0001-V3)

2002   Every Song Tells a Story (Ranbach RB-0122 CD; DR-4343 DVD)

2004   JazzThing (Maximum MAX14792)

2006   JazzThing Live in Toronto (Ranbach/Fontana RBFN001)

        Randy Bachman Anthology (Friday Music 829421-104827)

2007   JazzThing II (with New Guitar Summit) (Ranbach/Fontana RBFN003)

BACHMAN-CUMMINGS

2006   Bachman Cummings Songbook (Sony/BMG 82876 81247 2)

        The Thunderbird Trax (BC001)

        Bachman Cummings: First Time Around DVD (Sony/BMG 82876 82779-9)

2007   Jukebox (Sony 88697112982)

BACHMAN AND TURNER

2010   Bachman & Turner (E1/Box of Songs BOS CD 002)

ACKNOWLEDGMENTS

The list of thank-yous is like the music: a timeline of my life.

So from the very beginning, I thank my parents, brothers, bandmates, fans, Elvis, Nerky, Lenny Breau, The Shadows, The Beatles, Neil Young, Burton Cummings, Fred Turner, and my greatest accomplishments—my kids and grandkids.

To the now: my manager and best friend, Gilles Paquin, and his family and team; my bandmates Marc La France, Brent Knudsen, and Mick Dalla-Vee; my crew, Kevin Duffy, Daryl Chonka, Mick Schmidtmyer, Christian Stonehouse, Anthony Barreto; Gibson Guitars; CBC Radio; Tod Elvidge; and Winnipeg, which was the greatest place to be born and to be a teenager in the 60s. It was amazing!